PEOPLE AND CLIMATE CHANGE

People and Climate Change

VULNERABILITY, ADAPTATION, AND SOCIAL JUSTICE

Edited by Lisa Reyes Mason

and Jonathan Rigg

OXFORD
UNIVERSITY PRESS

OXFORD
UNIVERSITY PRESS

Oxford University Press is a department of the University of Oxford. It furthers
the University's objective of excellence in research, scholarship, and education
by publishing worldwide. Oxford is a registered trade mark of Oxford University
Press in the UK and certain other countries.

Published in the United States of America by Oxford University Press
198 Madison Avenue, New York, NY 10016, United States of America.

Library of Congress Cataloging-in-Publication Data
Names: Mason, Lisa Reyes, editor. | Jonathan Rigg, editor.
Title: People and climate change : vulnerability, adaptation,
and social justice / edited by Lisa Reyes Mason and Jonathan Rigg.
Description: New York, NY : Oxford University Press, [2019] |
Includes bibliographical references and index.
Identifiers: LCCN 2018045121 (print) | LCCN 2018050142 (ebook) |
ISBN 9780190886462 (updf) | ISBN 9780190886479 (epub) |
ISBN 9780190886486 (Online Component) | ISBN 9780190886455 (alk. paper)
Subjects: LCSH: Climatic changes—Social aspects.
Classification: LCC QC903 (ebook) | LCC QC903 .P444 2019 (print) |
DDC 304.2/5—dc23
LC record available at https://lccn.loc.gov/2018045121

9 8 7 6 5 4 3 2 1

Printed by Sheridan Books, Inc., United States of America

Contents

Foreword

⌒_____

CLIMATE CHANGE IS a social challenge. It threatens the social relationships, family stability, well-being, livelihoods, and sometimes the survival of people and communities worldwide. Common consequences include food and water insecurity, respiratory and other physical diseases, mental distress and emotional health problems, housing damage, unemployment, and asset depletion. Therefore, in the larger picture, the impacts of global environmental changes—including rising sea levels, freshwater decline, and habitat and biodiversity loss—are not just physical but also social and economic, and therefore political too.

MAJOR SOCIAL CHALLENGES IN CLIMATE CHANGE

Climate change presents three major types of social challenges: (1) Climate change is a social justice issue; (2) responding to it requires community, organizational, and policy solutions; and (3) humans must envision and create a new society not based on burning fossil fuels. The chapters in this book take up these issues.

Social Justice

Though climate change inevitably affects everyone, it is nevertheless a social justice issue. Impacts and effects of climate change are not equally distributed, creating a host of social, economic, and environmental inequalities. For those who are most impoverished and disadvantaged, consequences are far worse than they are for those who are wealthy and secure. People with less social, economic, and political resources and influence are more likely to bear the negative effects of floods, droughts, pollution, resource shortages, severe weather incidents, and other environmental problems. People from developing countries, coastal nations, indigenous groups, the poorest communities, subsistence farmers, racial and ethnic minorities, women and children, older adults, and other vulnerable populations are much more likely to suffer the harsh conditions and harmful impacts of climate change. The sources and burdens of climate change are very unequally distributed, placing the issue clearly in the realm of social justice. At a global level, well-off nations contribute far more than poor countries in greenhouse gas emissions. Even within individual countries, the rich can often shield themselves from the effects of climate change, whereas the poor have little choice but to face the hardships and "adapt" or "cope" as best they can. This major social justice aspect is a very compelling "people" issue in climate change—raising large moral questions—and is a recurring theme in the book.

Community, Organizational, and Policy Solutions

Following on from the previous point, responding to climate change requires more than just individual and household coping. It calls for both community and organizational innovations and also national and international policy solutions. The challenge is not simply to "adapt" but also to engage climate change with vision, direction, and efficacy. Social innovations for effective responses include strategies for advocacy, mitigation, adaptation, migration, resettlement, and a host of other issues. These may only be finding their footing, but they are underway and are reflected in the chapters in this volume.

A Different Society

Most profoundly, humans must envision and create a very different society—one not based on the massive burning of fossil fuels. To achieve such a social and economic transformation, technological changes will be required, but technology alone is not enough. Humans must also adopt and integrate new technologies into their daily lifestyles and social institutions and, importantly, play a direct role in shaping those technological innovations.

However, relying on individuals alone to make such necessary changes would be insufficient. For example, efficient and clean cooking stoves designed to reduce carbon burning, improve ventilation, and improve the health of people in developing nations have been available for decades. Although the technology has improved, and stoves are available at little or no cost, adoption has been slow (Ruiz-Mercado, Masera, Zamora, & Smith, 2011). Many people throughout the world, in nations across the economic spectrum, are reluctant to make even minor changes that would benefit the environment. Behaviors in wealthy countries are far more disappointing (e.g., the millions of oversized sport utility vehicles on U.S. roads with very low fuel mileage and the surfeit of "McMansion" houses in U.S. cities with many empty rooms that are heated or cooled on a daily basis).

Very often, humans do not "do the right thing" and can be very slow learners. These basic human tendencies highlight the limited potential of individual behavioral approaches to major social transformation. Therefore, on reflection, it is abundantly clear that innovations in social institutions will have to do the heavy lifting. Yet many of the required social innovations have not yet begun or are at best works in progress, including the shift to using solar and wind power, implementing more demanding fuel/mileage standards for transportation, discouraging excessive household size, and making household energy conservation more automatic. The imperative is to be clear that limiting harmful emissions and responding to climate change are not solely matters of perfecting and applying new energy technologies. The transition will also require massive social creativity and innovation. The social dimensions of climate change—what humans, communities, and societies must do—matter immensely yet are so far largely neglected.

However, the outlook is not all gloomy, and we have examples from which to learn. There are meaningful shifts toward renewable energy sources in Germany and elsewhere, more public utilities are incentivizing conservation, a "small house" or "right-sized house" movement is nascent but growing, and so on. No single social innovation will be a magic bullet—many must be imagined, designed, tested, and implemented. This book sharpens the focus on the human dimensions of climate issues, and it points to social responses that must be achieved for large-scale solutions, including policy implications—local, national, and international.

As one distinctive aspect of desirable social change, we are long overdue in recognizing the value of—and what we can learn from—indigenous people in their relationship to the environment. For millennia, humans lived in much greater harmony with other species of plants and animals. The value of these patterns and relationships has been largely ignored following the Enlightenment and Industrial Revolution. Across most of the planet, conquering nations and economic exploitation have killed and subjugated indigenous peoples and disregarded their knowledge. Yet even today, 6% of the global population (much of it indigenous) oversees 80% of global biodiversity (Galloway McLean, 2010). It would be very foolish to continue to ignore this massive stewardship and what indigenous populations may be able to teach the rest of us.

The People and Climate Change project takes up this challenge, but there is a risk that it will be perceived simply as "helping people" to adapt and survive. Although helping people is a fundamental goal, it is only one part of the social innovation that will be required. Equally or more important will be advocacy, action, and social development. Literally, the challenge is creating *a new kind of society*, one that is globally aware and sustainable for the long term.

PARTNERSHIPS FOR CLIMATE JUSTICE AND SOCIAL INNOVATION

Some of the work has begun. Through new applied research, the Environment and Social Development initiative at the Center for Social Development (CSD) at Washington University in St. Louis—in partnership with the University of Tennessee—examines social vulnerability to environmental change and strategies for social action and adaptation. At CSD, we partner with many other organizations in the United States and abroad. The chapters in this volume grew out of the November 2016 conference People and Climate Change: Vulnerability, Adaptation, Social Justice, which built on a partnership between Washington University in St. Louis and the National University of Singapore. This partnership, known as Next Age Institute, creates a global focus on evidence-based social innovations that can respond to 21st century challenges, such as climate change.

It is also noteworthy that "create social responses to a changing environment" has been identified as one of the Grand Challenges in Social Work in the United States. The Grand Challenges have been initiated by the American Academy of Social Work and Social Welfare in partnership with all the major social work organizations. This is the first time that social work scholars and the profession as a whole have formally identified people and environmental change as a core mission. Social work can contribute to evidence-based solutions. The profession has considerable experience taking on major social tasks: deinstitutionalization of children, protection from abuse, women's suffrage, maternal health, child welfare, labor protections and social security, civil rights and voting rights, behavioral health interventions, and more (for a summary of social work contributions to major social challenges, see Sherraden et al., 2013).

All of these have led to the creation of new social institutions that deliver public goods or other forms of general benefits. The long and meandering pathway of civilization is, in a practical sense, the eventual creation of public goods that save time and money and ensure greater human well-being. In the present case, a new public good might be discovery and delivery of cheap and clean energy to all. This will not be just a technological change; it must be accompanied by large-scale and multifaceted social innovations—for example, adoption of new equipment, willingness to change consumption patterns and/or amounts, and perhaps new strategies for sharing energy with others. These social innovations are never automatic; they have to be imagined, tested, refined, and implemented, all of which will require dedicated work.

In this regard, it is possible that a renewed social work may emerge in this century, addressing social organization and development that is responsive to new environmental and other challenges. I strongly suspect that this social work will be a partnership with other applied social sciences, in geography, anthropology, public health, public administration, and related fields. We will do much better if we work together.

It is clear that climate change will be a major challenge for much of the world's population. Evidence, advocacy, and action to mitigate environmental harm, protect the most vulnerable people, and adapt as successfully as possible are moral as well as practical priorities. The important work will be largely social. A redefined, renewed, and interdisciplinary social work for the 21st century can and must step up to this challenge. Perhaps this will be reconceived as *social development*, as a more forward-looking, purposeful, and positive social practice.

In closing, I appreciate and admire the intellectual and practical leadership of my colleagues Dr. Lisa Reyes Mason of the University of Tennessee and Professor Jonathan Rigg of the University of Bristol. Professors Mason and Rigg conceived and planned the remarkable conference that preceded this book.

I also thank my colleagues at CSD at Washington University in St. Louis, especially Lissa Johnson and Tanika Spencer for dedication and skill in implementing the conference, Jill Miller for conference communications, and John Gabbert for his editorial assistance with this excellent book. Finally, I am grateful to Senior Editor Dana Bliss and colleagues at Oxford University Press for their continuing and very productive collaboration.

Michael Sherraden
Washington University in St. Louis
March 6, 2018

REFERENCES

Galloway McLean, K. (2010). *Advance guard: Climate change impacts, adaptation, mitigation, and Indigenous Peoples—A compendium of case studies*. Darwin, Australia: UNU-IAS Traditional Knowledge Institution.

Ruiz-Mercado, I., Masera, O., Zamora, H., & Smith, K. R. (2011). Adoption and sustained use of improved cook stoves. *Energy Policy, 39*, 7557–7566.

Sherraden, M., Stuart, P., Barth, R. P., Kemp, S., Lubben, J., Hawkins, J. D., . . . Catalano, R. (2013). *Grand accomplishments in social work* (Grand Challenges for Social Work, Working Paper No. 2). Baltimore, MD: American Academy of Social Work and Social Welfare.

Acknowledgments

THIS BOOK IS based on the papers presented at the symposium People and Climate Change: Vulnerability, Adaptation, Social Justice, held at the Brown School of Social Work (Brown School), Washington University in St. Louis, in November 2016. We thank the Center for Social Development (CSD) at the Brown School, the National University of Singapore, and the University of Tennessee for their support. We also thank Lissa Johnson, Tanika Spencer, and Jill Miller for their assistance in organizing the event.

The symposium and this book would not have been possible without the leadership of Michael Sherraden, CSD Director, whose vision of applied research leads to social innovation and policy change. His work to expand the core areas of CSD's contributions to society inspired the symposium and, therefore, this book.

Finally, we are grateful to John Gabbert for his invaluable editorial work from start to finish of the project.

About the Editors

Lisa Reyes Mason is an Assistant Professor at the University of Tennessee College of Social Work and faculty director of the Environment and Social Development initiative at the Center for Social Development at Washington University in St. Louis. Her research centers on environmental change, social justice, and community engagement. She is an applied social scientist with a PhD in social work, and her work is transdisciplinary by nature. She collaborates regularly across disciplines and prioritizes working with community members to understand their experiences, priorities, and ideas for change. Her current research examines socially responsive stormwater management, access and response to severe weather warnings, and public preferences for neighborhood-level environmental data, with a focus on urban communities in the United States. Prior research examined seasonal water insecurity in the northern Philippines. She received her PhD and Master of Social Work (MSW) from the Brown School at Washington University in St. Louis.

Jonathan Rigg is Professor of Geography in the School of Geographical Sciences at the University of Bristol in the UK. Until the end of 2018 he was Professor of Geography and Director of the Asia Research Institute at the National University of Singapore, during which time this book was conceptualized and completed. He is a development geographer with a long-standing interest in understanding the human effects of social, economic, and environmental transformations in the Asian region. Initially, this focused on farming, later extending to migration, urban living, livelihoods, popular participation, and resilience. He has undertaken fieldwork in Laos, Nepal, Sri Lanka, Thailand, and Vietnam. He has published eight books, edited six, authored or co-authored 70 papers, and contributed approximately 50 chapters to edited volumes. His most recent book is *More Than Rural: Textures of Thailand's Agrarian Transformation* (Hawaii University Press, 2019).

About the Contributors

Margaret Alston is Professor of Social Work at Newcastle University. Previously, she was Professor of Social Work and head of the Department of Social Work at Monash University, where she established the Gender, Leadership and Social Sustainability research unit. In 2010, she was awarded an Order of Australia for her services to social work and to 20 rural women. She is a past chair of the Australian Council of Heads of Schools of Social Work and was appointed a foundation fellow of the Australian College of Social Work in 2011. She has completed projects on gender and climate change with Oxfam in Bangladesh, UNESCO in the Pacific, and the Australian Centre for International Agricultural Research in Laos. She was engaged as a United Nations (UN) gender expert by the Gender Division of the UN's Food and Agriculture Organization, studying gender and climate change in India. Most recently, she worked as a gender expert for the United Nations Environment Programme in Geneva, training field staff on gender-sensitive practice. She has published widely in the field of gender and climate change.

Lea Berrang-Ford is an Associate Professor in the Department of Geography at McGill University. Using spatial analyses and mixed methodologies, she researches the social and environmental determinants of global health and infectious disease, specifically investigating sleeping sickness in Uganda and climate change health impacts. She co-leads the international, interdisciplinary Indigenous Health Adaptation to Climate Change (IHACC) project, which investigates vulnerability and adaptation to the health effects of climate change among remote indigenous populations in the Canadian Arctic, Ugandan Impenetrable Forest, and Peruvian Amazon. She also launched the international

TRAC3: Tracking Research on Adaptation to Climate Change Consortium, and published an article pioneering systematic approaches for climate change adaptation tracking. She is co-editor of *Climate Change Adaptation in Developed Nations: From Theory to Practice* (2011), and she serves as a Canada Research Chair in Global Health and Environmental Change.

Shanondora Billiot (United Houma Nation) is an Assistant Professor at the University of Illinois. She earned her PhD in social work from Washington University in St. Louis and holds an MSW from the University of Michigan. Prior to entering a doctoral program, she had 10 years of experience working in the mental health field from the grassroots level to implementing and analyzing federal and international health and mental health policies. At the U.S. Departments of Veterans Affairs and of Health and Human Services, she analyzed programs that address health and mental health issues of veterans and victims of armed conflict. As an MSW student, she led a study in a small Ecuadorian parish to discover the incidence rates of persons living with disabilities who were exposed to volcanic ash. Her current research uses mixed methods to explore indigenous-specific sensitivities to global environmental change exposure and health outcomes among members of her tribal community currently located along the Gulf Coast of southeast Louisiana.

Ambrose Buyinza has a strong background and superior foundation in physical and spatial land use planning, geographical information systems (GIS), computer-aided design, and global positioning system skills. His undergraduate research focused on the implications of high-rise developments on the existing urban infrastructure (Jinja Municipality). He has worked with many organizations and national and local governments on a variety of projects specifically as a GIS specialist. He is currently undertaking his postgraduate research in seasonal variability of herbage biomass resources for grazers (cattle and sheep) in Karamoja subregion. His other fields of interest include disaster and risk management, risk assessment and analysis, advanced GIS, and architecture. He is part of the team building the information base at the UN HABITAT, Makerere University.

Cesar Carcamo is a Professor at the School of Public Health and Administration at Cayetano Heredia University. His research focuses on epidemiological methods, with emphasis on sexually transmitted diseases, global health, and health informatics. He is a co-investigator on the IHACC project. He has also consulted for numerous international organizations, including the World Health Organization and UNAIDS (the Joint United Nations Programme on HIV/AIDS), regarding sexually transmitted disease epidemiology and control.

Paul Chakalian is an environmental social science PhD student in Arizona State University's School of Human Evolution and Social Change. He studies how sociodemographic and economic indicators interact with exposure and sociopolitical structures to mediate health and well-being in complex hazardscapes. His dissertation research examines the causes of social vulnerability to environmental hazards with a focus on extreme heat and power failure in urban environments. He holds an MA in climate and society from Columbia University and has a BA in liberal arts with a concentration in sociology and philosophy from Evergreen State College.

April L. Colette is a geographer specializing in global environmental change and the political economy of the urban environment. Drawing on theories and methods from human geography, urban geography, cultural anthropology, political science, and urban studies, her research has focused on flood-related risk and vulnerability, climate change adaptation, and local politics in urban Argentina. Her work examines the following interlinked themes: vulnerability in the face of urban environmental change; historical perspectives on risk, hazards, and disasters; institutional and social practices around urban infrastructure; and the role of local actors in shaping local politics and practice. She is committed to conducting community-based research that aims to incorporate the community's goals for development while addressing the environmental challenges they face. Prior to receiving her PhD in geography from the University of Illinois at Urbana–Champaign, she completed her master's degree at the London School of Economics and Political Science and worked as an international development consultant on urban and environmental policy projects for the U.S. Agency for International Development, the Japan International Cooperation Agency, and the World Bank.

Ashlee Cunsolo is a researcher and environmental advocate, working with research and policy to make a difference in how we live with and in this world. As a community-engaged social science and health researcher working at the intersection of place, culture, health, and environment, she has a particular interest in the social, environmental, and cultural determinants of indigenous health; intercultural learning and dialogue; capacity development; environmental ethics; and the social justice implications of social, environmental, and health inequality. She works with indigenous communities and leaders throughout Canada on a variety of community-led and community-identified research initiatives. Before becoming Director of the Labrador Institute of Memorial University, she was the Canada Research Chair in Determinants of Healthy Communities and an associate professor in the Departments of Nursing and Indigenous Studies at Cape Breton University in Unama'ki/Cape Breton. In 2014, she released a documentary film collaboratively produced with the five Inuit communities in Nunatsiavut, Labrador, about the impacts of climate change on Inuit culture, livelihoods, and well-being.

Sarah Curtis is Professor Emeritus at Durham University, United Kingdom, where she previously held the position of Professor of Health and Risk, directing the interdisciplinary Institute of Hazard, Risk and Resilience. A specialist in health geography, she has led a range of research focusing on the social and physical environmental factors that are important for health inequality. She has worked collaboratively with a number of nonacademic agencies, making a significant contribution in various fields of health policy.

Juan Declet-Barreto is a geographer and a climate scientist at the Union of Concerned Scientists. His research maps, analyzes, and searches for solutions to the unequal human health and livelihood impacts of environmental hazards, particularly on communities affected by environmental injustices and other vulnerable populations on the front lines of climate change impacts. He has researched the historical–geographical, epidemiological, and microclimatological dimensions of extreme heat vulnerability and urban heat islands. He earned his PhD in environmental social sciences, master and bachelor of science degrees in geography, and an associate's degree in geographic information systems from Arizona State University.

Victoria L. Edge is a senior science advisor for the Public Health Agency of Canada and an adjunct professor in the Department of Population Medicine at the University of Guelph. Her research-related activities have focused on public health issues in northern Canadian communities. These activities have included efforts to enhance community health surveillance and investigate climate change health impacts related to infectious waterborne and foodborne illnesses. She is a co-investigator on the IHACC project. She is a Queen Elizabeth II Diamond Jubilee Medal winner (2012).

James D. Ford is an Associate Professor in the Department of Geography at McGill University, where he leads the Climate Change Adaptation Research Group. A leader in research on vulnerability and adaptation to climate change, he engages in a diversity of initiatives, including projects focusing on indigenous populations and climate change (with a major focus on the Arctic), developing adaptation plans with communities and industry, examining ways to create "usable" science, and developing novel approaches to tracking climate change adaptation at global and regional levels. He is a principal investigator on the IHACC project. He is editor-in-chief of the journal *Regional Environmental Change*, a board member at the Canadian Institutes of Health Research's Nasivvik Centre for Inuit Health, and Applied Public Health Chair with the Canadian Institutes of Health Research.

Sharon L. Harlan is a Professor in the Department of Health Sciences and the Department of Sociology & Anthropology at Northeastern University. Her research explores the human impacts of urban climate change that are dependent on people's positions in social hierarchies, places in built environments of unequal quality, and policies that improve or impede human adaptive capabilities. She is currently engaged in multi-university, collaborative, and comparative projects on excessive heat and water problems as significant and increasingly critical threats to human health and well-being in cities. She was previously a professor of sociology at Arizona State University, and she received her PhD from Cornell University.

Sherilee L. Harper is an Associate Professor in the School of Public Health at the University of Alberta. Her research investigates associations among weather, environments, and indigenous peoples' health in the context of climate change. She collaborates with indigenous partners to prioritize climate-related health actions, planning, interventions, and research. She is a principal investigator on the IHACC project. She is also a co-investigator on the Indigenous Peoples Adapting to the Health Effects of Climate Change project, which works with indigenous communities and knowledge users in the Canadian Arctic.

David M. Hondula is an Assistant Professor of Climatology and Atmospheric Science in the School of Geographical Sciences and Urban Planning at Arizona State University. His research interests include natural hazards, urban climate, climate change, and heat exposure. At Arizona State University, he is a senior sustainability scientist and holds affiliations with the Urban Climate Research Center as well as the Center for Policy Informatics. He is also a volunteer faculty affiliate of the Maricopa County Department of Public Health. He received his PhD in 2013 from the Department of Environmental Sciences at the University of Virginia.

G. Darrel Jenerette is a Professor of Landscape Ecology in the Department of Botany and Plant Sciences and Director of the Center for Conservation Biology at the University of California, Riverside. He has studied social segregation of urban ecosystem services throughout the southwestern United States. This work increasingly is directed to evaluating the health consequences of increasing heat and the role of vegetation for reducing heat stress. He received his PhD in 2004 from the Department of Plant Biology at Arizona State University.

Alejandro Llanos is a physician and specialist in infectious and tropical medicine, with emphasis in vector-borne diseases such as leishmaniasis and malaria. He is the founder and former dean of the School of Public Health at Cayetano Heredia University and also founded and led a malaria control program in Andean countries. The program was recognized by the Pan American Health Organization in 2009 as the best malaria control intervention. He is a principal investigator on the IHACC project. His research specifically focuses on the parasitological epidemiology, environmental and social determinants, prevention, and control of vector-borne diseases in Andean countries, especially in rural communities.

Shuaib Lwasa is an Associate Professor in the Department of Geography, GeoInformatics, and Climatic Sciences at Makerere University. He has more than 15 years of experience in university teaching and research working on interdisciplinary projects. Recent works are in the fields of climate change mitigation, climate change and health, adaptation of cities to climate change, urban environmental management, spatial planning, disaster risk reduction, climate change vulnerability, and urban sustainability with links to livelihood systems. He has published on topics of cities and adaptation to climate change, health impacts of climate change, drought, flooding risk, land and property rights, land use and landscape ecology, resource efficiency, and spatial planning for sustainability. He coordinates the Habitat University Climate Change and Disaster Hub at the Department of Geography. He also serves on the science steering committees of Integrated Research on Disaster Risk and the Urbanization and Global Environmental Change project. He is a lead author of the *Fifth Assessment Report of the Intergovernmental Panel on Climate Change* (2014).

Benon Nabaasa is an outgoing MA Geography student at Makerere University. He graduated with a Bachelor's of Science in Conservation Forestry and Products Technology with a first class honors. He has a strong background and good grounding in natural resources, specifically forest and rangeland resources. His undergraduate research findings on the role of wood fuel in climate change mitigation in rural and urban areas in Uganda were published as a conference proceeding at the Tharandt "Welcome to Africa Workshop" in Germany. He worked with BRACED MercyCorps Uganda as a field supervisor during the BRACED Baseline Survey in Karamoja. In his MA thesis, he explores the patterns and dynamics of browse forage in the drought-stricken Karamoja subregion of Uganda, the nature and dynamics of grazing lands in pastoral communities, and risk assessment and analysis of communities to climate extremes and shocks. His fundamental interests include permaculture, ecology of natural forests, and biodiversity of cities.

Didacus B. Namanya is a geographer at the Ugandan Ministry of Health. In this capacity, he gathers and analyzes information regarding population distributions, economic activities, disease distributions, and health infrastructure. He also offers part-time lectures in geographic information science to students of public health at Makerere University Institute of Public Health and Uganda Martyrs University Nkozi. He is a co-researcher on the IHACC project. He was also a co-researcher in a consortium that conducted a study on health, environmental change, and adaptive capacity related to water- and vector-borne diseases in eastern Africa. He serves as a member of several policy-related committees, including the Uganda Foodborne Disease Burden Epidemiology Reference Group, the National Climate Change Policy Committee, and the National Adaptation Programmes of Action.

Katie Oven is a research associate with leading responsibility for work packages in major research projects at the Universities of Durham and Hull in the United Kingdom. A geographer working at the interface between physical and social science, her interests include disasters and development in the Global South, particularly the social production of vulnerability and resilience to natural hazards. She is engaged in applied research and works closely with a number of government and nongovernment partners within the United Kingdom and internationally.

Rita Padawangi is a senior lecturer at the Singapore University of Social Sciences. She received her PhD in sociology from Loyola University Chicago, where she was also a Fulbright Scholar for her master of arts studies. She holds a Bachelor of Architecture degree from the Parahyangan Catholic University. Her research interests include the sociology of architecture and participatory urban development. She is a member of the collaborative research group Governing Compound Disasters in Urbanizing Asia at ARI-NUS, focusing on the relationship between urban development and disasters in cities and metropolitan areas of Jakarta, Surabaya, and Metro Manila.

Jessica Parfait, of the United Houma Nation, is working toward her master's in anthropology at Louisiana State University, where she also earned a bachelor's of arts degree in anthropology. She is currently working as an archivist for United Houma Nation. Having created her tribe's first digitized system, she ensured many cultural items and critical documents are safe. Archival research also influenced her interest in environmental racism and its history in coastal Louisiana. Her thesis will evaluate the effects of multiple forced migrations on the culture of her tribe. Having lived in Louisiana all her life, witnessing the effects of multiple hurricanes, Jessica will focus her thesis on a holistic approach to evaluate the issues tribal people face.

Bernadette P. Resurrección is a senior research fellow at the Stockholm Environment Institute (SEI) and Adjunct Associate Professor of Gender and Development at the Asian Institute of Technology, Thailand. SEI is an international research institute committed to bridging research with policy. For many years, she has researched gender, environment, and development. She has participated in efforts ranging from field-based studies to critical policy analyses. Her work has focused specifically on themes such as livelihoods, disasters, and climate change in peri-urban areas; migration and displacement; and water governance in river basins. She co-leads the global Gender and Social Equity Programme of SEI and is exploring ways in which gender and development practices can address complex and grounded realities that feminist political ecology research can richly capture. Her current research is on gender professionals in environment and development organizations. She completed her doctoral and master's degrees in development studies at the International Institute of Social Studies of Erasmus University in The Hague.

Michael Sherraden is the George Warren Brown Distinguished University Professor and founding director of the Center for Social Development at Washington University in St. Louis. He is a leading scholar in asset building, with authored or edited books including *Assets and the Poor* (1991), *Inclusion in the American Dream* (2005), *Can the Poor Save?* (2007), *Asset Building and Low-Income Families* (2008), and *Asset-Building Policies and Innovations in Asia* (2014). He is also engaged in research on civic service and engagement, with books including *National Service* (1982), *The Moral Equivalent of War* (1990), *Productive Aging* (2001), and *Civic Service Worldwide* (2007). His research focuses on testing social innovations, with impacts on policy in the United States and many other countries. In 2010, *Time* magazine named him among the 100 most influential people in the world. He is a fellow in the American Academy of Social Work & Social Welfare and serves as co-chair of the Grand Challenges for Social Work Steering Committee.

Jonathan Wistow is a lecturer in the School of Applied Social Sciences at Durham University, United Kingdom. His interest in health inequalities centers on the implications of both methodological and ideological framings for how such inequalities are understood and addressed. His research in this area focuses on the application of both complexity theory and qualitative comparative analysis to health inequalities and links to broader debates about governance and public policy implementation.

PART I

Introduction and Overview

1

Climate Change, Social Justice

MAKING THE CASE FOR COMMUNITY INCLUSION

Lisa Reyes Mason and Jonathan Rigg

CLIMATE CHANGE IS a physical process but also a profoundly social and political challenge. It is a global issue that affects the distribution of rights, resources, and opportunities that people need to live healthy, productive, and meaningful lives.

When it comes to climate change, there are social justice issues around every corner. People who have contributed the least to climate change—indigenous groups, people in poverty, and children, to name a few—already suffer the worst consequences. Questions such as who is required to adapt, what is their adaptive capacity, who is compensated, and to what degree are questions of justice. Also, there is the question of who bears responsibility and how the burden should be shared internationally and within nations.

This book pays particular attention to the social justice dimensions of climate change. Its main purpose is to look closely at the lived experiences of people, the inequities that some groups experience more than others, the underlying reasons why, and the policy changes that should be pursued. To do this, we draw on a geographically diverse set of community-based examples that examine wider debates about vulnerability and adaptation to climate change. Throughout, we take climate change out of the realms of the physical and technical (or to some, the "natural") to ask a series of "why" questions. Our responses to these questions are far less clear-cut and require us to think socially and politically and, therefore, to make social and political judgments about the processes we are seeking to understand.

3

Rather than focusing on the rate of climate change, how it manifests in physical terms, and the distribution and costs of those physical changes, we focus instead on how climate change comes to rest, so to speak, in people's lives and why it comes to rest in the ways that it does. Of utmost importance, we also ask what can be done about the unequal consequences of climate change through transformation of social institutions and arrangements—guided by values that prioritize the experience of affected groups and the inclusion of diverse voices and communities in the policy process.

In this chapter, we make the case for our focus on community inclusion by first grounding the work in social justice principles. We then describe five intersecting dimensions of "climate reductionism" that must be addressed to articulate why climate change must be contextualized and understood through the lens of local social, economic, and political contexts. Next, we discuss vulnerability and how it is often reproduced through market-oriented policies that overlook the needs of the most vulnerable. Finally, we highlight the guiding questions and organization of the book's chapters, and we conclude with a call to address the "wicked problem" of climate change in partnership with communities and in ways that value local expertise in policy pursuits.

CONCEPTUALIZING SOCIAL JUSTICE

What do we mean by "social justice"? There is no single definition of the term, and it is often interpreted and used in different ways. At its most basic level, social justice is a philosophical construct "used to determine what mutual obligations flow between the individual and society" (Almgren, 2018, p. 1). Different theories or perspectives of social justice—such as libertarianism, utilitarianism, Rawlsian, and a capabilities approach—can reach different conclusions of what these mutual obligations should be and how they should be structured (Almgren, 2018; Lowery, 2007).

In this book, we are primarily concerned with a social justice ideal of equal and fair access to rights, resources, and opportunities that reduce people's vulnerability—in part by increasing their capacity to adapt—to the consequences of climate change, with an emphasis on historically and currently marginalized groups. This view is most in line with an egalitarian approach that includes elements of Rawlsian (or "justice as fairness") and capabilities (Sen, 2005) thinking in how obligations between individuals and society should be constructed (Johnson, Penning-Rowsell, & Parker, 2007; Thaler & Hartmann, 2016). Central to this book, and like other scholarship at the nexus of environment and justice (e.g., Schlosberg & Carruthers, 2010, p. 17), is our focus on "justice for communities," not just for individuals alone.

Two underlying principles—or types of social justice—that thread through this book are *distributive justice* (e.g., the distribution of environmental goods or of the social and economic capital needed to adapt to a changing environment) and *procedural justice* (e.g., the process of decision-making about distribution and the inclusion or exclusion of groups in that process). From Phoenix, Arizona in the United States (Chapter 2) to Candioti Sur in Santa Fe, Argentina (Chapter 5), we see how historical patterns of social, economic, and political marginalization have contributed to today's unequal access to safety and security in a changing environment. Indeed, many chapters in this book carry a theme of how groups with lower socioeconomic standing are segregated, with their lands and communities becoming "sacrifice zones" at the hands of policies that prioritize other social groups.

Procedurally, we find examples as different as planned relocation of United Houma Nation tribal members in the United States (Chapter 6) to large-scale economic development in Indonesia (Chapter 7) that fail to involve local residents in the relocation or land reclamation decision-making process, in some cases literally taking land away from under people's feet. We cannot emphasize enough how central this theme of participation—of community engagement and inclusion—is to this book as a whole; in other words, how important we view the pursuit of procedural justice in an effort to secure distributive justice as communities throughout the world grapple with the consequences of climate change.

Key concepts from the *capabilities approach* (e.g., capacities to live self-determined lives of meaning and value) are another thread in this book—and ones that are still underapplied in climate scholarship (Schlosberg, Collins, & Niemeyer, 2017). If we are sincere in our approach to community inclusion and valuing local experience and expertise, then we must begin where our community members are—steeped in their own visions of what a healthy, productive, and meaningful life would look like—and with the awareness that climate or environmental change may be just one of many influences on realizing those visions.

CONTEXTUALIZING CLIMATE CHANGE

The chapters that follow dive deeply into community experiences of climate change and its consequences in diverse global settings. Though present conditions and inequities within and between communities are described, the historical, spatial, temporal, and political drivers of these inequities must be understood to understand the "why" of vulnerability and to identify appropriate policies (Ribot, 2010). In other words, what are the root causes of vulnerability for individuals and social groups, how do these shape adaptive capacity and adaptation pathways, and what does this mean in terms of policy response (Agrawal, Lemos, Orlove, & Ribot, 2012, p. 319)?

Five Dimensions of Climate Reductionism

Illuminating these questions is, as we see it, a key challenge for scholars in the social sciences and for policymakers. The difficulty in moving such questions forward is in many ways a product of five intersecting dimensions of *climate reductionism*. This term was coined by Mike Hulme (2011b) to refer to the extraction of climate from "the matrix of interdependencies that shape human life within the physical world" (p. 247). We use it here as a springboard to think about a broader set of reductionisms in climate change science. These all arise from the absence or marginalization of the social sciences and humanities (Table 1.1). Each privileges a certain way of thinking about or approaching climate change, which has the effect of narrowing the scope of view and possibilities for action. This book is a deliberate effort to "un-narrow" the debate and widen the lens of how climate change and its consequences are understood, discussed, and addressed.

First, there is a degree of *disciplinary* climate reductionism. As Dispesh Chakrabarty (2009) writes, the "crisis of climate change calls on academics to rise above their disciplinary prejudices, for it is a crisis of many dimensions" (p. 215). Scholars from all quarters need to engage in climate change research because the questions and challenges it raises are at once political, moral, socioeconomic, cultural, psychological, and historical—as well as scientific and technical (Agrawal et al., 2012, p. 330). Though the humanities and social sciences have engaged with climate change, and are doing so increasingly, it is the predictive natural sciences that still largely set the terms of the debate (Malm & Hornborg, 2014, p. 63). This has tended to lead to global approaches to climate change with "indexes" of vulnerability, an emphasis on "data" collected through quantitative scientific methods, standardized and linear policy prescriptions, and toolboxes of transferable technologies, all underpinned by a faith in market forces, human ingenuity, and techno-managerial solutions (Tanner & Allouche, 2011). Why is the need to broaden the debate from the positivist (i.e., the natural sciences) to the interpretative (i.e., the social sciences and humanities) disciplines, or to collaborate among them, so important? Because such positivist assessments, which have dominated not least the work of the Intergovernmental Panel on Climate Change, "determine the framing of what exactly is the climate change 'problem' that needs to be 'solved,' and they set the tone for the human imaginative engagement with climate change" (Hulme, 2011a, p. 177). Scientific knowledge is both partial and political. Issues are framed in particular ways, and evidence takes a certain form, is collected using approved protocols and methodologies, and is given intellectual gravitas through accepted framings.

In 2002, Paul Crutzen—who 2 years earlier with Eugene Stoermer coined the term the *Anthropocene* (Crutzen & Stoermer, 2000) to describe and demarcate a new geological era in which the human imprint on the earth is evident in the geological record—argued that "a daunting task lies ahead for scientists and engineers to guide society towards environmentally sustainable management during the era of the Anthropocene," going on to suggest that "this will require appropriate human behaviour at all scales, and may well involve internationally accepted, large-scale geo-engineering projects, for instance to 'optimize' climate" (Crutzen, 2002, p. 23). This process of rendering technical (Li, 2011), or the tendency to reduce complex problems and frame solutions so that they are amenable to technical fixes, has been noted previously in other fields, including the science and

TABLE 1.1

Five Climate Reductionisms

Reductionism	Privileging	Narrowing effect	Sample "un-narrowing" contributions of this book
Disciplinary	Privileging of natural or predictive disciplines over the interpretative disciplines in the social sciences and humanities	Value given to hard data and statistical methods, modeling, and approaches that "render technical" climate change	Social science or interdisciplinary inquiry with diverse methods and "ways of knowing" (Chapters 2–10).
Participatory	Privileging of expert knowledge over "everyday" people's local and indigenous knowledge	Treatment of people as objects for top-down policy intervention; marginalization of communities, community action, and participation	Importance of valuing expertise of older adults (Chapter 4), women (Chapters 3 and 9), and indigenous groups (Chapter 10).
Experiential	Privileging climate change over other threats, risks, and vulnerabilities in people's lives	Failure to view climate change in a hierarchy of risk with the result that people's everyday risks or concerns are shaded from view	When people's priorities are brought into view, it becomes evident that these may differ from researchers' or planners' priorities (Chapters 2 and 7).
Teleological	Privileging of a singular future based on climate modeling, with prescriptive transition pathways	Limiting of alternative futures; climate change becomes the new environmental determinism; policies are shaped to fit with this singular vision	Policies shaped by deterministic model-based assumptions have led to maladaptation among some Ugandan groups (Chapter 8).
Species	Privileging of an undifferentiated humanity, equally susceptible to the effects of climate change, over a differentiated humanity with levels of varying vulnerability	Tendency to view climate change as a global process with indiscriminate effects	Detailed description and understanding of how climate change impacts different groups, in different ways (Chapters 2–10).

social science of disasters (O'Keefe, Westgate, & Wisner, 1976; Wisner et al., 2004) and soil erosion (Blaikie, 1985). In each instance, the root causes—whether of "natural" disasters, soil erosion, or climate change—are overlooked, with the result that the field of view is narrowed and, in the process, so are the solutions.

The second dimension, *participatory* climate reductionism, follows closely from disciplinary reductionism and the rendering technical argument—namely that climate change is for experts. Let us be clear: This is not to disparage experts and expert (i.e., scientific) knowledge. Rather, it is to note how people's knowledge and science, and the participation of laypeople, are marginalized to become objects for intervention. Thus, we see in some of the literature a set of linked, and to our mind problematic, propositions: that the application of science is the answer; that experts (i.e., scientists and engineers) can and should lead this effort and are best equipped to do so; and that all this can be done *to* people, who become grateful targets for and recipients of such interventions. This marginalizes or rules out most community knowledge, experience, and action, sometimes because it is devalued and sometimes because it never enters the frame of valuation in the first place. This might include, for example, non-capitalist subsistence and other alternative practices. As a result, assessments of "adaptive capacity" are structured and measured according to set criteria, leading to the characterization of certain individuals and groups as of "low adaptive capacity."

Such omission or marginalization of alternative actors and knowledge(s) is both normatively (Few, Brown, & Tompkins, 2007) and practically (Shaw et al., 2009; Stringer, Scrieciu, & Reed, 2009; Wachsmuth, 2015) problematic. Participatory approaches often reveal that the priorities and concerns that researchers assume are important, and on which policies are then based, do not reflect people's felt needs and priorities. Simply stated, for many of the world's poor, who are just "one illness away from poverty" (Krishna, 2010), climate change is not at the top of their lists of concerns. We term this *experiential* climate reductionism: the tendency to shade from view the wider lived and everyday context within which people experience climate change. Communities, groups, and individuals face myriad challenges to their livelihoods and well-being—and have always done so. The challenge of climate change may be new in terms of its global footprint, but it is not necessarily different. Take, for instance, R. H. Tawney's (1932) reflections on China in the early 1930s: "There are districts [in China] in which the position of the rural population is that of a man standing permanently up to the neck in water, so that even a ripple is sufficient to drown him" (p. 77). For many vulnerable societies and peoples, then, climate change may still be a ripple in the choppy waters they have always had to navigate to survive in the face of a capricious environment, an unequal society, a volatile economy, or an overbearing or inefficient state. When we start to ask questions at the personal and local levels, it quickly becomes clear that in many instances climate change is a second-, third-, or even fourth-order issue for people from historically marginalized groups. When climate change comes to rest in communities' and people's lives, any solution needs to be about much more than "just" climate change.

The fourth dimension has been notably explored by Mike Hulme (2011b) and is termed here *teleological* climate reductionism. This pays attention to the way in which climate change science creates a unilinear pathway, with a defined telos (i.e., outcome or end), that limits our ability to think about and map out alternative futures: "The openness, contingency, and multiple possibilities of the future are closed off as these predicted virtual climates assert their influence over everything from future ecology, economic activity, and social mobility to human behavior, cultural evolution, and geosecurity" (Hulme, 2011b, p. 249; see also Barnes et al., 2013). Climate reductionism of this type becomes the new environmental determinism. It is used as a predictor for mass species extinctions, global conflict, famine, massive flows of climate refugees, and more. In so doing, it leaves little room for imagining—and pursuing—alternative futures.

Finally, the fifth dimension is *species* climate reductionism: the notion that climate change is a global challenge affecting all of humanity equally, and humans particularly (not the rest of the living world). Tacitly, the assumption is that we can view humans in the singular when it comes to climate change (Chakrabarty, 2012, p. 2; Moore, 2016, p. 82). Of course, this is true at one level: We all live with the specter of climate change. But it is also clear that it does not, and will not, affect everyone to the same degree. Humanity's future is not undifferentiated, except insofar as we will all be inhabiting a changed planet. This is why Chakrabarty's (2009) claim that "unlike in the crises of capitalism, there are no lifeboats here for the rich and the privileged (witness the drought in Australia or recent fires in the wealthy neighborhoods of California)" (p. 221) was critiqued so vehemently because it "blatantly overlooks the realities of differentiated vulnerability on all scales of human society" (Malm & Hornborg, 2014, p. 66). Climate change exaggerates that which already exists, and therefore there is a need to view climate change not only operating in an already highly unequal and differentiated world but also, in all likelihood, accentuating those inequalities and inequities. Climate change discriminates, and it is the usual suspects who suffer most—for example, poor people and poor countries, women (Arora-Jonsson & Sveriges, 2011; Djoudi et al., 2016), the old and young (Carter et al., 2016), and minorities and indigenous groups (Wildcat, 2013).

Repositioning Climate Change

Given the elisions that arise from the five intersecting forms of climate reductionism, efforts to understand and address vulnerability and enable socially just climate change adaptation depend crucially on a full understanding and appreciation of the societies and social contexts in which such efforts are being made (Barnes et al., 2013, p. 541). This demands comparison to illuminate difference, rather than aggregation to arrive at generalization. Decades of failure with top-down efforts to promote new technologies or engender change in directions that experts and policymakers deem to be desirable make it clear that local people must be involved, from beginning to end. Of course, there have been trenchant critiques of the participatory approach in international development—the "tyranny of participation," as it has been termed (Cooke & Kothari, 2001)—but this does not negate the broader point that local, everyday people must normatively be part of such efforts (for reasons of procedural justice), and practically too, because without their involvement such efforts will, in all likelihood, fail (and thus not address distributive justice).

These tendencies highlight that climate change, though not disputed in the sense that anthropogenic climate change is very broadly accepted, nonetheless remains highly contested. This extends from how it is assessed, how we come to see and interpret its effects, and what actions are taken (or, equally important, *not* taken). When climate change affects people, as it surely does, then it stops being (just) a physical process amenable to measurement and interpretation by the positivist disciplines or natural sciences, and addressed or neatly solved through technological action, and becomes social and political, and therefore a matter of rights and justice. This repositioning of climate change does not devalue the importance of understanding the process and its consequences; rather, it resituates and places climate change within a nexus of other competing processes, impediments, and opportunities—that is, the fuller context of people's lives that we must understand if we are to engage in participatory planning, social change, and institutional transformation.

Re-placing climate change in this manner leads to a reframing of the questions posed. Thus, rather than asking, "Who is exposed to the effects of climate change?" we might instead more provocatively ask, "Why do people find themselves marginalized or exposed to climate change in the first place?" Just as critical scholars of "natural" disasters have sought to understand the reasons that lead people to build their homes on hillsides exposed to landslides, even when they appreciate the risks of so doing, likewise critical scholars of climate change seek to understand how broader conditions of vulnerability are produced and reproduced.

VULNERABILITY, PRECARITY, AND LIBERAL RESILIENCE

Reframing questions about climate change requires that we ask about the production and reproduction of vulnerability and reflect on how the making of vulnerability has traditionally been conceptualized. Often, the same policies that have provided prosperity for some groups have increased vulnerability, or produced precarity, for others.

Like defining social justice, though, what do we mean by "vulnerability"? In the broadest sense, vulnerability is the potential to suffer harm, experience loss, or be "wounded by the world" (Turner, 2006, p. 28). In climate change discourse, vulnerability refers more specifically to the likelihood of experiencing harm from exposure to socioenvironmental stress and from insufficient capacity to adapt to change (Adger, 2006). Discussion of social vulnerability to the consequences of climate change emphasizes the structural or systemic reasons for which exposure is higher, and adaptive capacity lower, for some groups of people more so than others (Ribot, 2010).

Often, vulnerability is viewed as an inheritance of the past. People are vulnerable because of a set of preexisting conditions, whether physical (e.g., isolation), social (e.g., gender inequalities), environmental (e.g., unimproved soils), technological (e.g., traditional seeds), or economic (e.g., lack of credit). Groups often characterized as highly vulnerable include women, children and youth, older adults, racial and ethnic minorities, indigenous peoples, and people in poverty. In this book, we find detailed descriptions of such vulnerability—from women in Southeast Asia and Australia (Chapters 3 and 9) to older adults in England (Chapter 4) and minority groups in Uganda (Chapter 8), with each case steeped in descriptions of how people experience the impacts of climate change or how historic and current social institutions and arrangements have influenced and produced such vulnerability.

To reduce vulnerability and promote resilience, mainstream approaches rely heavily on market integration and economic diversification to draw people and societies into the mainstream, decrease deficiencies, and increase material prosperity. Rigg and Oven (2015) term this the discourse of *liberal resilience*. What this mainstream approach tends to gloss over, however, is the extent to which market integration has mixed vulnerability effects. Certainly, it tends to generate economic growth and therefore reduce absolute income poverty, in aggregate terms. But it also creates new articulations of vulnerability. One way of distinguishing between inherited and produced vulnerability is to term the latter *precarity*. Late capitalism produces conditions of precarity, even while it might reduce vulnerability, complicating our understanding of how to address the inequitable consequences of climate change.

This means that we need to be careful in assuming that policies that generate economic growth will also raise adaptive capacity and, in the process, make people less vulnerable and more resilient to climate change, and much else besides. The evidence is that market-based economic expansion eases some aspects of vulnerability but accentuates and produces other vulnerabilities (i.e., precarity). For instance, when subsistence farmers lose their land to corporations or the state through processes of "land grabbing")—well documented across Asia, Africa, and Latin America (see, for example, numerous papers in the *Journal of Peasant Studies*)—this may very well contribute to raising aggregate economic production or gross domestic product but likely renders those displaced farmers yet more vulnerable.

The essential question is why some groups have the necessity to adapt to climate change thrust upon them. This is partly about wealth; however, it is mainly about power and, therefore, about injustice. There is a need to examine more closely community experiences with mainstream policies—whether they truly address vulnerability or whether they instead generate new forms of precarity. The growing interest in community economies that, hitherto, have been hidden points to an alternative way of looking and valuing (Gibson, Hill, & Law, 2018). As Anna Tsing (2015) writes, "There is a rift between what experts tell us about economic growth on the one hand, and stories about life and livelihood on the other" (p. 132), and this has a bearing on how we view, think about, and address matters connected to climate change.

GUIDING QUESTIONS AND ORGANIZATION OF THE BOOK

The chapters that follow, in their different ways, address and challenge aspects of the five climate reductionisms outlined in this introductory chapter. The chapters are valuable in three notable respects. First, they are disciplinarily diverse and are authored by scholars from both the "Global North" and the "Global South" and First Nations peoples. Second, they detail the risks of climate change reductionism through their deep inquiry into the local social, political, and environmental contexts that shape the consequences of climate change and the temporal and spatial scales that they cover. Third, and more practically, they detail potential social policy responses that point the way toward solutions that are equitable and inclusive. Guiding questions for each chapter include the following:

1. What is the local social, economic, political, and environmental context in which the case is situated?
2. Who is vulnerable to the processes and events discussed?
3. Why are these groups and individuals vulnerable or exposed?
4. What does this mean for social or climate justice, whether local, national, or global?
5. How are people, communities, and organizations adapting, and how effective are these adaptations? What novel or innovative adaptations are evident?
6. What policy interventions and "solutions" present themselves, and at what scales? Who are the critical actors in devising and implementing these solutions?

The main chapters of the book are divided into three parts titled "Weather," "Land," and "Comparisons." As will be evident to those who read chapters across these parts, however, the contributions raise concerns and debates that cross-cut between each. The sectional divides merely highlight the entry points for discussion: weather extremes in Part II; questions of land access and dispossession in Part III; and comparison, whether between countries or communities, in Part IV.

Part II describes vulnerability and adaptation to extreme weather—heat waves, dry spells, extreme rainfall, and cold weather—in detailed case studies from developed and developing countries. Sharon Harlan and her co-authors (Chapter 2) examine extreme heat and water scarcity in Phoenix, Arizona, the so-styled "hottest city" in the United States. With a public health perspective, they link social vulnerabilities to individual and community capacity to adapt, while tracing the historical development of vulnerability via political ecology, shedding light on the legacies of environmental injustice in the metropolitan Phoenix area. They argue, persuasively and in detail, that residential—in other words, spatial—patterns of vulnerability to climate change have a lineage that can be traced historically. Their chapter speaks directly to the general point that climate change exaggerates the inequalities that already exist, with a legacy of poverty and environmental degradation spatially manifested that makes these neighborhoods and their residents vulnerable to extreme heat. A second theme is the way that even grassroots activists view climate change (and extreme heat) as a second-order problem to the many other priorities they face. Public health and pro-poor adaptation pathways are described, and the authors call for policy change that explicitly values equity and justice for the most vulnerable, while exposing the "roadblocks" to pro-poor adaptation pathways.

Bernadette Resurrección (Chapter 3) draws on fieldwork in the Philippines, Vietnam, and Thailand to critically examine gendered vulnerability to water insecurity with a feminist political ecology lens. Public policies and decisions that commodify water (Philippines), allow pollution of drinking water (Vietnam), or sacrifice some communities to save others (Thailand) are critiqued and illuminated through the lived experiences of women, with implications for how climate adaptation policy should transform structural power relations in society. This chapter shows how "natural" events, when examined in detail, are found to be profoundly "non-natural"—"entwined," as Resurrección puts it, "with deliberate political–economic decisions." The chapter also convincingly grounds the point made in this introductory chapter that the richer and more powerful can often insulate themselves from the effects of climate change, whether through deploying their wealth (in the case of Vietnam) or their power (in the case of Thailand). It is not just that some people are wealthier than others; they, and their activities, are also often valued more highly so that they are protected (from floods) while others are sacrificed. Resurrección ends her chapter by arguing that from "this study of women's lives, it is apparent that vulnerabilities are complex, contingent, and embedded in structural, embodied, and emotional everyday experiences that require hybrid and nuanced solutions."

Katie Oven, Jonathan Wistow, and Sarah Curtis (Chapter 4) focus on older adults in England, using complexity theory to analyze adequacy of the health and social care sectors to protect this population during extreme weather events. Though older adults have unique vulnerabilities to climate change, they also have sources of strength and resilience, which can inform public policy planning in these sectors. The chapter demonstrates the need to view climate change operating against a dynamic sociodemographic context, namely an aging population. The authors also argue strongly in favor of drawing on local knowledge and actors when planning for enhanced resilience to extreme weather. Even in high-income countries, then, failures emerge when local knowledge is overlooked and local actors are ignored.

Part III examines climate-related change in land use and related policy choices that governments make and the efforts of communities to reimagine their futures within environmental and policy constraints. April Colette (Chapter 5) uses rich archival and ethnographic methods to critically examine flooding and infrastructure planning in Santa Fe, Argentina. She argues that flood risk is unevenly distributed due to discourse that normalizes risk for marginalized groups and policy choices that intentionally sacrifice the land, homes, and well-being of some groups for the benefit of others. She is interested in the "nitty-gritty" of risk—not just the materiality of risk, but its discursive character too. Her subjects have become inured to risk; it has become normalized—something that arises from their personal decisions rather than government action and inaction, thus shifting responsibility and hiding the historical injustices that explain risk exposure. Higher ground was reserved for the rich and middle classes, whereas the lower classes were made to live on riskier lower ground. Echoing Resurrección (Chapter 3), this historical inheritance is maintained through the elite's economic resources and political connections. "Sacrifice zones" exist in Santa Fe, just as they do in Bangkok's periphery. That this does not lead to greater anger is because risk and flooding, as the former Mayor told Colette, is "culturally accepted." This generates a false consciousness about Sante Fe's risk environment. The chapter also speaks directly to the general point that the risk reduction paradigm focuses on technological fixes to physical problems that "occlude social and political causality," as Colette states. They are rendered technical.

Shanondora Billiot and Jessica Parfait (Chapter 6) confront the planned and forced relocation of United Houma Nation (UHN) tribal members from their own lands in coastal Louisiana. The authors highlight the place attachment of indigenous peoples such as the UHN and how the environment suffuses their traditions and cultures, as well as their livelihoods. A government policy pursued without consensus from tribal members, the plan re-inflicts the historical trauma of indigenous peoples in the United States. In response, some tribal members have informally organized and used their influence, but they have tended to avoid using more formal channels of power and communication. A particular challenge in this case is a lack of federal recognition of the tribe's sovereignty. The authors conclude with policy comparisons of what tribes with and without federal recognition can do to protect their members, their lands, and their ways of living in the face of a changing climate.

Rita Padawangi (Chapter 7) confronts the nexus of sea level rise, land reclamation, and economic development in two Indonesian settings, Jakarta and Bali. She describes how social justice has been sidelined by developers' pursuit of profit and how some communities have organized in resistance and pursued legal recourse to protect their livelihoods and land. For Padawangi, disaster justice and climate justice need to be set in the wider context of urban development justice. Any attempts at solution, she argues, that ignore this wider field will likely perpetuate, rather than ameliorate, such injustices. Like Colette (Chapter 5), Padawangi refers to normalization tendencies, but in this instance in relation to the cost of economic growth, so often viewed as a "price to be paid": "Social injustices are normalized as the requirement of progress through urban development." What is striking in her chapter is the manner in which environmental threats, partially created by development processes, are harnessed as opportunities for further development and justified as such. Here, the notion that the poor are used to floods is also taken one step further, and the poor become the cause of floods. Victims become acculturated to floods and then redrawn as the cause of flooding. The solution to these shifting sands of injustice, for Padawangi, is action research and a social movement against land reclamation.

Part IV takes an explicitly comparative approach, examining similar climate phenomena in different community contexts as well as across regions and levels of development. Shuaib Lwasa and his co-authors (Chapter 8) compare historical and contemporary resilience among two social groups in Uganda: Karamojong pastoralists and Batwa forest pygmies. Government policies have compromised the traditional livelihoods of both groups, undermining food security in particular, by promoting sedentary cropping to pastoralists despite water scarcity in the region and by the forced relocation of forest pygmies away from their traditional sources of food. Lwasa and colleagues argue that the indigenous, local knowledge of these groups—built up over long histories of living with and adapting to environmental change—has been ignored. As a result, government policies that are justified as adaptation measures to support food security have, in fact, led to maladaptation with worse social outcomes, furthering injustices and deepening inequities. "Development" in Uganda is viewed by both the agencies of the state and most nongovernmental organizations in terms of a prescriptive transition path that all communities are expected to follow and according to which policies are molded. Alternatives adaptation pathways do not sit easily in this vision.

Margaret Alston (Chapter 9) compares gender and water insecurity in Australia and Bangladesh, two markedly different countries. She identifies several ways in which climate impacts and adaptations are gendered in both settings, with women often experiencing harmful outcomes that are largely invisible to broader society due to patriarchal norms and power relations. Like Oven, Wistow, and Curtis (Chapter 4), Alston argues that local knowledge must not be overlooked—in this case, gendered knowledge in particular. Her work challenges the technical- and expert-driven dimension of climate reductionism by emphasizing the need for women to have greater access to water policy decision-making. Alston's chapter also extends the neoliberal critique in this introduction and other chapters, demonstrating how market-oriented policies set in consultation with technical experts, in many cases, have rendered women's lives more vulnerable—precarious, even—by overlooking how their workloads and burdens are exacerbated by water problems and top-down policy solutions. Her recommendations include cultural challenge of patriarchal norms, more inclusive and participatory decision-making at all scales of governance, and policy change in the many social areas that climate change affects—from health and education to child care and transportation.

Sherilee Harper and co-authors (Chapter 10) examine the climate, health, and food security nexus among three different groups of indigenous peoples: the Inuit in Arctic Canada, the Batwa in Uganda (examined through another lens by Lwasa and colleagues in Chapter 9), and the Shawi in the Peruvian Amazon. The authors prioritize community participation in all phases of research and argue that much more value should be placed on indigenous knowledge and practices in adaptation policymaking. Though we need to be careful not to view past experience as a simple analogue for the future, Harper and colleagues argue that such knowledge and practice have played a critical role in securing food security to date, will continue to be important, and therefore their erosion should be a source of concern. "Indigenous knowledge, values, and practices," they say, "must be at the heart of successful health-related climate change policy interventions decision-making."

Finally, to conclude the book (Chapter 11), we synthesize how the chapters of the book address themes of vulnerability and adaptation in deeper context and how they go some way to addressing the five climate reductionisms outlined above. We also summarize policy implications of the chapters across different scales of influence and governance, emphasizing how what we learn from this book points us toward even deeper commitment to purposeful, inclusive, impactful work with communities.

SOLVING AND RE-SOLVING CLIMATE CHANGE

In 1973, Rittel and Webber coined the term *wicked problem*. They sought to distinguish between problems in the natural sciences, which they characterized as "definable and separable and may have solutions that are findable," from solutions in social and policy planning, which they suggested are "ill-defined" and "rely upon elusive political judgment for resolution." They added that "social problems are never solved. At best they are only re-solved—over and over again" (p. 160).

Some scholars have argued that climate change is the wicked problem par excellence—even a "super wicked" problem because of the way the passage of time makes addressing the problem ever more difficult and ever more expensive (Lazarus, 2009, p. 1160). For some (Grundmann, 2016), climate change is not, in fact, a scientific problem at all. As a process, we may need to analyze it scientifically, but it needs to be addressed as a social problem, much like crime or education. Polemically, Grundmann argues that "climate science provides no help to meet this challenge [of climate change], once it has been acknowledged. The essential expertise for making progress with climate change mitigation and adaptation lies in the social sciences" (p. 563).[1]

Though we are not unappreciative of the role for hard sciences, and often the importance of collaborating together, the chapters in this volume emphasize throughout how the "essential expertise" must come from social and policy efforts, in close partnership with the people and communities themselves that are affected by the wicked problem of climate change. A top-down, exclusive approach to solving and re-solving climate change risks the persistent ignorance of social injustice, the reproduction of vulnerability, and the saving or privileging of few at the expense of many. To solve and re-solve climate change and its consequences, we must place it and understand it deeply in time and place, critically question the historical patterns and current policies that create and

---

[1] This contention is echoed by Hulme (2011a): "The STEM [science, technology, engineering, and mathematics] disciplines by themselves carry a hubris that they seemingly cannot shake off. On their own they are inadequate for tackling 'wicked' problems such as climate change" (p. 178).

maintain exposure and vulnerability, and keep questions about the pursuit of social justice at the fore. We must ask *Why?* And from there, we must pursue the policy changes that matter most.

REFERENCES

Adger, W. N. (2006). Vulnerability. *Global Environmental Change, 16*(3), 268–281.

Agrawal, A., Lemos, M. C., Orlove, B., & Ribot, J. (2012). Cool heads for a hot world—Social sciences under a changing sky. *Global Environmental Change, 22*(2), 329–331.

Almgren, G. (2018). *Health care politics, policy, and services: A social justice analysis* (3rd ed.). New York, NY: Springer.

Arora-Jonsson, S., & Sveriges, L. (2011). Virtue and vulnerability: Discourses on women, gender and climate change. *Global Environmental Change, 21*(2), 744–751.

Barnes, J., Dove, M., Lahsen, M., Mathews, A., McElwee, P., McIntosh, R., . . . Yager, K. (2013). Contribution of anthropology to the study of climate change. *Nature Climate Change, 3*(6), 541.

Blaikie, P. (1985). *The political economy of soil erosion in developing countries.* Harlow, UK: Longman.

Carter, T. R., Fronzek, S., Inkinen, A., Lahtinen, I., Lahtinen, M., Mela, H., . . . Terama, E. (2016). Characterising vulnerability of the elderly to climate change in the Nordic region. *Regional Environmental Change, 16*(1), 43–58.

Chakrabarty, D. (2009). The climate of history: Four theses. *Critical Inquiry, 35*(2), 197–222.

Chakrabarty, D. (2012). Postcolonial studies and the challenge of climate change. *New Literary History, 43*(1), 1–18.

Cooke, B., & Kothari, U. (2001). *Participation: The new tyranny?* New York, NY: Zed Books.

Crutzen, P. J. (2002). Geology of mankind. *Nature, 415*(6867), 23.

Crutzen, P. J., & Stoermer, E. F. (2000). The Anthropocene. *IGBG Newsletter, 41,* 17–18.

Djoudi, H., Locatelli, B., Vaast, C., Asher, K., Brockhaus, M., & Basnett Sijapati, B. (2016). Beyond dichotomies: Gender and intersecting inequalities in climate change studies. *Ambio, 45*(S3), 248–262.

Few, R., Brown, K., & Tompkins, E. L. (2007). Public participation and climate change adaptation: Avoiding the illusion of inclusion. *Climate Policy, 7*(1), 46–59.

Gibson, K., Hill, A., & Law, L. (2018). Community economies in Southeast Asia: A hidden economic geography. In A. McGregor, L. Law, & F. Miller (Eds.), *Routledge handbook of Southeast Asian development* (pp. 131–141). London, UK: Routledge.

Grundmann, R. (2016). Climate change as a wicked social problem. *Nature Geoscience, 9*(8), 562–563.

Hulme, M. (2011a). Meet the humanities. *Nature Climate Change, 1*(4), 177–179.

Hulme, M. (2011b). Reducing the future to climate: A story of climate determinism and reductionism. *Osiris, 26*(1), 245–266.

Johnson, C., Penning-Rowsell, E., & Parker, D. (2007). Natural and imposed injustices: The challenges in implementing "fair" flood risk management policy in England. *Geographical Journal, 173*(4), 374–390.

Krishna, A. (2010). *One illness away: Why people become poor and how they escape poverty.* Oxford, UK: Oxford University Press.

Lazarus, R. J. (2009). Super wicked problems and climate change: Restraining the present to liberate the future. *Cornell Law Review, 94*(5), 1153.

Li, T. M. (2011). Rendering society technical: Government through community and the ethnographic turn at the World Bank in Indonesia. In D. Mosse (Ed.), *Adventures in Aidland: The anthropology of professionals in international development* (pp. 57–80). Oxford, UK: Berghahn.

Lowery, C. T. (2007). Social justice and international human rights. In M. A. Mattaini & C. T. Lowery (Eds.), *Foundations of social work practice* (4th ed., pp. 63–92). Baltimore, MD: NASW Press.

Malm, A., & Hornborg, A. (2014). The geology of mankind? A critique of the Anthropocene narrative. *Anthropocene Review, 1*(1), 62–69.

Moore, J. (2016). The rise of cheap nature. In J. W. Moore (Ed.), *Anthropocene or capitalocene? Nature, history, and the crisis of capitalism* (pp. 78–115). Oakland, CA: Kairos.

O'Keefe, P., Westgate, K., & Wisner, B. (1976). Taking the naturalness out of natural disasters. *Nature, 260*(5552), 566–567.

Ribot, J. (2010). Vulnerability does not fall from the sky: Toward multi-scale, pro-poor climate policy. In R. Mearns & A. Norton (Eds.), *Social dimensions of climate change: Equity and vulnerability in a warming world* (pp. 47–74). Washington, DC: World Bank.

Rigg, J., & Oven, K. (2015). Building liberal resilience? A critical review from developing rural Asia. *Global Environmental Change, 32*, 175–186.

Rittel, H. W. J., & Webber, M. M. (1973). Dilemmas in a general theory of planning. *Policy Sciences, 4*(2), 155–169.

Schlosberg, D., & Carruthers, D. (2010). Indigenous struggles, environmental justice, and community capabilities. *Global Environmental Politics, 10*(4), 12–35.

Schlosberg, D., Collins, L. B., & Niemeyer, S. (2017). Adaptation policy and community discourse: Risk, vulnerability, and just transformation. *Environmental Politics, 26*(3), 413–437.

Sen, A. (2005). Human rights and capabilities. *Journal of Human Development, 6*(2), 151–166.

Shaw, A., Sheppard, S., Burch, S., Flanders, D., Wiek, A., Carmichael, J., . . . Cohen, S. (2009). Making local futures tangible—Synthesizing, downscaling, and visualizing climate change scenarios for participatory capacity building. *Global Environmental Change, 19*, 447–463.

Stringer, L. C., Scrieciu, S. S., & Reed, M. S. (2009). Biodiversity, land degradation, and climate change: Participatory planning in Romania. *Applied Geography, 29*, 77–90.

Tanner, T., & Allouche, J. (2011). Towards a new political economy of climate change and development. *IDS Bulletin, 42*(3), 1–14.

Tawney, R. H. (1932). *Land and labour in China.* London, UK: George, Allan & Unwin.

Thaler, T., & Hartmann, T. (2016). Justice and flood risk management: Reflecting on different approaches to distribute and allocate flood risk management in Europe. *Natural Hazards, 83*(1), 129–147.

Tsing, A. L. (2015). *The mushroom at the end of the world: On the possibility of life in capitalist ruins.* Princeton, NJ: Princeton University Press.

Turner, B. S. (2006). *Vulnerability and human rights.* University Park, PA: Pennsylvania State University Press.

Wachsmuth, J. (2015). Cross-sectoral integration in regional adaptation to climate change via participatory scenario development. *Climatic Change, 132,* 387–400.

Wildcat, D. R. (2013). Introduction: Climate change and indigenous peoples of the USA. *Climatic Change, 120*(3), 509–515.

Wisner, B., Blaikie, P., Cannon, T., & Davis, I. (2004). *At risk: Natural hazards, People's vulnerability and disasters.* New York, NY: Routledge.

PART II
Weather

In ancient Egyptian mythology and in myths derived from it, the phoenix is a female mythical sacred firebird with beautiful gold and red plumage. Said to live for 500 or 1461 years (depending on the source), at the end of its life-cycle the phoenix builds itself a nest of cinnamon twigs that it then ignites; both nest and bird burn fiercely and are reduced to ashes, from which a new, young phoenix arises.

—*LEGEND OF THE PHOENIX* (N.D.)

2

Pathways to Climate Justice in a Desert Metropolis

Sharon L. Harlan, Paul Chakalian, Juan Declet-Barreto, David M. Hondula, and G. Darrel Jenerette

FUTURE SOCIETIES WILL face many uncertainties in a rapidly warming and urbanizing world. One of the most critical challenges is how cities will adapt to new local temperature regimes projected to occur in this century, including more frequent and intense episodes of extremely hot weather. Exposure to high temperatures currently causes a large number of weather-related deaths throughout the world (Gasparrini et al., 2015). The temperature regime shifts caused by climate change—higher daily maximums, warmer nights, and longer warm seasons—are projected to increase heat-related deaths in the absence of sufficient adaptation measures (International Panel on Climate Change, 2014). By altering food sources, fresh water availability, the spread of vector-borne diseases, and energy demands, these shifts are also projected to change ecosystem behaviors and strain urban infrastructure that indirectly affects human health (Luber & Lemery, 2015). Moreover, higher temperatures relate to higher rates of interpersonal and intergroup conflicts worldwide (Hsiang & Burke, 2014). Thus, changes in the physical and social worlds are intertwined, requiring adaptations that are complex and multidimensional.

A "pathways" metaphor for adaptation to climate change can help communities visualize their options for the future, plan for uncertainties in interactions and feedback loops in socioecological systems, and grasp the extensive nature of changes required to reduce vulnerability (Maru & Smith, 2014). An adaptation pathway is "a dynamic, long-term transitory and transformative process that involves repeated decisions" (Maru & Smith, 2014, p. 322). An example of an adaptation pathway is New York City's response to

Hurricane Sandy, which Rosenzweig and Solecki (2014) describe as *dynamic robustness*—having both short-term plans that reduce immediate risks and long-term plans that can evolve as conditions change over time. Other important advantages of the adaptation pathway approach include addressing the root causes and social contexts of vulnerability, employing cross-scale applications, and being open to participation from diverse communities—including vulnerable groups—in decision-making.

Different disciplines and authors define vulnerability to climate hazards in various ways (O'Brien, Erikson, Nygaard, & Schjolden, 2007). We employ a definition that separates exposure and sensitivity to hazards from adaptive capacity. High exposure and sensitivity are the reasons that entities are potentially vulnerable to harm, whereas *adaptive capacity* is the availability of resources to avoid, reduce, or recover from the effects of short-term heat disasters and long-term climate pressures (Moser, Norton, Stein, & Georgieva, 2010). Climate vulnerability is framed as both a direct outcome of heat-related health hazards and an indirect outcome of the socioecological context within which heat hazards exist (O'Brien et al., 2007).

Adaptation pathways should incorporate climate justice principles into climate change action. Broadly speaking, *climate justice* is concerned with human causes of climate change and the impacts and policy choices that are made to mitigate and adapt to it on both local and global scales. The four principles of climate justice for designing policies that reduce impacts on vulnerable populations are (1) fair distribution of material burdens and benefits; (2) recognition of inequality in status between developed and developing nations and among social class, race, age, gender groups within individual societies, as well as the institutional structures that oppress groups in subordinate positions; (3) advancing the social position of subordinate groups so that they have the capabilities—resources, opportunities, and freedoms—to exist as full members of society; and (4) meaningful participation of those groups in decision-making bodies and institutions (Harlan, Pellow, & Roberts, 2015). Pathways and justice frameworks thus share important precepts, especially their incorporation of historical narratives, cross-scale linkages, and inclusiveness of affected communities in power sharing.

This chapter examines the climate hazard of extreme heat. Some heat hazards are acute, short-term extreme heat events (i.e., heat waves) when weather conditions greatly exceed normal temperatures.[1] Heat waves often cause a public health crisis that requires emergency response to protect lives. Other heat hazards are chronic pressures, such as global and urban warming trends that result in prolonged exposure to higher

---

[1] Note that there are many definitions of heat waves, such as multiple consecutive days on which temperatures exceed the 95th percentile of normal temperatures. (For a detailed assessment of different definitions, see Smith, Zaitchik, & Gohlke, 2013.) Exceptional heat waves have resulted in hundreds to tens of thousands of excess deaths over periods of time ranging from days to weeks (e.g., the 1995 Chicago heat wave [Semenza et al., 1996] and the 2003 European heat wave [Conti et al., 2005]).

than optimal temperatures, which have long-term effects on people and socioecological systems.

The chapter then discusses two different but overlapping types of vulnerability and the potential pathways for adaption to extreme heat. First, a heterogeneous mix of residents are physiologically susceptible to heat for reasons as varied as age, illness, or finding themselves in situations of acute and intense heat exposure, such as working outdoors. For the public health community, the challenge is to protect those individuals and educate them about how to avoid situations that are dangerously hot. Public health adaptation pathways that align with achieving better health outcomes in Arizona are ongoing and can be improved.

Second, historical processes of uneven economic development and continuing social discrimination in metro Phoenix, Arizona, have produced a large bottom stratum of the population—mostly poor and disproportionately minorities—that is residentially vulnerable to climate change. This population generally lives in low-income neighborhoods chronically exposed to the highest temperatures that lack access to social resources, ecological benefits, and technological means to cope with heat. The challenge here is that local and state elected governments have not developed pathways to address the broader unequal social contexts in which vulnerabilities have evolved over time. There are roadblocks to creating pro-poor adaptation pathways, but we recommend aspirational pathways that would embody principles of climate justice for vulnerable neighborhoods in metropolitan Phoenix.

THE CLIMATE HAZARD OF EXTREME HEAT IN PHOENIX, ARIZONA

Phoenix is located in the northern Sonoran Desert at the confluence of the Salt and Gila River channels. The subtropical hot desert climate was inhabited for centuries by the Hohokam prehistoric people, who created an extensive network of irrigation canals to support their subsistence farms. More recently, the Akimel O'odhom (or O'otham) native people continuously farmed this area for several centuries. Phoenix has a relatively short 150-year history as an Anglo-American settlement.

Modern Phoenix is one of several rapidly growing post-World War II suburban cities in the semi-arid West that came of age in the era of automobiles, air conditioning, and affluence sufficient for the middle class to afford more living space (Gammage, 2016). The city of Phoenix is physically indistinguishable from more than 20 contiguous municipalities that stretch 100 km from east to west and approximately 80 km from north to south. Only the tribal communities and some other croplands and desert remnants stand apart from the urban sprawl. Among 382 U.S. metropolitan statistical areas, Phoenix–Mesa–Scottsdale ranked 12th in 2015 with a population of 4.75 million. Hereafter, we refer to this entire region as *metro Phoenix* or simply *Phoenix* and to the older, pre-Anglo settlement as *the Salt River Valley*, the historical cultural label for the region.

Climate hazards in metro Phoenix have both natural and human drivers related to its location in a semi-arid desert biome and a trajectory of rapid urban development that has independently contributed to rising temperatures. Everyone who lives in this region is potentially vulnerable to the risk of extreme heat that is innate to the desert climate and amplified by water scarcity and human modifications in the natural and social environments. Though the mild winter climate is a major attraction for tourists and part-time residents, the entire area is chronically hot from May through September. On average during the period 1981–2010, the season with daytime maximum temperatures exceeding 32.2°C (90°F) extended for more than 160 days; during a typical year, there are more than 100 days with daytime highs above 37.8°C (100°F) (Arguez et al., 2012). Within this long warm season, acute heat events occur with some regularity; temperatures higher than 43.3°C (110°F) are not uncommon and are projected to become even more common. Prolonged periods of especially high temperatures motivated the National Weather Service to issue extreme heat warnings that were in effect an average of 18 days each year during the period 2011–2015.[2]

Rising temperatures in the region due to global climate change are distributed evenly over the urbanized area of central Arizona, but urban-generated heat is unevenly distributed and varies spatially with topography, wind patterns, and land covers. The effect of urbanization on metro Phoenix temperatures, known as the urban heat island or urban heat, is evident in Figure 2.1, which compares time series of minimum and maximum temperatures from two weather stations located in the inner city and in the desert on the far edge of urban development. Figure 2.1 shows that average monthly summer minimum temperature increased by more than 6°C (10.8°F) in the urban core between a baseline period spanning the 1930s and 1940s and present day. On the edge of development, this increase was less than 3°C (5.4°F) (Georgescu, Moustaoui, Mahalov, & Dudia, 2013; Ruddell, Hoffman, Ahmad, & Brazel, 2013).

Regarding the future, modeled climate scenarios suggest that the relative contributions of global warming and urbanization to future warming in Phoenix could be of approximately the same order of magnitude in the 21st century (Georgescu, Morefield, Bierwagen, & Weaver, 2014). Ensembles of global and urban climate model simulations project that metro Phoenix could experience 42.2 extreme heat days per summer in mid-century (2041–2070) compared to 10.6 in the reference period 1971–2000 (Grossman-Clarke, Schubert, Clarke, & Harlan, 2014).

---

[2] During that time, warnings were issued as early in the year as May 13 and as late as September 26. The second half of the warm season each year brings the added stressor of elevated atmospheric humidity, when shifts in regional wind patterns advect moisture from the Pacific Ocean and Gulf of Mexico into the region (Adams & Comrie, 1997). The decision to issue a heat warning depends on multiple factors, including maximum and minimum temperature, event duration, and seasonality. During the hottest 3 months of the year, forecasts for daily maximum temperatures higher than 43.3°C (110°F) for 2 or more consecutive days will often activate a warning.

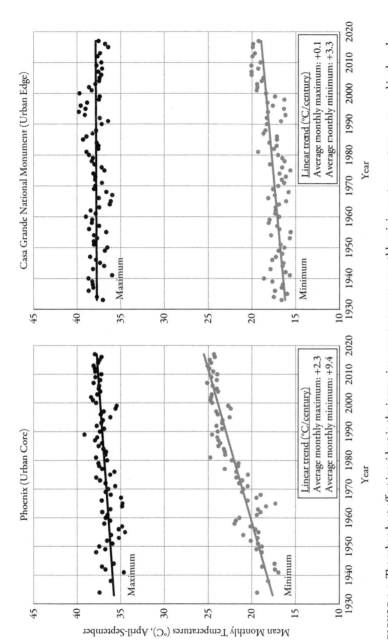

FIGURE 2.1 The urban heat effect is evident in the increasing average summer monthly minimum temperatures measured in the urban core of Phoenix (left panel) compared to a station on the edge of urban development (right panel).

Risks to the Socioecological System

The viability of the entire socioecological system in metro Phoenix rests upon delicately balanced technological modifications of the built environment to make it habitable for a large urban population. To moderate heat risks, Phoenix relies on the nexus of water, energy, and vegetation, which forms a coupled human and natural system. This cooling system exhibits vulnerabilities to both external and internal pressures that could potentially cascade into life-threatening system shocks for the whole population. Increasingly hot weather, including warmer nights, has the potential to permanently alter the ecology, economy, and water use in metro Phoenix (Ruddell et al., 2013). Failures in any of the water, energy, or vegetation subsystems may translate into rapidly changing distributions of heat vulnerability.

Water Scarcity

Water scarcity is an ever-present hazard that poses an independent threat to climate vulnerability in semi-arid lands. Phoenix has made strides in water management and use reduction, but there are still many challenges with regard to adequate supply to support the rising population and the economic base, water quality, and food security for the future under climate change. Having access to water is directly related to the mitigation of heat for illness prevention and increased comfort. Also, the efficient use of water is essential for future energy production and the availability and distribution of surface water for irrigated green landscapes.

Energy Consumption

From the 1970s onward, the population of Phoenix has grown exponentially, largely because of the technological capability for widespread use of air conditioning. Adopting modern Anglo-American architecture and construction materials used in temperate climate zones rather than traditional styles from desert cities has contributed to energy demand for cooling indoor environments. Energy delivery for air conditioning is subject to failures that can immediately limit the coping capacity of people to manage high heat. Failures in the energy grid can occur in response to unpredictable events, such as storms, but also can occur due to high-load demands associated with widespread air conditioning use during above normal temperatures. The efficiency of energy production by thermoelectric plants, which require intake of water for operation, will be challenged by increasing water temperatures in intake source and environmental requirements to limit the temperature of water released from the plants (Frumhoff et al., 2015; Garfin, LeRoy, McMahan, Black, & Roh, 2015). Reliable energy supply is also essential to maintain water infrastructure in the region; in the southwestern United States, approximately 20% of the energy supply is used directly for water pumping and transportation (Garfin et al., 2015).

Thus, the future viability of the entire socioecological system under climate change depends on balancing the trade-offs among interactions between energy and water.

Vegetation Cover

In metro Phoenix, the largest driver of microclimate variability is land cover—more abundant vegetation is associated with cooler temperatures (Declet-Barreto, Brazel, Martin, Chow, & Harlan, 2013; Jenerette et al., 2007). Variation in vegetation cover is associated with more than 20°C (68°F) variability in land surface temperatures across the region during summer at midday (Jenerette, Harlan, Stefanov, & Martin, 2011), which in turn is associated with large differences in neighborhood heat exposure (Jenerette et al., 2016). When the weather is hotter, vegetation provides even more cooling (Jenerette et al., 2011), suggesting a possible negative feedback on urban climate changes that may enhance the effectiveness of vegetation in response to warming from urban-generated heat and global sources.

Many cities throughout the world have invested in urban greening programs to moderate local climate conditions and improve human comfort and well-being, including to minimize heat exposure (Pearlmutter et al., 2017). Doing so in arid or semi-arid climates, however, requires irrigation, and outdoor water use is the largest component of residential consumption in metro Phoenix. An important question, then, is how to use water-efficient green infrastructure to cool the urban environment in a manner that will reduce both energy use and heat exposure for people indoors and outdoors (Pataki et al., 2011). Enhancing the resilience of green infrastructure is crucial to reduce human heat vulnerability in Phoenix, but at the same time, the region must avoid water shortages and plant disease that could cause widespread tree mortality leading to rapid outdoor warming, increasing energy demand, and human heat vulnerability.

THE PUBLIC HEALTH PERSPECTIVE ON RISKS OF HIGH TEMPERATURES

When exposed to hot environments, the human body undergoes significant physiological stress to keep the internal temperature near 37.0°C (98.6°F). Heat stress causes discomfort and fatigue and exacerbates preexisting medical conditions. When unable to keep itself cool, the body can experience heat exhaustion and cramps, from which short-term recovery is possible with modest care, or heat stroke, a very dangerous condition in which body temperature exceeds 40°C (104°F). Heat stroke has a high fatality rate; individuals who do not immediately perish from it often suffer long-term complications and disabilities. Hot weather also poses indirect threats to human health, including impacts on mental state (Berry, Bowen, & Kjellstrom, 2010; Noelke et al., 2016), physical activity levels (Baranowski, Thompson, Durant, Baranowski, & Puhl, 1993; Graff Zivin & Neidell, 2014), and other determinants of well-being.

In Maricopa County, where metro Phoenix is located, 10 years of detailed reporting on heat-related deaths from the Maricopa County Department of Public Health (MCDPH) has created a good understanding of the populations most susceptible to heat exposure. In 2016, there were 130 confirmed deaths from heat exposure. Of these, 72% were male and 76% were aged 50 years or older. People experiencing homelessness, those without a functioning air conditioner at home, and individuals abusing substances are disproportionately represented in the heat mortality statistics (MCDPH, 2016a).

In addition to human fatalities, extreme heat significantly increases hospital admissions and emergency room visits: For the period 2008–2011, there were 10 times as many heat-related hospitalizations and 40 times as many heat-related emergency visits as there were heat deaths in Maricopa County (Petitti, Hondula, Yang, Harlan, & Chowell, 2016). A substantial portion of the county's population suffers from symptoms of heat illness and thermal discomfort for which they do not seek medical treatment (Jenerette et al., 2016). From discomfort to mortality, negative heat-related health outcomes fall disproportionately on vulnerable populations. These groups include adults who are older or chronically ill with cardiovascular or respiratory disease; people living in poverty; socially isolated individuals; those with low educational levels; racial and ethnic minorities; and those, for any reason, who are unable to access cool indoor environments when it is hot (Petitti, Harlan, Chowell-Puente, & Ruddell, 2013; Reid et al., 2009; Stafoggia et al., 2006).

Adaptation Pathways to Protect Heat-Sensitive Populations

The negative effect of high temperatures on human health necessitates the public health sector's participation to achieve sustainable climate justice. Public health promotes and protects "the health of people and the communities where they live, learn, work and play" (American Public Health Association, 2016). The public health sector spans federal, state, and local public health agencies; social service providers; policymakers; researchers; weather forecasters; the broadcast media; and the public at large. Health professionals treat heat-related conditions, educate patients about heat risks, and can be advocates for policies that mitigate heat risks. All of these actors play a role in public health preparedness, response, and recovery efforts concerning extreme heat.

In metro Phoenix, entities already taking such a role include the Centers for Disease Control and Prevention, the Arizona Department of Health Services, MCDPH, the City of Phoenix and other municipalities, the Maricopa Association of Governments, forecasters at the National Weather Service Phoenix forecast office, and university researchers. We draw from our own engagement with these organizations, their publicly available resources, and the scientific literature to map how the public health sector in metro Phoenix is developing pathways for increasing adaptive capacity to extreme temperatures in 3 of the 10 essential services of public health defined by the American

Public Health Association (Frumkin, Hess, Luber, Malilay, & McGeehin, 2008): (1) Monitor health status to identify and solve community health problems; (2) inform, educate, and empower people about health issues; and (3) evaluate effectiveness, accessibility, and quality of personal and population-based health services.

Monitor Health Status to Identify and Solve Community Health Problems

In 2005, a severe heat wave resulted in dozens of homeless people suffering heat-related deaths. In response, MCDPH deployed a comprehensive advanced heat mortality surveillance program. Using real-time surveillance methods from this program, MCDPH and Arizona Department of Health Services officials also now lead a national working group developing guidelines for the detection of both heat-related death and heat-related illnesses. Data collected through these approaches provide a more comprehensive accounting of the populations affected by heat compared to national statistics. For example, the crude heat-associated death rate for Maricopa County in 2015 was approximately 1.5 deaths per 100,000 residents (MCDPH, 2016a), whereas the national-level crude heat-related death rate is estimated at only 0.2 deaths per 100,000 residents (Berko, Ingram, Saha, & Parker, 2014).

The detailed inventory of heat-related deaths in metro Phoenix enables MCDPH to publish annual reports about the residency status, demographics, place of injury, residential characteristics, substance abuse, and living situation of those most severely affected by heat. This information is especially important for detecting the most sensitive populations and shaping preparedness and response strategies to reduce the disproportionate burden of heat incurred by some groups in the region. Thus, such reports are crucial to tracking the success of metro Phoenix's efforts to build adaptive capacity and pursue climate justice.

Inform, Educate, and Empower People About Health Issues

Efforts to engage and empower the public regarding issues surrounding heat and health take many forms in central Arizona. In recent years, the local National Weather Service has partnered with health agencies to disseminate public early warnings of acute heat conditions. The warnings aim both to reduce exposure and to connect people to community resources such as cooling centers. A high percentage of the population receives and is aware of these warnings (MCDPH, 2015).

A challenge facing the region is to determine how these systems should evolve as heat events becomes more chronic. Public agencies and researchers are responding by considering alternative alerting systems in which risk could be communicated more frequently without fatiguing the public.

Health authorities and the National Weather Service partner on educational and messaging campaigns to build community knowledge about best practices to avoid heat-related illnesses and how to recognize early symptoms of heat stress. Specialized messaging tool kits are provided for certain populations and sectors, including schools, outdoor workers, older adults, and Spanish speakers (Arizona Department of Health Services, 2016).

Informational and educational programming have the potential to both reduce adverse health events and promote equity. However, digital communication may not reach some of the most vulnerable populations, such as socially isolated, elderly, and homeless individuals. Though existing efforts largely focus on enabling people to recognize symptoms of heat-related illness and be aware of available resources, there may be good opportunities to promote the participation element of climate justice in the diagnosis of health hazards through citizen science and community engagement. For example, it is now possible for individuals to wear low-cost sensors to monitor ambient or body temperature in different environments (Kuras et al., 2017).

More widespread educational efforts are critical in the Phoenix region to ensure that the public, which has traditionally been dismissive of extreme heat, has a better grasp of the severity of health risks associated with heat.

Evaluate Effectiveness, Accessibility, and Quality of Personal and Population-Based Health Services

Frameworks to evaluate the effectiveness of climate adaptation strategies have been proposed (e.g., Ebi, Kovats, & Menne, 2006), and some formal adaptation plans have been evaluated (e.g., Baker, Peterson, Brown, & McAlpine, 2012); however, there is little specific evidence regarding the benefits to human health (or avoided costs and burdens) of adaptation measures that have been implemented. This lack of evidence limits the ability of public health agencies and other organizations to adopt effective adaptive management or evidence-based approaches to minimize risk and pursue equity (Hess, Eidson, Tlumak, Raab, & Luber, 2014). Health agencies in metro Phoenix recognize this shortcoming and have begun to invest in the evaluation of heat adaptation activities.

A critical service in Phoenix for heat adaptation is the provision of cooled space. Publicly operated cooling centers are a necessity for people who cannot afford air conditioning in their homes. For those without cooled space, the regional Heat Relief Network coordinated by the Maricopa Association of Governments and the City of Phoenix plays an essential role. The Network is composed of several dozen facilities that provide free access to cooled space for anyone in need during the summer months. Some facilities provide additional services, including water distribution, overnight shelter, food provision, and counseling, as part of other programs they operate. Network coordinators are considering expanding the hours and improving the signage for the cooling centers (Berisha et al., 2017).

In 2015, MCDPH organized a large-scale household survey to better understand community needs related to heat preparedness. In 2017, it began pursuing new projects related to the survey findings, including more targeted efforts to understand the needs of homebound individuals when extreme heat occurs. These examples provide early evidence of an iterative, evidence-based approach toward a more sustainable and equitable society. More evaluation efforts are expected in the immediate future because the state health department has adopted the Centers for Disease Control and Prevention's Building Resilience Against Climate Effects framework under the auspices of the Climate-Ready Cities and States Initiative (Marinucci, Luber, Uejio, Saha, & Hess, 2014). This framework similarly champions an iterative approach toward reducing adverse health outcomes associated with atmospheric hazards and climate change.

Evaluation programs thus far in metro Phoenix are top-down measures that blend elements of autonomous and planned adaptation. Future projects will be in part motivated by anticipated future threats. Evaluation programs can provide critical guidance for the promotion of climate justice by forming an evidence base about the successes and challenges of implementing different types of adaptation programs in various communities.

Increasing Adaptive Capacity and Improving Health Outcomes

Agency-based governance in the public health sector is a successful example of an ambitious, planned effort to combat heat-related health problems in Arizona. Though climate change was not the original motivation for heat surveillance, warning, and outreach programs, the state and county agencies are developing iterative pathways based on evidence, evaluation, and improvement. As the health departments strengthen their alliance with the federal Building Resilience Against Climate Effects program, they build their capacity to deal with the increasing magnitude of heat hazards.

With respect to health surveillance, continued allocation of public resources toward these programs is essential for long-term monitoring and analysis that can accelerate assistance to the most in-need populations and for circumstances that present the greatest risk. Health surveillance and threat identification efforts such as public warning systems may be supplemented with new data sources from increasingly available low-cost, portable, and digitally connected devices, such as smartphones or the sensors mentioned above (Hondula, Kuras, Longo, & Johnston, 2018). More information about the thermal environment can be collected from distributed stationary or mobile sensor networks in the community. These devices also provide a potential platform for communication to the public: Extreme heat, for example, is not one of the hazards for which wireless emergency alerts are currently issued through mobile phones.

Though all the public health programs themselves are not yet fully effective— people continue to die from heat or suffer heat-related illness—our assessment is that the trajectory of this sector's response to extreme heat is very positive. It is also important to continue to spread the knowledge that the burden of heat is experienced disproportionately by impoverished groups in the region, many of which fall into the target population of public health initiatives. Most of the messaging about the dangers of extreme heat emphasizes actions that individuals should take to protect their bodies (e.g., hydration, shade, avoidance of the sun) and their kin (e.g., checking on older relatives and neighbors during heat waves). Public health needs to be more vocal about the barriers impoverished people face in undertaking these protective measures. This sector understands health disparities and could take a more explicit and much needed advocacy position in the state for developing the capabilities of the lowest income groups.

THE PRO-POOR PERSPECTIVE ON CLIMATE CHANGE VULNERABILITY

In studies of climate change and vulnerable populations throughout the world, poverty is a key socioeconomic indicator of vulnerability (Mearns & Norton, 2009). In the United States, there is also a strong case for the independent effect of race on vulnerability to extreme events and the longer term effects of climate change (Congressional Black Caucus, 2004). The entire stratum of the lowest income population in metro Phoenix is vulnerable to climate change in part because the places in which they are most likely to live are especially hazardous.

Microclimates, measured as air or land surface temperatures, are highly variable across neighborhoods and residential parcels (yards) during the hot months (Harlan, Brazel, Prashad, Stefanov, & Larsen, 2006; Jenerette et al., 2007). Lower income neighborhoods (as measured by lower median household income) have significantly less vegetation and higher daily maximum and minimum temperatures compared to higher income neighborhoods (Harlan et al., 2006; Jenerette et al., 2007; Larsen & Harlan, 2006; Ruddell, Harlan, Grossman-Clarke, & Buyantuyev, 2009). The positive relationship between vegetation abundance and neighborhood income is increasing over time in metro Phoenix (Jenerette et al., 2011). During heat waves, threshold temperatures are exceeded for many more hours in lower income neighborhoods, exposing residents to dangerous levels of outdoor heat for longer periods (Harlan et al., 2006; Ruddell et al., 2009). Moreover, the cost of electricity, broken equipment, and the cost of repairs prevent lower income people from using air conditioners to cool indoor temperatures in their homes (Jenerette et al., 2016).

Higher proportions of residents in poorer, hotter neighborhoods report experiencing symptoms of heat-related illnesses. Spatial epidemiology shows that probabilities of death and hospitalization directly caused by high temperature are significantly higher in these neighborhoods (Harlan, Declet-Barreto, Stefanov, & Petitti, 2013). Overcoming such health disparities requires an explanation and awareness of the local drivers of historical entrenched social inequalities that are beyond the reach of traditional public health remedies.

In this section, we recount a brief political ecological history of a misdirected pathway that has led to the entrapment of climate-vulnerable people in hazard-prone neighborhoods in South Phoenix. Racial discrimination is linked to ways in which these neighborhoods are vulnerable to increasing temperatures today because there has been a failure to develop or support community adaptive capacities that would reduce their risks from extreme heat. We discuss the most important roadblocks to climate adaptation and offer recommendations for moving forward with pro-poor adaptation pathways.

Historical Origins of Residential Segregation in Phoenix

In 2013, metro Phoenix had one of the highest poverty rates among the largest U.S. metro areas, with 17.4% of the population living below the federal government's poverty line, and this population is increasingly concentrated in the poorest neighborhoods (Cortright & Mahmoudi, 2014). Central City South (neighborhoods just south of downtown Phoenix) is one of the most impoverished areas of metro Phoenix, with a 61% poverty rate and a population that is 95.8% Latino, African American, Native American, and Asian/Pacific Islander (PRC Quality of Life Plan, 2008).[3]

The creation of this disenfranchised, low-income, and climate-vulnerable community can be traced to three distinct moments in the regional political economy (Declet-Barreto, 2013).[4] The first was the resurgence of agriculture in the Salt River Valley (SRV) in the late 1800s when White settlers rebuilt the abandoned Hohokam irrigation canals to create profitable businesses in export agriculture (Luckingham, 1989; Whitaker, 2000). Agricultural development set the conditions for sociospatial segregation of minorities (mostly Native Americans and Mexicans) through various forms of land fraud, which decreased the economic standing of minorities as they were forced to give up subsistence farming and turn to wage work. This created a highly racialized socioeconomic hierarchy, gradually relegating minorities to the hottest and lowest portion of the SRV (Bleasdale, 2015). A catastrophic flood of the Salt River in 1891 stranded minorities there while Anglos relocated to northern higher elevation areas, creating the first lineaments of race-based geographic segregation in South Phoenix (Bolin, Grineski, & Collins, 2005). By the 1900s, many Mexican farmhands and their families lived in makeshift housing along the Salt River irrigation canals (Figure 2.2).

The Great Depression of the 1930s signaled the second moment in Phoenix's urban expansion, characterized by a shift toward industrial development. New Deal funds modernized infrastructure, including elimination of streetside irrigation ditches in favor of concrete canals. Until then, many people in South Phoenix relied on the water, shade, and food sources provided by their proximity to the dirt-lined irrigation ditches. Lining,

---

[3] The population of metro Phoenix in 2015 was 30% Latino, 57% non-Hispanic White, 5% African American, 4% Asian, 2% Native American, and 2% mixed race and other (Census Reporter, 2015).
[4] The history and geography of extreme heat vulnerability in the Phoenix region summarized in this section are explored at length in Declet-Barreto's (2013) doctoral dissertation.

FIGURE 2.2 In the early 1900s, Mexican laborers and their families lived in slums in makeshift housing near the Salt River irrigation canals.
Source: Barry M. Goldwater Historic Photograph Collection, Arizona State University Libraries.

piping, and the burial of *acequias* (hand-dug irrigation canals) eliminated water seepage through the soil—a technical efficiency aggressively sought by the Salt River Project.

As metro Phoenix industrialized, agricultural land gave way to factories, warehouses, waste disposal, and transportation corridors. Residential segregation was codified during this time through the adoption of zoning regulations that protected single-family residential property values (i.e., affluent White neighborhoods) by explicitly forbidding industrial land uses there while allowing them in multifamily housing neighborhoods (i.e., populated by low-income minorities; York et al., 2014). Race-based redlining further reinforced residential segregation by disqualifying minorities from residential mortgages and through race-restrictive covenants in single-family neighborhoods that prevented non-Whites from living in more affluent suburbs (Bolin et al., 2005).

The post-World War II period ushered in the third moment of modern development in the SRV, characterized by suburban expansion and the annexation of previously isolated agricultural communities into metro Phoenix. During this period, water and land uses transitioned from mostly agricultural to more industry and suburban residential development. The spatial footprint of the urban heat island grew larger because of the preference for low-density, automobile-centric lifestyles. To make the region more economically competitive, Phoenix elites created a business-friendly form of municipal government, effectively decreasing the political power of minorities.

The history of South Phoenix is one example in the metro area of how legacies of poverty and environmental degradation have shaped the social and built environments of lower income neighborhoods, making them more vulnerable to extreme heat and many other environmental hazards in the 21st century. In 2017, the very low-income, predominantly minority population was concentrated near the downtown areas of larger central cities (e.g., Phoenix, Mesa, Chandler, Scottsdale) in substandard housing and mobile home parks, along industrial corridors, and in the far western and far eastern suburbs where land values are lower. Low-wage, outdoor industries and occupations are still prevalent in the local economy, and minorities are overrepresented in the lowest wage jobs, including outdoor work in construction and landscaping, where they are exposed to high temperatures. From 2006 to 2010, 60.3% of workers in metro Phoenix construction and extractive occupations were non-White, whereas only 21.9% of workers in management, business, and financial occupations were non-White (U.S. Census Bureau, n.d.).

Misdirection: The Fallacy of Relying on Individual Climate Adaptation in Poor Neighborhoods

Residents in historically segregated, poor neighborhoods often do not have enough money to afford the same adaptations available to higher income households. Such adaptations include irrigation for residential landscaping, electricity for air conditioning, secure housing, and mobility to escape the heat. Publicly funded heat-coping resources, such as trees, parks, and open spaces, are also scarcer in those neighborhoods. Though the public health establishment is developing pathways to address individual heat-related health issues, many limitations in the capacity of low-income households to protect themselves are linked to larger systems of structural inequalities. Moreover, substantial barriers prevent systemic changes that would reduce present and future heat risks, including substandard housing with unaffordable cooling, top-down cooling policies that do not benefit vulnerable people, politicians oppositional to climate change policy, and grassroots organizations with other priorities.

Substandard Housing and Unaffordable Indoor Cooling Are Widespread

To build adaptive capacity for climate change, people need access to secure housing with adequate temperature regulation, but housing quality in older areas of metro Phoenix is notoriously substandard. Though federal expenditures in the 2000s have made selective improvements in the quality of housing stock (Dantico, Guhathakurta, & Mushkatel, 2007), not enough affordable homes are available (Reagor, 2015). The Phoenix metro area has one of the lowest availabilities of affordable rental homes for low-income households in the country (National Low Income Housing Coalition, 2017). Public housing is concentrated in relatively few neighborhoods, with the vast majority of city-subsidized, project-based, and Section 8 housing located in the same 15 census tracts (Guhathakurta & Mushkatel, 2000).

Air conditioning is essential during Phoenix summers, but rising prices and lack of assistance mean that electrical rates are unaffordable for many poor people in metro

Phoenix; moreover, utility companies disconnect summertime electrical service for nonpayment (Joffe-Block, 2013). Enrollments in two main federal energy assistance programs, the Weatherization Assistance Program and the Low Income Home Energy Assistance Program (LIHEAP), are very low nationally (7%–24% of the eligible population in six states evaluated [Landey & Rzad, 2014]) and in Arizona, where households under 60% of the state median income are eligible for LIHEAP and both funding and enrollments have decreased since 2010 (LIHEAP, 2014).

Under Arizona state law, air conditioning is deemed an essential service, and landlords have a legal responsibility to maintain healthy livable buildings, which includes working heating, cooling, and ventilation. However, many landlords do not uphold their responsibilities, and there are local news reports of tenants' complaints every summer (Rivas, Cervantes, & Ducey, 2016). Tenants have legal options to ensure that landlords comply with their responsibilities. However, they cannot typically exercise these rights until at least 5 days after notifying their landlords, which can be a dangerous amount of time without air conditioning in Phoenix (Arizona Department of Housing, 2015). The Maricopa County Residential Tenant Landlord Act leaves most tenant–landlord conflict resolution up to the judgment of courts, which have traditionally placed the burden of proof on tenants (Anglen, 2013; Arizona Department of Housing, 2015). Ultimately, a large proportion of heat deaths each year occur inside dwellings in which the air conditioning is either not functional or not operating (MCDPH, 2016b).

City Heat Island Moderation Misses Many Neighborhoods

Measures to moderate the urban heat island are top-down policies not motivated by the needs of vulnerable communities for cooler outdoor spaces. For example, downtown Phoenix's Urban Form Project planted street trees to create a more pleasant pedestrian environment in the central business district (Chow, Brennan, & Brazel, 2012). Rather than benefitting vulnerable populations, this project was motivated by the desire to revitalize the economy through business and tourism. Subsequent spin-off initiatives (e.g., the Tree and Shade Master Plan, Free Tree program, coverings at bus stops) have given more consideration to shade in public places for some residents; however, none feature explicit language to reduce heat risks for vulnerable populations (City of Phoenix, 2008, 2010).

These urban greening projects come with trade-offs. In desert cities lacking rain-fed vegetation, the water costs of using irrigated vegetation to reduce temperatures are a concern. To promote water conservation, the Salt River Project (SRP) partners with seven cities in metro Phoenix to offer rebates to residents who convert mesic (turf grass) to xeriscape (dry land cover and drought-tolerant plants). The costs and benefits of irrigated vegetation in public and private landscaping are an active research area in the West, but evaluations to date have not reached firm conclusions (Seapy, 2015). What is clear from research in Phoenix, however, is that drier landscapes without vegetation create hotter microclimates, and poorer neighborhoods have less vegetation, fewer trees, and hotter temperatures compared to wealthier ones (Harlan et al., 2006; Jenerette et al. 2007). Municipal policy-driven adaptations subsidize only homeowners who can afford to have landscapes and maintain them. Thus, municipal governments have not adequately taken into account a key principle of climate justice—fairness—in access to housing and energy and in distributing benefits of environmental resources for outdoor heat moderation.

State Politics Disregard Climate Change and Sustainability

The Republican-controlled Arizona State Legislature is not supportive of climate change mitigation or adaptation measures. The Republican governor as of 2017, Doug Ducey, and former governors are on record as either denying that climate change is occurring or unsure that humans are responsible for causing it. Consistent with their party platform, they have thwarted policy initiatives that would promote environmental protection, climate change justice, and sustainable development in the state. For example, the state legislature banned making any law that would implement Agenda 21, the United Nations sustainability program, and has petitioned the U.S. Environmental Protection Agency not to tighten standards on ground-level ozone emissions. The legislature and the governor received poor marks from the Sierra Club (2016) on environmental protection measures. With a fiscally conservative government committed to low taxes and private property rights, the chances of Arizona passing state laws that protect renters' rights to safe housing, expand social entitlements, or create any other policies to advance climate change justice are minimal.

Arizona gives mixed signals on promoting clean and affordable energy, which are complicated by legitimate debates about the best ways to do so. Elections also play an important role in the energy politics of the state's largest electrical and water utility, SRP, which serves nearly all of metro Phoenix. Though it is beyond the scope of this chapter to examine energy and water politics, it is notable that SRP has approved rate hikes for residential solar customers, asserting that they benefit from reverse metering and are not paying their fair share for the operational costs of maintaining the electrical grid. This frustrates clean energy advocates who want a rapid transition to renewable energy (Harelson, 2018; Randazzo, 2015). Two advocates of home rooftop solar power won seats in 2016 on the 14-member SRP board, but their reform agenda faces intense opposition from other members of the board and council.

The Arizona state government's opposition to environmentally friendly and income redistributive policies leaves efforts for climate change mitigation and adaptation largely to municipalities, where there is a brief history of very select climate initiatives. Thirteen cities in Arizona, including several of the larger ones in metro Phoenix, have signed on to the U.S. Mayors Climate Protection Agreement, under which they have committed to mitigate carbon dioxide emissions. As noted above, some cities in the region have undertaken downtown or citywide urban greening projects. Still, overall, Arizona elected officials have made it difficult for significant policy progress toward climate justice or social adaptations to climate change.

Grassroots Activists Have More Pressing Issues

Local activists in Phoenix have stepped up to protect their communities' interests on many issues. These communities have mobilized their assets to address social and environmental injustices, such as high crime rates and air pollution. Many residents of Central City South, for example, reject the label "vulnerable" and work to shape their own future through a process of inclusion and meaningful participation of grassroots groups with other state and municipal stakeholders, decision-making bodies, financial institutions, and businesses.

After many years of neglecting crime and blight in South Phoenix, the city funded "Fight Back" grants to neighborhoods. With support from city and business leaders, the local nonprofit Phoenix Revitalization Corporation (PRC) then began to develop a Quality of Life Plan (QLP) for several neighborhoods (Central City South, 2010). Continually seeking residents' input, PRC focused on a QLP blueprint for a sustainable community, using their assets (e.g., schools, churches, libraries, parks) to create a grassroots, resident-driven vision for the neighborhoods. Residents' goals included recreation, health, services, housing, economic development, transportation, and a sense of community spotlighting their historical "points of pride." The QLP envisioned a healthier community with "less crime, and blight, more amenities that meet the needs of all who live in it, safe affordable mixed income housing, a healthier environment and a recognition and celebration of its rich cultural history" (Central City South, 2010). In addition, PRC recruited outside stakeholders to their cause, including local foundations, businesses and banks, the police, and Arizona State University.

Preparing for the physical consequences of climate change has not emerged as a grassroots priority of the neighborhoods in Central City South. Over the course of 6 years, we (i.e., a small group of faculty and students at Arizona State University, including two authors of this chapter) were deeply involved with PRC. Though PRC was politely receptive to our agenda for climate change adaptation, it never adopted the agenda as part of its QLP. Adaptation was subsumed under its goal of neighborhood "beautification," which included planting trees. The heat-mitigating benefits of trees eventually became part of its neighborhood improvement narrative, but the residents were much more interested and engaged with projects that we undertook at their request, such as community gardens, a food access survey, successfully advocating for a neighborhood park, and creating a community museum exhibit about residents' "environmental memories" of their old barrios.

In 2014, the Sonoran Institute undertook a survey of more than 20 Latino leaders in Arizona about their beliefs, concerns, and engagement with activities to address climate change (Culp, Oliver, & Gonzalez Patterson, 2014). Consistent with national surveys that show Latinos are more likely than Whites to believe climate change is real, the results also illustrate the underlying tensions and cautious approach to climate change among some minority activists. Latino leaders broadly acknowledged worsening and unpredictable local weather, its probable connection to climate change, and the likely adverse financial and health impacts on future generations of Latinos in Arizona; however, they were hesitant to embrace this issue as a core part of their own agenda. Though they supplied useful suggestions about how to engage, educate, and support their community in better planning for climate change, some made a very important point about adaptation: They have more important priorities that affect the lives of Latinos today, such as the anti-immigration legislation in Arizona (SB 1070), voting rights, and economic stability. Climate adaptation, some said, does not address the root causes of environmental injustices, such as power plant placement and other facilities, which cause serious health problems in Latino neighborhoods. One participant forthrightly asked the organizers, "Are you [Sonoran Institute] using the Latino community to rally people around your cause?"

Aspirational Pro-Poor Pathways to Climate Adaptation

Understanding the relationships between climate vulnerability and the larger cultural, economic, and political landscape in which it exists allows us to more accurately pinpoint opportunities for intervention that can reduce extreme heat vulnerability for the poor, who are most at risk. Moser and colleagues (2010) used a pro-poor adaptation framework to analyze the *assets*—the physical, financial, human, social, and natural capital of poor individuals, households, and communities—of the poorest urban areas in developing nations. They argue this is a missing component of studies that label vulnerable places but do not engage with local residents to help them identify and build upon their assets. Our research points to aspirational pro-poor pathways for interventions in metro Phoenix, including reordering state and local governmental social priorities, increasing public subsidies for cooler indoor and outdoor environments, and support for bottom-up initiatives to community problems.

Reorder State and Local Government Social Priorities

As a starting point, state and local governments must do a better job of fulfilling their obligations to meet the population's basic needs for food, shelter, education, health care, and living wage employment. In Phoenix, environmental degradation and the lack of socioeconomic opportunity further impoverish people who live in historically exploited areas of the city. It is clear that disadvantaged populations suffer negative health outcomes from their social and physical environments (Mechanic & Tanner, 2007). Government deficiencies in meeting social needs are a large part of the climate vulnerability gap between rich and poor households. Therefore, state and local governments must enhance access to market-based goods and services that affect adaptive capacity (e.g., decent housing, affordable utilities, health care, food security, and transportation) in low-income neighborhoods. Otherwise, intersecting deficits place cumulative burdens on communities, forming a substructure of vulnerability that, when aggravated by extreme weather events, can manifest as new and more severe burdens. The extreme temperatures from global climate change will continue to make these problems worse.

After meeting those basic needs, state and local governments must redirect the benefits of climate adaptation resources to the most underserved neighborhoods first, not last. Currently, the balance is strongly in favor of people taking care of themselves and an individual household's ability to pay. Likewise, improving the heat-resistance capacity of homes (e.g., insulation, upgrading windows and doors, shades and shutters, fans, air conditioning, trees and plants) mostly depends on homeowners' ability to pay for implementation and maintenance.

Public Subsidies for Cooler Indoor and Outdoor Environments

Public environmental benefits, such as green parks, urban agriculture, and restored canals and waterways, should be strategically located in and near low-income neighborhoods. The amount of public resources for weatherization programs and energy subsidies needs to be increased, and legal protection for renters should be enforced. In communicating with low-income communities about the benefits of climate adaptation, the government should emphasize that a major co-benefit of supporting the energy transition will be better health through less air pollution, meaning less asthma and respiratory illnesses. At the same time, however, the public utilities need to get fully onboard with making clean energy affordable and accessible.

Support for Bottom-Up Initiatives to Solve Community Problems

Procedural justice in climate adaptation through the meaningful involvement of vulnerable groups in decision-making is essential for pro-poor pathways. Yet this appears to be surprisingly complex in Phoenix because grassroots leadership is wary of being co-opted into supporting long-term goals at the expense of distraction from immediate needs. Phoenix Latino leaders are highly in favor of the government taking action to mitigate greenhouse gas emissions, but the leaders themselves are more focused on addressing social and environmental problems that have been neglected by government and perceived by their communities as paramount (e.g., civil rights, voter rights, jobs, cleaning up pollution). This raises essential questions about pro-poor adaptation strategies and a community's interests. By inadequately meeting responsibilities to protect the global environment and fulfill the social contract, governments have forced difficult choices on local communities and their leaders. What are their priorities: reducing global hazards, equitable distribution of local ecosystem benefits, publicly subsidizing goods and services that are unaffordable to poor households, better legal protection for the poor, or changing broader social policies that will create more stable and stronger communities? This dilemma also brings to the fore the rights of vulnerable communities to self-preservation and resident-driven visions for the quality of life. For example, do they have the right to decide which assets they want to develop, or the right to speak with diverse viewpoints rather than being simply labeled a "community perspective"? Based on a long history of economic exploitation and serving as research subjects, communities have well-deserved skepticism in dealing with government and other stakeholders that wish to impose their own agendas on the poor. Thus, a pro-poor climate adaptation pathway in metro Phoenix has encountered, and will continue to encounter, many twists and turns if the agenda moves forward.

CONCLUSION

The founders of modern Phoenix named it for the firebird that rose from the ashes of an ancient civilization. They may have overlooked the lesson that the original settlement probably disappeared because of climate change, so let us hope that history does not repeat itself in the second coming. The hottest city in the United States seems to excite the popular imagination, and nearly everyone has an opinion: The city of extremes inspires admiration from its boosters (e.g., 19th-century "Garden City of America") and ridicule from its tormentors, who call it "The World's Least Sustainable City" (Ross, 2011) and ask, "Could Phoenix Soon Become Uninhabitable?" (deBuys, 2013). Sensationalist titles sell books and magazines, but they do not create solutions to managing climate change.

As pragmatic, long-term, current and past residents of the Southwest, we believe that sounding the death knell is premature for desert cities such as Phoenix, Las Vegas, and Los Angeles. The region is not doomed, despite having a long way to go to overcome its past deficiencies, reduce its vulnerability to climate change, and achieve just solutions for its social and environmental problems.

Due to knowledge about weather, climate, past disasters, and the prospects for technological and engineering innovations, modern cities have many options for increasing their adaptive capacity to projected extreme temperatures and water scarcity. Hot cities have been some of the first responders to mitigating temperatures. In many ways, Phoenix is an exemplar of both the positive steps that cities can take and the need to redirect a historically unjust development pathway toward more socially equitable solutions for mitigating heat and climate extremes. Cities of the future, including metro Phoenix, will have to adapt to a much warmer climate, more heat waves, and long-term drought if they are to remain places where a broad economic spectrum of people, not only the wealthy, can survive and enjoy living.

Securing a sustainable future for the region will require a large investment in the region's infrastructure and a new development paradigm aimed at mitigation of the urban heat island in low-income neighborhoods, using water more efficiently for outdoor cooling, and reducing dependence on fossil fuel energy for indoor cooling. The public health sector in Arizona has already embarked on an ambitious pathway to reduce heat deaths in susceptible populations through better surveillance, more public outreach, and extended services. Pursuing climate justice is the cornerstone of a potential pro-poor adaptation pathway for this region that requires paying more attention to increasing the adaptive capacity of the bottom income strata. Achieving just outcomes at the regional scale requires rallying political will to assume collective responsibility for the health and well-being of those least able to adapt autonomously.

Given the planetary scale of the climate system, and sociospatial variability in the impacts of climate change, local adaptation policies must acknowledge the first principle of climate justice, calling for a fair distribution of environmental and social burdens and benefits that affect an individual's or group's ability to cope with climate change. Fair distribution is achieved through a process that incorporates the other climate justice principles of recognition, enhanced capabilities, and meaningful participation. Hence, good governance at all levels is the most effective—perhaps only—arena in which climate change can be functionally and fairly addressed.

ACKNOWLEDGMENTS

This work was supported in part by National Science Foundation grants GEO-0816168, GEO-0814692, BCS-1026865, and DEB-0423704; Hazards SEES Award 1520803; and the Sustainability Research Network Cooperative Agreement 1444758. The authors thank the editors and Diana B. Petitti for thorough reviews that improved the chapter.

REFERENCES

American Public Health Association. (2016). *What is public health?* Retrieved from https://apha. org/what-is-public-health

Anglen, R. (2013, June 30). Law gives landlords advantage in disputes. *Arizona Republic.*

Arguez, A., Durre, I., Applequist, S., Vose, R. S., Squires, M. F., Yin, X., ... Owen, T. W. (2012). NOAA's 1981–2010 U.S. climate normals: An overview. *Bulletin of the American Meteorological Society, 93,* 1687–1697.

Arizona Department of Health Services. (2016). *Extreme weather & public health: Heat safety.* Retrieved from https://www.azdhs.gov/preparedness/epidemiology-disease-control/extreme-weather/index.php#heat-home

Arizona Department of Housing. (2015). Arizona Residential Landlord and Tenant Act: Arizona revised statutes, Title 33, Chapter 10, pp. 3–28.

Baker, I., Peterson, A., Brown, G., & McAlpine, C. (2012). Local government response to the impacts of climate change: An evaluation of local climate adaptation plans. *Landscape and Urban Planning, 107,* 127–136.

Baranowski, T., Thompson, W. O., Durant, R. H., Baranowski, J., & Puhl, J. (1993). Observations on physical activity in physical locations: Age, gender, ethnicity, and month effects. *Research Quarterly for Exercise and Sport, 64*(2), 127–133.

Berisha, V., Hondula, D., Roach, M., White, J. R., McKinney, B., Bentz, D., . . . Goodin, K. (2017). Assessing adaptation strategies for extreme heat: A public health evaluation of cooling centers in Maricopa County, Arizona. *Weather, Climate, and Society, 9,* 71–80.

Berko, J., Ingram, D. D., Saha, S., & Parker, J. D. (2014). Deaths attributed to heat, cold, and other weather events in the United States, 2006–2010. *National Health Stat Report, 76,* 1–15.

Berry, H. L., Bowen, K., & Kjellstrom, T. (2010). Climate change and mental health: A causal pathways framework. *International Journal of Public Health, 55*(2), 123–132.

Bleasdale, T. H. (2015). *Gardens of justice: Food-based social movements in underserved, minority communities* (Doctoral dissertation). Retrieved from Arizona State University Library Digital Repository (2958).

Bolin, B., Grineski, S., & Collins, T. (2005). The geography of despair: Environmental racism and the making of South Phoenix, Arizona, USA. *Human Ecology Review, 12,* 156.

Census Reporter. (2015). *Phoenix–Mesa–Scottsdale, AZ metro area.* Retrieved from https://censusreporter.org/profiles/31000US38060-phoenixmesascottsdale-az-metro-area

Central City South. (2010). *Our community, our vision, our quality of life plan.* Phoenix Revitalization Corporation. Retrieved from http://www.phxrevitalization.org/ccsqlp/CCS_Quality_of_%20Life_Plan_2010.pdf

Chow, W. T. L., Brennan, D., & Brazel, A. J. (2012). Urban heat island research in Phoenix, Arizona: Theoretical contributions and policy applications. *Bulletin of the American Meteorological Society, 93,* 517–530.

City of Phoenix. (2008). *Downtown Phoenix Urban Form Project.* Retrieved from https://www.phoenix.gov/pdd/pz/downtown-phoenix-urban-form-project-2008

City of Phoenix. (2010). *Tree and Shade Master Plan.* Retrieved from https://www.phoenix.gov/parkssite/Documents/PKS_Forestry/PKS_Forestry_Tree_and_Shade_Master_Plan.pdf

Congressional Black Caucus. (2004). *African Americans and climate change: An unequal burden.* Retrieved from http://rprogress.org/publications/2004/CBCF_REPORT_F.pdf

Conti, S., Meli, P., Minelli, G., Solimini, R., Toccaceli, V., Vichi, M., . . . Perini, L. (2005). Epidemiologic study of mortality during the summer 2003 heat wave in Italy. *Environmental Research, 98*(3), 390–399. doi:10.1016/j.envres.2004.10.009

Cortright, J., & Mahmoudi, D. (2014). *Lost in place.* City Observatory. Retrieved from http://cityobservatory.org/wp-content/uploads/2014/12/LostinPlace_12.4.pdf

Culp, S., Oliver, H., & Gonzalez Patterson, N. (2014). *Survey on the impact of climate change on Latino communities in Arizona: Perspectives from civic & community leaders*. Sonoran Institute. Retrieved from https://sonoraninstitute.org/files/pdf/survey-on-the-impact-of-climate-change-on-latino-communities-in-arizona-01212015.pdf

Dantico, M., Guhathakurta, S., & Mushkatel, A. (2007). Housing quality and neighborhood redevelopment: A study of neighborhood initiatives in Phoenix, Arizona. *International Journal of Public Administration, 30*, 23–45.

deBuys, W. (2013, March 14). Could Phoenix soon become uninhabitable? *The Nation*. Retrieved from https://www.thenation.com/article/could-phoenix-soon-become-uninhabitable

Declet-Barreto, J. (2013). *A socio-ecological understanding of extreme heat vulnerability in Maricopa County, Arizona* (Doctoral dissertation). Retrieved from Arizona State University Library Digital Repository (20820).

Declet-Barreto, J., Brazel, A. J., Martin, C. A., Chow, W. T. L., & Harlan, S. L. (2013). Creating the park cool island in an inner-city neighborhood: Heat mitigation strategy for Phoenix, AZ. *Urban Ecosystems, 16*, 617–635.

Ebi, K. L., Kovats, R. S., & Menne, B. (2006). An approach for assessing human health vulnerability and public health interventions to adapt to climate change. *Environmental Health Perspectives, 114*, 1930–1934.

Frumhoff, P. C., Burkett, V., Jackson, R. B., Newmark, R, Overpeck, J., & Webber, M. (2015). Vulnerabilities and opportunities at the nexus of electricity, water and climate. *Environmental Research Letters, 10*(8). Retrieved from http://iopscience.iop.org/article/10.1088/1748-9326/10/8/080201/meta

Frumkin, H., Hess, J., Luber, G., Malilay, J., & McGeehin, M. (2008). Climate change: The public health response. *American Journal of Public Health, 98*, 435–445.

Gammage, G. (2016). *The future of the suburban city: Lessons from sustaining Phoenix*. Washington, DC: Island Press.

Garfin, G., LeRoy, S., McMahan, B., Black, M., & Roh, B. (2015). *Preparing for high consequence, low probability events: Heat, water & energy in the Southwest*. Tucson, AZ: Institute of the Environment.

Gasparrini, A., Guo, Y., Hashizume, M., Lavigne, E., Zanobetti, A., Schwartz, J., . . . Armstrong, B. (2015). Mortality risk attributable to high and low ambient temperature: A multicountry observational study. *Lancet, 386*, 369–375.

Georgescu, M., Morefield, P. E., Bierwagen, B. G., & Weaver, C. P. (2014). Urban adaptation can roll back warming of emerging megapolitan regions. *Proceedings of the National Academy of Sciences, 111*, 2909–2914.

Georgescu, M., Moustaoui, M., Malhalov, A., & Dudhia, J. (2013). Summer-time climate impacts of projected megapolitan expansion in Arizona. *Nature Climate Change, 3*(1), 37–41.

Graff Zivin, J., & Neidell, M. (2014). Temperature and the allocation of time: Implications for climate change. *Journal of Labor Economics, 32*(1), 1–26.

Grossman-Clarke, S., Schubert, S., Clarke, T. A., & Harlan, S. L. (2014). Extreme summer heat in Phoenix, Arizona (USA) under global climate change (2041–2070). *DIE ERDE: Journal of the Geographical Society of Berlin, 145*, 49–61.

Guhathakurta, S., & Mushkatel, A. H. (2000). Does locational choice matter? A comparison of different subsidized housing programs in Phoenix, Arizona. *Urban Affairs Review, 35*, 520–540.

Harelson, S. (2018, October 1). *SRP board approves price reduction*. Retrieved from https://www.srpnet.com/newsroom/releases/100118.aspx

Harlan, S. L., Brazel, A. J., Prashad, L., Stefanov, W. L., & Larsen, L. (2006). Neighborhood microclimates and vulnerability to heat stress. *Social Science & Medicine, 63*, 2847–2863.

Harlan, S. L., Declet-Barreto, J. H., Stefanov, W. L., & Petitti, D. B. (2013). Neighborhood effects on heat deaths: Social and environmental predictors of vulnerability in Maricopa County, Arizona. *Environmental Health Perspectives, 121*, 197–204. doi:10.1289/ehp.1104625

Harlan, S. L., Pellow, D. N., & Roberts, J. T. (2015). Climate injustice and inequality: Insights from sociology. In R. E. Dunlap & R. J. Brulle (Eds.), *Climate change and society: Sociological perspectives* (pp. 127–163). Oxford, UK: Oxford University Press.

Hess, J. J., Eidson, M., Tlumak, J. E., Raab, K. K., & Luber, G. (2014). An evidence-based public health approach to climate change adaptation. *Environmental Health Perspectives, 122*, 1177–1186.

Hondula, D. M., Kuras, E. R., Longo, J., & Johnston, E. W. (2018). Toward precision governance: Infusing data into public management of environmental hazards. *Public Management Review, 20*, 746–765. doi:10.1080/14719037.2017.1320043

Hsiang, S. M., & Burke, M. (2014). Climate, conflict, and social stability: What does the evidence say? *Climatic Change, 123*, 39–55.

International Panel on Climate Change. (2014): *Climate change 2014: Impacts, adaptation, and vulnerability*. Retrieved from http://www.ipcc.ch/report/ar5/wg2

Jenerette, G. D., Harlan, S. L., Brazel, A., Jones, N., Larsen, L., & Stefanov, W. L. (2007). Regional relationships between surface temperature, vegetation, and human settlement in a rapidly urbanizing ecosystem. *Landscape Ecology, 22*, 353–365.

Jenerette, G. D., Harlan, S. L., Buyantuev, A., Stefanov, W. L., Declet-Barreto, J., Ruddell, B. L., . . . Li, X. (2016). Micro-scale urban surface temperatures are related to land-cover features and residential heat related health impacts in Phoenix, AZ USA. *Landscape Ecology, 31*, 745–760.

Jenerette, G. D., Harlan, S. L., Stefanov, W. L., & Martin, C. A. (2011). Ecosystem services and urban heat riskscape moderation: Water, green spaces, and social inequality in Phoenix, USA. *Ecological Applications, 21*, 2637–2651.

Joffe-Block, J. (2013, June 12). *Keeping up with A/C costs a struggle for many*. National Public Radio Fronteras Desk. Retrieved from http://www.fronterasdesk.org/content/keeping-ac-costs-struggle-many

Kuras, E. R., Bernhard, M., Calkins, M., Ebi, K., Hess, J., Kintziger, K., . . . Uejio, C. (2017). Opportunities and challenges for personal heat exposure research. *Environmental Health Perspectives, 125*(8), 085001.

Landey, A., & Rzad, Y. (2014). *Approaches to low-income energy assistance funding in selected states* (APSE Policy Brief). U.S. Department of Health & Human Services. Retrieved from https://aspe.hhs.gov/basic-report/approaches-low-income-energy-assistance-funding-selected-states

Larsen, L., & Harlan, S. L. (2006). Desert dreamscapes: Residential landscape preference and behavior. *Landscape and Urban Planning, 78*, 85–100.

Legend of the Phoenix. (n.d.). Retrieved from http://www.labyrinthina.com/legend-of-the-phoenix.html

Low Income Home Energy Assistance Program. (2014). *Arizona LIHEAP facts*. Retrieved from http://liheap.org/states/az

Luber, G., & Lemery, J. (2015). *Global climate change and human health: From science to practice.* Hoboken, NJ: Wiley.

Luckingham, B. (1989). *Phoenix: The history of a southwestern metropolis.* Tucson, AZ: University of Arizona Press.

Maricopa County Department of Public Health. (2015). *Community Assessment for Public Health Emergency Response (CASPER) "Heat vulnerability and emergency preparedness needs assessment" report.* Retrieved from http://www.maricopa.gov/publichealth/Services/EPI/pdf/heat/Special/2015-CASPER-Report.pdf

Maricopa County Department of Public Health. (2016a). *Heat-associated deaths in Maricopa County, AZ, final report for 2015.* Retrieved from http://www.maricopa.gov/publichealth/Services/EPI/pdf/heat/2015annualreport.pdf

Maricopa County Department of Public Health. (2016b). *Heat-associated deaths in Maricopa County, AZ, multi-year report for 2006–2013.* Retrieved from http://www.maricopa.gov/PublicHealth/Services/EPI/pdf/heat/2006-2013MortalityReport.pdf

Marinucci, G. D., Luber, G., Uejio, C. K., Saha, S., & Hess, J. J. (2014). Building resilience against climate effects—A novel framework to facilitate climate readiness in public health agencies. *International Journal of Environmental Research and Public Health, 11*, 6433–6458.

Maru, Y. T., & Smith, M. S. (2014). GEC special edition—Reframing adaptation pathways. *Global Environmental Change, 28*, 322–324.

Mearns, R., & Norton, A. (2009). *Social dimensions of climate change: Equity and vulnerability in a warming world.* Washington, DC: World Bank.

Mechanic, D., & Tanner, J. (2007). Vulnerable people, groups, and populations: Societal view. *Health Affairs, 26*, 1220–1230.

Moser, C., Norton, A., Stein, A., & Georgieva, S. (2010). *Pro-poor adaptation to climate change in urban centers: Case studies of vulnerability and resilience in Kenya and Nicaragua.* The World Bank Sustainable Development Network. Retrieved from http://siteresources.worldbank.org/EXTSOCIALDEVELOPMENT/Resources/244362-1232059926563/5747581-1239131985528/ESW_propoorurbanadaptationReport4947GLBweb2.pdf

National Low Income Housing Coalition. (2017). *The gap: A shortage of affordable homes.* Retrieved from http://nlihc.org/sites/default/files/Gap-Report_2017_interactive.pdf

Noelke, C., McGovern, M., Corsi, D. J., Jimenez, M. P., Stern, A., Wing, I. S., & Berkman, L. (2016). Increasing ambient temperature reduces emotional well-being. *Environmental Research, 151*, 124–129.

O'Brien, K., Eriksen, S., Nygaard, L. P., & Schjolden, A. (2007). Why different interpretations of vulnerability matter in climate change discourses. *Climate Policy, 7*, 73–88.

Pataki, D. E., Boone, C. G., Hogue, T. S., Jenerette, G. D., McFadden, J. P., & Pincetl, S. (2011). Socio-ecohydrology and the urban water challenge. *Ecohydrology, 4*, 341–347.

Pearlmutter, D., Calfapietra, C., Samson, R., O'Brien, L., Ostoić, S. K., Sanesi, G., & del Amo, R. A. (2017). *The urban forest: Cultivating green infrastructure for people and the environment.* New York, NY: Springer.

Petitti, D. B., Harlan, S. L., Chowell-Puente, G., & Ruddell, D. (2013). Occupation and environmental heat-associated deaths in Maricopa County, Arizona: A case–control study. *PLoS One, 8*, e62596.

Petitti, D. B., Hondula, D. M., Yang, S., Harlan, S. L., & Chowell, G. (2016). Multiple trigger points for quantifying heat-health impacts: New evidence from a hot climate. *Environmental Health Perspectives, 124*, 176–183. doi:10.1289/ehp.1409119

PRC Quality of Life Plan. (2008). Retrieved from http://www.phxrevitalization.org/ccsqlp/

Randazzo, R. (2015, January 11). SRP's proposed solar rate hikes draw ire. *The Arizona Republic.* Retrieved from http://www.azcentral.com/story/money/business/2015/01/12/srp-proposed-solar-rate-hikes-draw-ire/21618141

Reagor, C. (2015, March 27). Metro Phoenix needs more affordable housing. *The Arizona Republic.* Retrieved from http://www.azcentral.com/story/money/real-estate/catherine-reagor/2015/03/27/metro-phoenix-needs-affordable-housing/70544580

Reid, C. E., O'Neill, M. S., Gronlund, C. J., Brines, S. J., Brown, D. G., Diez-Roux, A. V., & Schwartz, J. (2009). Mapping community determinants of heat vulnerability. *Environmental Health Perspectives, 117*, 1730.

Rivas, R., Cervantes, R., & Ducey, J. (2016, August 4). Woman found dead in 113-degree Tempe apartment. *ABC15 Arizona.* Retrieved from http://www.abc15.com/news/region-southeast-valley/tempe/pd-woman-found-dead-in-113-degree-tempe-apartment

Rosenzweig, C., & Solecki, W. (2014). Hurricane Sandy and adaptation pathways in New York: Lessons from a first-responder city. *Global Environmental Change, 28*, 395–408.

Ross, A. (2011). *Bird on fire: Lessons from the world's least sustainable city.* New York, NY: Oxford University Press.

Ruddell, D., Hoffman, D., Ahmad, O., & Brazel, A. (2013). Historical threshold temperatures for Phoenix (urban) and Gila Bend (desert), central Arizona, USA. *Climate Research, 55*, 201–215.

Ruddell, D. M., Harlan, S. L., Grossman-Clarke, S., & Buyantuyev, A. (2009). Risk and exposure to extreme heat in microclimates of Phoenix, AZ. In P. S. Showalter & Y. Lu (Eds.), *Geospatial techniques in urban hazard and disaster analysis* (pp. 179–202). New York, NY: Springer.

Seapy, B. (2015). *Turf removal & replacement: Lessons learned.* California Urban Water Council. Retrieved from http://cuwcc.org/Portals/0/Document%20Library/Resources/Publications/Council%20Reports/Turf%20Removal%20_%20Replacement%20-%20Lessons%20Learned.pdf

Semenza, J., Rubin, C., Falter, K., Selanikio, J., Flanders, W., Howe, H., & Wilhelm, J. (1996). Heat-related deaths during the July 1995 heat wave in Chicago. *New England Journal of Medicine, 335*(2), 84–90.

Sierra Club. (2016, May 23). *Sierra Club releases 2016 report card for Arizona legislature and governor.* Retrieved from http://www.sierraclub.org/arizona/blog/2016/05/sierra-club-releases-2016-report-card-for-arizona-legislature-and-governor

Smith, T., Zaitchik, T., & Gohlke, B. (2013). Heat waves in the United States: Definitions, patterns and trends. *Climatic Change, 118*(3), 811–825.

Stafoggia, M., Forastiere, F., Agostini, D., Biggeri, A., Bisanti, L., Cadum, E., . . . Perucci, C. A. (2006). Vulnerability to heat-related mortality: A multicity, population-based, case-crossover analysis. *Epidemiology, 17*(3), 315–323.

US Census Bureau. (n.d.). *2006–2010 American community survey 5-year estimates: EEO occupational groups by sex and race/ethnicity, Phoenix–Mesa–Glendale, AZ metro area.* Retrieved February 5, 2018, from https://factfinder.census.gov/bkmk/table/1.0/en/EEO/10_5YR/EEOALL3R/310M100US38060

Whitaker, M. C. (2000). The rise of Black Phoenix: African-American migration, settlement and community development in Maricopa County, Arizona 1868–1930. *Journal of Negro History, 85*, 197–209.

York, A., Tuccillo, J., Boone, C., Bolin, B., Gentile, L., Schoon, B., & Kane, K. (2014). Zoning and land use: A tale of incompatibility and environmental injustice in early Phoenix. *Journal of Urban Affairs, 36*(5), 833–853.

3

Water Insecurity in Disaster and Climate Change Contexts

A FEMINIST POLITICAL ECOLOGY VIEW

Bernadette P. Resurrección

GLOBAL CLIMATE CHANGE and climate disasters are significant issues that affect contemporary politics, policy action, and academic research. Centuries of neoliberal development that relied on fossil fuels have resulted in a changing global climate and both extreme and slow-onset weather events. The effects and damage are not uniform, whether delineated in spatial (i.e., geographical), social, or economic terms. Researchers and policymakers need to address their complex manifestations and learn from those who are experiencing such changes and events.

Given combined climate-related pressures and other anthropogenic processes such as industrialization, agricultural intensification, and urbanization, water security for human communities throughout the world is declining. Such strain underscores social and gender inequalities, a fundamental idea crystallized by earlier disaster scholars (Bankoff, Hilhorst, & Frerks, 2004; Wisner, Blaikie, Cannon, & Davis, 2004). The growing gender, climate change, and disaster literature advances the idea that gender inequality is one of the drivers of vulnerability and risk of climate change and disasters (Bradshaw, 2001; Denton, 2002), demonstrating adverse effects for certain groups of women and men. Throughout the 2000s, institutions have sought to marshal evidence (Neumayer & Plümper, 2007) that disasters and climate change affect specific groups of women[1] more

---

[1] This work is often cited in advocacy activities to make the case that women are hardest hit by disasters. However, the results of the research show more complex configurations than how it is often invoked.

acutely than others to make the case for including gender in climate change and disaster action agreements at national and international levels.[2]

Gendered vulnerability to disasters and climate risk does not derive from a single factor such as "being a woman" (Enarson, 1998). Instead, vulnerability indicates historically and culturally specific patterns of practices, processes, and power relations that render some individuals or groups more disadvantaged than others. A differentiating process, vulnerability is a dynamic condition shaped by inequities in resources distribution and access. It represents the control individuals have over choices and opportunities. Vulnerability involves the historical patterns of social domination and marginalization in addition to the embodied experience of disadvantage (Bankoff et al., 2004; Eakin & Luers, 2006). Vulnerability is not, then, a set of intrinsic, or fixed, properties that individuals or groups possess. Rather, it is about how people are gendered, disciplined, and regulated as women or men—and as a result, differentially vulnerable—under varying conditions of climate change stresses and disaster risks (Enarson, 1998). These ideas also align with political ecology's growing concern with socio-natures (Castree & Braun, 2001), where in particular, disasters and climate change are viewed as socially, politically, and biophysically produced and instantiated.

This chapter employs a feminist political ecology (FPE) lens to demonstrate how gendered, emotional, and lived experiences offer alternative ways of understanding people's vulnerability to disasters and climate change. It examines how the neoliberal and market-oriented conditions responsible for the world's heavy reliance on fossil fuels continue to intensify through the example of the privatization of water distribution to drive economic growth. Rather than an economistic take on climate change-related water stresses, this chapter departs from a view of water as purely harnessed for production purposes but in which people—through the genderedness of their everyday lives—attach meanings and experience emotions as they go about and live with shifting conditions of water shortages, pollution, and floods.

Water insecurity is the state of people not having rights or access to sufficient water of adequate quality for productive or consumption purposes, or being made increasingly vulnerable to unacceptable levels of water-related risks, such as flooding (Bakker, 2012). Specific social groups of women and men—marked by their class, ethnicity, age, geographical location, and social standing—experience water insecurity in ways that exacerbate and prolong their economic and social disadvantage. This chapter explores water insecurity in disaster and climate change contexts through people's emotional, everyday, and lived experiences (Carney, 2014; Harris, 2015; Tschakert, Tutu, & Alcaro, 2013).

In the sections that follow, the features of an FPE of climate and disaster risks are reviewed. Thereafter, the chapter examines three case studies in Vietnam, Thailand, and

---

[2] A case in point is the 2015 Sendai Framework on Disaster Risk Reduction.

the Philippines to illustrate the workings of FPE in climate change and disaster contexts of water insecurity. The final section offers conclusions and reflects on a few pathways for change.

THE FEMINIST POLITICAL ECOLOGY OF CLIMATE AND DISASTER RISKS

Political ecology, the discipline from which FPE originated, argues that environmental degradation is not an "unfortunate accident under advanced capitalism, but instead a part of the logic of that economic system . . . a consistent symptom of various logics and trajectories of accumulation" (Peet, Robbins, & Watts, 2011, p. 26). In addition to degradation, political ecology addresses current neoliberal efforts to "green" the economy, governance, and environment through conservation, clean technologies, carbon trade and offsets, and techno-managerial approaches to climate change mitigation and adaptation (Fairhead, Leach, & Scoones, 2012; Peet et al., 2011).

Like political ecology, the core defining feature of FPE is its critique of neoliberal drivers that appropriate resources and heighten people's gendered and social risks to development-induced disasters. As a subfield of political ecology, FPE recognizes gender as power relations that are a "critical variable in shaping resource access and control interacting with class, caste, race, culture, and ethnicity to shape processes of ecological change" (Rocheleau, Thomas-Slayter, & Wangari, 1996, p. 4). Since its inception in the 1990s, when it aimed to highlight the women's political struggles around resources and rights (Moeckli & Braun, 2001), FPE has shown strong poststructuralist leanings that question received wisdoms on the production of gender and other social identities. The poststructuralist view posits that those who fit into discrete gender roles are at all times engaged in oppositional relations with men. Through the workings of power, women (and men) constantly reproduce or acquire new identities, which are often intersections of gender with other social differences, such as class, ethnicity, race, or age, that eventually mark their disadvantage or privilege (English, 2010; Sachs, 1997). Feminist political ecology also staunchly critiques neoliberal and patriarchal power structures and advocates for environmental justice and sustainable development (Buechler, 2009; Carney, 2014; Elmhirst, 2011; Harcourt & Nelson, 2015; Harris, 2006; Hawkins & Ojeda, 2011; Leach, 2015; Nightingale, 2006; Rocheleau & Nirmal, 2015). As Rocheleau (2015) notes, 20 years after its beginnings,

> FPE is more about a feminist perspective and an ongoing exploration and construction of a network of learners than a fixed approach for a single focus on women and/or gender. This constant circulation of theory, practice, policies and politics, and the mixing of various combinations of gender, class, race, ethnicity, sexuality, religion, ontologies and ecologies, with critique of colonial legacies and neoliberal designs, has characterized many feminist political ecologists. It is a work in process. (p. 57)

To highlight the political aspects of resource use and access, FPE analyzes the growing commercialization of water in neoliberal development processes. It questions the reliance on technoscientific solutions, which sidestep holistic and grounded approaches. Acknowledging that women are not one unified, coherent group with a single identity, FPE studies their subjective, constantly changing identities as they relate to a changing climate and more frequent disasters. Given the dire need to address climate change and disaster policy discourse, FPE offers valuable insights into the relationship between humans and nature that can contribute to more grounded analyses and better solutions.

In emerging disaster and climate change contexts and in this chapter, FPE focuses on three dimensions of gendered and social experiences of water insecurity, disadvantage, and displacement. First, FPE focuses on an intersectional analysis of people as they experience climate change that re/creates new gender subjectivities as they intersect with class and age. Second, FPE examines people's embodied experiences of affect in water pollution, disasters, and displacements, or shifting livelihoods as these connect with other scales of neoliberal and political economic power and decision-making (Hanson, 2015; Harding, 2008). Third, FPE scrutinizes knowledge production, governance, and policymaking as they sidestep the drivers of vulnerability created by differentiated, unjust life opportunities, vulnerable places, and social exclusions.

A FEMINIST POLITICAL ECOLOGY PERSPECTIVE OF WATER INSECURITY IN THREE SOUTHEAST ASIAN PERI-URBAN AREAS

This chapter applies an FPE lens to episodes of water insecurity in sites affected by flooding and water shortages and pollution induced by long dry spells and heavy precipitation from a 3-year research project, "Adapting to Climate Change in Peri-urban Southeast Asia in the Philippines." The three study sites are Laguna, Philippines; Pathumthani, Thailand; and Van Mon Commune, Vietnam. These sites were studied from 2013 to 2015, with support provided by the International Development Research Centre (IDRC).[3] The following sections are taken from 26 in-depth interviews with women from the project's study sites. The interviewees were randomly selected from sampled household survey respondents in the three study sites, and their names have been changed in this chapter to protect their privacy.

From an FPE perspective, the following sections present highlights from the everyday lives of five women in the three study sites as they "deal with water" in the context

[3] The author co-led the IDRC project together with a colleague from the Asian Institute of Technology, Thailand, and worked with research partners, the Social Development Research Center, De La Salle University, Manila, and the Center for Natural Resources and Environmental Studies, Vietnam National University, Hanoi. I am deeply indebted to Edsel E. Sajor, Rutmanee Ongsakul, Le Thi Van Hue, and Antonio Contreras for their generous contributions of time and ideas to this project.

of increasing water pollution, water scarcity, and flooding compounded by climate change and neoliberal socioeconomic conditions. These accounts show that in water contexts, the neoliberal logics of privatization, commercialization, and reified separation between "nature," "disasters," and "society" engage closely with emotions and intersectional gender subjectivities (Ahlers & Zwarteveen, 2009; Harris, 2009). In Santa Rosa, Laguna, Philippines, women from drought-beleaguered informal settlements make claims to increasingly scarce water supply in a peri-urban village, where water access shapes them as clients instead of users, complicated by the water competition they face with growing industrial and recreational plants within close proximity of their neighborhoods. In the villages of Van Mon Commune, Vietnam, women cope with increasingly polluted water sources as their communities prosper with the wealth generated from recycling metal plants and the aluminum trade. Their intimate and occupational lives coalesce with their abilities to access clean water, marking them as topping or failing the bar of success and dignity in their villages. Finally, in Pathumthani, Thailand, flood-displaced women anchor their identities with home. They emote strong desires to return despite severe flood damage to their homes and property, a result of the government's flood management regime that opted to keep the city core of Bangkok dry while inundating peri-urban places that lie on the city's periphery. What seemed to be an event caused by nature is tightly entwined with deliberate political–economic decisions. This exemplifies that nature and people's emotions from climate change experiences are not isolated events but, rather, occur in relation with specific social, political, and economic forces at play.

Reluctant Clients and Illegal Connections: Water Scarcity in the Time of Drought and Industrial Growth in the Philippines

Santa Rosa, Laguna, is a low-lying municipality at the peri-urban fringes of metro Manila, the Philippines. It has a mix of formal and informal water distribution institutions that rely on groundwater extraction through deep wells. Exclusive gated residential communities, high-end shopping malls, theme parks, and huge industrial complexes have their own independent deep wells and distribution systems. The top 5 of 45 companies account for 68% of industrial demand for water. The dense clustering of wells, especially among residential and industrial wells, may result in the lowering of the water table in the long term (World Wide Fund, 2011). The local government monitors the extraction behavior of a private local water service provider but not the massive extraction from independent commercial and private users with their own deep wells. The unregulated extraction from these privileged water users is the major driver for water shortages that poor communities living at the periphery of industrial and commercial complexes experience. To make matters worse, Laguna Province was listed as a drought-affected province in 2015, and there were longer dry spells in 2016; Philippine meteorologists refer to this as the "El Niño" effect, "where rainfall assessment showed that parts of the country experienced below to way below normal rainfall condition" (Philippine Atmospheric Geophysical and Astronomical Services Administration, 2015).

Women in an informal settlement of 4,240 households, Barangay Sinalhan, manage the supply and distribution of water in their households. They rely heavily on pumping water from their deep artesian wells to meet their daily requirements. Water for the area is obtained mainly from underground sources, and the recharge zone for the aquifer is located upstream, outside the jurisdiction of the local government unit. In 2013, however, the water began drying up, and the little that was extracted emitted a foul smell. To cope, the women purchased water from neighbors who had access to pipe water at 2 PhP ($0.04 USD) per pail. Obtaining this water required huge amounts of time given that the women had to make several trips during the day, stand in queues, and ferry the pails of water back home. The women interviewed, however, did not have jobs and were usually young mothers who had to wash household items used by their very small children and husbands, who worked in nearby firms.

A private local piped water service provider, Laguna Water, supplies mainly the middle- and low-class neighborhoods around the vicinity of Barangay Sinalhan. Ana lives in Barangay Sinalhan and purchases water from Mrs. Cruz, a market stall owner who lives outside the informal settlement and whose water supply comes from Laguna Water. This is done by connecting a pipeline to Mrs. Cruz's Laguna Water pipe, beginning a string of undocumented pipe connections between Mrs. Cruz and Ana's neighbors. Mrs. Cruz provides her clients with water meters, visits every month to collect fees, and bills them 32 PhP ($0.61 USD) for every cubic meter of water consumed. Ana pays approximately 1,600 PhP ($30 USD) a month for her household's consumption.

Another woman, Sarah, who purchases water by the pail, reports that connecting to Mrs. Cruz's pipeline is beyond her means. Her husband has irregular income and she is unemployed, staying home most of the time to care for their four young children. This embarrasses her because unlike her neighbors who have easier access to clean water through Mrs. Cruz, she has to boil the water that she buys and takes home every day from a neighbor who has access to piped water—one of Mrs. Cruz's clients.

Laguna Water is unable to offer legal connections to households in Barangay Sinalhan because the land these households occupy is privately owned by a local resident of Santa Rosa; therefore, the residents are considered illegal dwellers. Water and power services are tied to private and statutory land tenure rights, and none of these women can show official land titles. Thus, "illegal" water connections can be dismantled at any time local authorities choose. In addition to the problems with access to household water supply, most existing wells are poorly maintained; located in flood zones; beside canals; or near toilets, piggeries, and other sources of pollution. This is worsened by more frequent flooding due to typhoons and heavier precipitation occurring in this low-elevation zone. Because Barangay Sinalhan is a flood-prone, low-lying area and serves as a catchment basin of surface run-offs from the upper interior slopes of Laguna Province, it is prone to flash floods. The research project's household survey shows that 10% of the village's residents are exposed to water shortages, 93% to floods, and 47% to water contamination due to floods.

The relationship that people have with water in this settlement is therefore fraught with tension, hardship, and insecurity. It is apparent that women having access to water does not by itself fully ensure their well-being or sense of water security. The conditions that push them to engage in illegal transactions go beyond the technical issues of water access and security alone; they involve larger questions of privatized land tenure and water rights and also competition with huge commercial water users for water use supported by a growth-driven economy of Santa Rosa, Laguna, planners and the Philippines as a whole.

The privatization and commodification of water indicates the decline of real and direct democracy and compromises the public good (Wichterich, 2015), compelling people such as Ana and her neighbors to resort to insecure means of accessing safe water and Sarah's self-exclusion and embodied hardships of fetching water daily. The neoliberal construction of water use and its linkage with private land tenure has shaped them to be reluctant clients and squatters, making do in an increasingly industrialized peri-urban area. Women's embodied, everyday, and emotional experiences in the risky access to water—worsened by drought, less rainfall, and drier wells—interweave with other wider scales of commercializing water commons identified with neoliberal economic growth (Harris, 2015).

Experiences of Water Pollution in Vietnam

Vietnam's economic reforms since 1986 have dramatically expanded industrial and agricultural development, resulting in an overall reduction of poverty since the 1990s. Rapid growth has occurred in both industrial and agricultural sectors, which contribute more than half of the country's gross domestic product, averaging approximately 8% yearly (Dang, 2009; Hue, 2015). Since then, living standards have improved gradually, both in urban and in rural lowlands. One of the key features of Vietnam's ongoing fast-track economic growth reforms has been private sector development and its integration with the global economy.

Such rapid economic development and integration, however, has created serious environmental concerns. This is in large part due to a drive toward increased use of the country's natural resources for fast-track economic growth and the subordination of long-term environmental concerns. Vietnam is thus forced to strike a delicate balance between economic growth and environmental concerns (Di Gregorio, Rambo, & Yangisawa, 2003; O'Rourke, 2002; Sinh, 2004). Economic growth often becomes the overriding priority, and a case in point is the craft industry in Vietnam today.

For example, approximately 1,480 craft villages in Vietnam, a majority of which (up to 80%) are home to household-based artisanal production units, export goods to nearly 100 countries throughout the world. The total nationwide revenue generated from exported products from these craft villages was $650 million USD and $730 million USD in 2006 and 2007, respectively (Ministry of Natural Resources and Environment, 2008). The expansion of these craft industries has led to the pollution of water sources, exacerbated further by the effects of climate change, especially more frequent flooding and run-offs from heavier rainfall.

Van Mon Commune, a peri-urban area, is approximately 21 km northeast of the capital Hanoi and has five villages (Quan Do, Quan Dinh, Man Xa, Phu Xa, and Tien Thon) with a total population of 2,244 households. Of economically active adults, 75%–80% are engaged solely in farming rice, whereas 20%–25% are engaged in artisanal craft production and petty trade. The total income in 2012 was 184,335 million dollars ($7,912,396 USD), of which the total income from artisanal production and related commercial services (selling of scrap) was 135,486 million dollars ($5,815,601 USD), accounting for 73.5% of the total income of the commune. The annual income was 17.7 million dollars ($760 USD) per capita, which had increased by 0.1 dollars million ($4.29 USD)/year compared with 2011 income levels (Van Mon People's Committee, 2012). The figures reveal that households engaged in artisanal production earn much more than those engaged in agricultural production. The number of wealthy families is also increasing as residents find ways to join the artisanal craft industry's economic workforce either as recycle workers or as traders.

The craft industry involves metal junk trade for metal scrap melting, where melted scrap is reprocessed into aluminum bars for the export and domestic markets, notably for the manufacturing of motorbikes and car accessories. In melting metal scrap, oil and mercury compounds are washed away from parts of old transformers, aircraft parts, and transmitter receivers. These compounds and residue from melted aluminum, copper, and iron equipment, together with chemical and agricultural waste from hog raising, discharge into the open common canals from which water is used to irrigate existing rice farms and into groundwater sources.

Local people are increasingly aware of such pollution, especially during the rainy season, which appears to have become increasingly longer. The average rainfall in the area varies between 1,224.4 and 1,639.4 mm per year in Van Mon Commune. Quan Do's villagers recall that normally floods occur in the rainy season from June to August, but recently flooding episodes have occurred unexpectedly during the dry season. The lowest average rainfall, 6.8 mm on average, occurs in October. Informants recall that in the fall of 2008, almost 2 weeks of continuous heavy rainfall seriously damaged 40% of total rice fields in the Commune. According to residents of Quan Do and Man Xa villages, other less intense but unexpected flooding events have occurred, and they recall not being able to protect their fields and homes.

Key informants in Man Xa village observe that polluted wastewater—both from the craft industry and from household waste—emerges from the open drainage system that flows as surface run-off throughout the village during intense rainy periods and floods.

Currently, locals usually dig deeper wells to extract and filter out clean groundwater for household needs. In the Commune, wealthy and middle-income households have three sources of water: a government water supply project, stored rainwater, and water pumped from their own wells that are approximately 50 m deep. Poorer households have only one source: the public water supply station, which has been known to carry a foul odor.

Ha and Phuong are women who work in the metal recycling craft industry. Ha scavenges residual metal scrap from a nearby recycling plant, melts it down herself in a furnace in her backyard, and sells it back to the plant. She also works as hired labor for a rice farm within the Commune during two harvest seasons annually. She is often tired, and she was exposed to unsafe water and high temperatures throughout two pregnancies. She states, "I worry that I am getting weaker and will not be able to do this job any longer to feed my children for a long time. I often feel dizzy and weak, but it somehow gets better the next day."

Phuong, meanwhile, has accumulated wealth by starting a business of buying premium metal scrap from Hanoi junkyards, which she then sells to the recycling plants in her village. Like the affluent 30% of the Commune who have regular sources of income from professional employment or stable enterprises, and who own relatively newly constructed spacious concrete two-story homes and at least one car, Phuong sunk a deep well approximately 100 m deep in her home that uses filtering tanks of sand, for which she paid $750 USD. She does not use the water from the public water supply stations for fear of contamination. Ha, like other poor women, has access only to the public water supply station. She reports feeling older than her age. Referring to women such as Phuong who have become successful metal scrap traders, accumulating sufficient capital, and who command prestige in their community, Ha reports, "I am not lucky as other women who can do business like buying and selling metal. I have no other choice but to do this kind of [melting] job."

Both Ha and Phuong have had husbands who were violent toward them. Visibly emotional, Phuong describes her torment at the hands of two former husbands who both tried to extort her enterprise-created wealth. She does not hesitate to openly narrate details of her experience, whereas Ha only whispers that her husband now lives apart from her and is silent about the causes of their separation. Phuong is less embarrassed by her status as a divorcee and a victim of domestic violence, perhaps because of her evident business success and social stature within the commune, whereas the research team discovered Ha's experiences, quite well known in her neighborhood, from other informants. Ha's reluctance to disclose that part of her life underscores that gendered violence induces shame and also has a class basis.

Ha and Phuong's access to water also reflects their standing in a social hierarchy in which the most well-off, such as Phuong, paradoxically have daily access to efficiently filtered and unpolluted water despite being those most involved in the water-polluting craft industry. Ha, meanwhile, uses her meager earnings from farming and small-scale metal recycling to pay for state-provisioned water, which is scarce and generally unsafe for drinking.

Access to safe water is a differentially embodied experience for the women, where the affluent also have safe water and better health. Water access is embedded in a context in which climate change worsens water pollution levels through unregulated economic growth strategies. This reality intersects gender with class markers of disadvantage, such as shame from gender-based violence and weakening health due to the demands of single parenthood and manual labor. The intersectionality of gender, class, shame, and social standing highlights elements of privilege and marginalization for both Ha and Phuong. Thus, the drivers of vulnerability in the case of Ha are a complex mix of intersecting gender (i.e., shame), class (i.e., poverty), and health (i.e., frequent exposure to metal furnace temperatures and unsafe water). Moreover, an FPE lens can shed light on how community prestige can diminish the shame of gender-based violence in the case of Phuong. Conversely, Ha's low status and lack of prestige aggravate her shame. The women's water practices also demonstrate that water is tied to power, social standing, and inequality that go beyond differences in its distribution and access (Truelove, 2011).

Emotional Geographies of Returning Home After Disaster in Thailand

Lying along the path of the sprawling floodplains north of Bangkok, Thailand's Pathumthani Province was heavily flooded in November and December 2011. As the Chao Phraya River swelled to its highest levels recorded since 1997, residents in canal settlements abandoned their homes. It was no longer tenable for residents to remain home and wait for the waters to recede as they normally do during regular annual flooding.

Unusually heavy rainfall from the La Niña effect caused the great 2011 flood of Thailand, which was exacerbated by the mismanagement of upstream dams and reservoirs that reached their maximum storage levels. Sluice gates were lifted to release vast amounts of excess reservoir water, causing flooding downstream and southward toward the deltaic areas and floodplains of the central region. This was compounded by the high tide and rising water level of the Chao Phraya River basin (Thailand Integrated Water Resource Management, 2012).

In contrast, the inner-city core of Bangkok remained dry. The government decided to divert floodwaters to localities in the urban fringe to preserve the political, financial, and business capital of the country. Then Prime Minister Yingluck Shinawatra insisted that the overflow should only affect the edge of the metropolitan area (MacKinnon, 2011). The director of the government's flood relief center responded that "it was necessary to save places of economic significance while sacrificing less important areas" (British Broadcasting Corporation, 2011). The Thai government directed the Royal Thai Army to repair the flood barriers in Pathumthani to shield Bangkok from the flood ("Government Moves to Protect Inner City," 2011). By manipulating flood gates and packing in sandbags as embankments along the flooded canal systems of the Bangkok Metropolitan Region,[4] floodwaters were diverted to the western and eastern peripheries of the city. This led floods to flow very slowly and last 6–8 weeks instead of flowing through the shortest and most direct route—via the city core of Bangkok—to drain into the Chao Phraya River toward the Thai Gulf.

Peri-urban areas including the Kracheng subdistrict of Pathumthani Province were among the hardest hit, marginalized and not a priority in the government's protection plan. The run-off water from the north reached Pathumthani Province in mid-October, and the flood lasted until early January 2012. The water level was 2 or 3 m deep on average. All households in Kracheng were inundated, and most residents abandoned their homes.

Kracheng subdistrict exhibits peri-urban characteristics that in part render its residents vulnerable to flooding and other types of water stresses. Conflicting urban and rural land and water uses in this area have also increasingly polluted water sources. Industrialization and urbanization have eliminated former waterways and natural wetlands. Political jurisdictions with unclear or overlapping boundaries also cripple the smooth availability of water-related and flood mitigation services. To exacerbate matters, the subdistrict is located on a low-lying and flood-prone area on the Chao Phraya Delta; thus, floods occur yearly, although the November 2011 flood was exceptional in its damage to homes and displacement of people. Finally, water management in the upstream dams and reservoirs also affects the Chao Phraya River's water levels that flow through the Kracheng subdistrict, compounding the risk of flooding. The remainder of this section recounts the stories of two women who experienced the effects of the November 2011 flood, through the prism of their emotions and displacement.

With a heavy heart, 85-year-old Khun La-ong left her old teakwood home of 65 years by the Chao Phraya River when water 2 or 3 m deep swirled inside her living room. Khun La-ong is used to the annual ebb and flow of the river's tides and floods but was unprepared—as were most of the population of the area—for the inundation of her entire home. She and her husband left for their daughter's house in Nakhon Pathom, leaving behind their only adult son. They stayed away for 6 weeks. While gone, Khun La-ong greatly missed her home, calling her son daily to find out when she and her husband could possibly return. She missed being in a familiar place; it was very strange for her to live in the city, far from any river. To cope, she kept herself strenuously busy, cleaning, cooking, and caring for her daughter's three children. Khun La-ong and her husband squeezed themselves into a small house in which six people lived—a difficult adjustment.

---

[4] Since the 1980s, the Bangkok Metropolitan Region has encompassed five adjacent provinces (Nakhon Pathom and Samut Sakhon in the west, Nonthaburi and Pathumthani in the north, and Samut Prakan in the east), which together with the city core of Bangkok constitute one of the world's largest urban agglomerations and the large floodplain north of the Chao Phraya River. It is home to more than 14 million people and has dominated Thailand's economy, outpacing other urban regions in the country in terms of importance.

She constantly worried that the flood would destroy her own home, as she knew that the government would not provide adequate compensation for their losses. She also worried about her husband's declining health, as he was stricken with diabetes. After their return home, her husband fell sick and had to be confined in a hospital. Khun La-ong believes stress from evacuating their home worsened her husband's condition. She began to experience heart problems and was likewise hospitalized. Despite the trauma of evacuating, Khun La-ong believes she is still strong enough to cope with more floods, and she claims that she will never leave her home of 65 years.

Khun Namwun, aged 60 years, lives with two of her three children in Kracheng subdistrict. The annual floods used to sow fears of drowning and snakes entering her home. The flood of 2011 was the most fearful moment of her life, despite having long experienced the annual floods. She was constantly watching the floodwaters rise, afraid that they would claim and sweep away her house. Her fears were worse when darkness fell, given the snakes and possibility of thieves. To calm herself, she resolved to fully accept the situation. She refused to evacuate to a drier, safer place because of her fear that nothing would be saved from her home if she abandoned it. She stated, "I could not show my fear to my daughters, or else they would lose their courage to weather through the flood." Her blood pressure rose, but she kept herself calm, aware that any display of fear would cause all of them to panic. Because of the flood, she began to consider moving elsewhere permanently. However, she decided to remain in the house because it belonged to her husband's relative, who charged her low rent, and because her daughters' wages were too low to cover rental rates elsewhere. Khun Namwun hesitated to stay with her eldest daughter Tuk, who lived with her in-laws in the city of Ayutthaya. Tuk visited Khum Namwun during the major flood. The only time Khun Namwun showed any fear or anxiety was when Tuk compelled her to move in with her and her husband's family. "They are not my family," Khum Namwun said, "This is my house, and I will not leave."

The previous stories demonstrate that emotions about home indicate the depth of these women's disaster experiences as they entangle with their decisions—fraught with fear and ambivalence—to return or remain home (Morrice, 2012). Disasters threaten people's personal possessions, sense of home and refuge, stable social networks, and, ultimately, their identities. Disasters damage material structures but also unsettle and trigger people's emotions that are tied to places, such as "home." The flood management authorities, for their part, made a deliberate choice of assigning the urban core as a privileged place by retaining and diverting water to peri-urban areas, thus sparing the urban core from inundation. The homes of these two women and many others' homes in peri-urban spaces are not considered significant in the minds of flood managers. "Place" is thus a social, political, and emotional construct. Places are invested by individuals and by collectives with meanings, beliefs, desires, and emotions that give them sufficient "permanence" as a locus of institutionalized social power or marginalization (Harvey, 1996). The women's experiences also demonstrate that emotions and illnesses as felt by women and their families are not isolated mental or physical states but, rather, relationally produced as lived and embodied experiences (Morales & Harris, 2014)—in this case, they were experienced in the intersection between disasters, the broader political economy of Thailand, and the hierarchical values assigned to peri-urban areas and the city core. Finally, emotions and lived experiences remind us that flood disasters and climate change reveal the tight connections between "nature" and "society." Despite the neoliberal logic that disaster and climate change are natural phenomena disentangled from society, flooding requires technical and management decisions that consider people, their sense of place, or their emotions tied to it.

CONCLUSION: RECEIVED WISDOM ON PARTICIPATION AND ENGAGEMENT

This chapter has employed an FPE lens to examine some of the fundamental logics and binaries of neoliberalism as they are applied to contexts of vulnerability and climate change.

Women's everyday lived experiences of climate change manifested by water scarcity, pollution, and flooding interweave with wider neoliberal dynamics of water commercialization in most areas of Southeast Asia today. Through their stories, it is apparent how the shifting subjectivities relate to climate change: how clean water access in Vietnamese craft villages marks gendered subjectivities, stratifying women in ways that keep them silent or willing to disclose the violence that they once lived through; how water shortages during dry spells and in competition with the use of water by industrial giants in Philippine peri-urban areas push some women to become reluctant clients or "market citizens" to an illegal system of water provision; and how women experience complicated emotions when leaving or returning to their homes ravaged by flooding in Thailand. These accounts demonstrate that the binary between "the private" and "the public" is a tenuous one. People's vulnerabilities to climate change are multidimensional.

Vulnerability to climate and disaster risks is often defined in terms of physical sensitivity to hazards such as floods, and their solutions are often represented and designed to reduce physical vulnerability. However, as the Thai case most glaringly demonstrates, flood management and post-disaster solutions often lean toward protecting the emblems of power, marshaling an assembly of physical solutions—with tacit, yet serious social intent and implications—to the 2011 flood problem. This disputes the view that climate change and disasters are discretely natural occurrences, thus dismantling the reified binary between "the natural" and "the social."

The use of an FPE lens offers more holistic and grounded ways of probing into people's experiences of climate-related water insecurity and stresses, aspects of which are often missed: gendered violence, hierarchies of place, affect, and insecurity in everyday life in growth-driven economies. People's relationship with water is not just about its utilitarian function and efficient distribution for productive uses—the neoliberal principle of optimal utility—but also about how people view themselves and feel emotions as they "deal with water." In the climate change and disaster literature, vulnerability has been narrowly defined as exposure to risk, whereas from this study of women's lives, it is apparent that vulnerabilities are complex, contingent, and embedded in structural, embodied, and emotional everyday experiences that require hybrid and nuanced solutions.

Resilience-building in disaster and climate change contexts should be able to address complex and multidimensional drivers of vulnerability in people's everyday lives. Indeed, resilience is not only about the need to govern, discipline, or live with water insecurity by a set of adaptation or disaster risk reduction measures but also about how we can "produce ourselves differently" (Taylor, 2015, p. xvi) and transform relations of power that cause risky environments to expand and prevail in the first place.

As a feminist project, "producing ourselves differently" fundamentally means to explicitly situate our analysis in the structural transformations currently taking place, sensitive to the gender and social dynamics in processes of (water) privatization. In concrete terms, this means that efforts by communities to challenge structural transformations and decision-making should not be hollow forms of participatory engagement that has often been applied at micro scales through devolution schemes or applying principles of subsidiarity (e.g., community water user groups or community adaptation). Past experiences have shown that it is not enough to simply have more people from diverse gender, class, or ethnic groups attend meetings to form resource care groups and raise their voices: "Unless broader social, cultural, and institutional structures also shift to support that engagement, participation will be superficial, short-lived, or even deeply frustrating" (Morales & Harris, 2014, p. 705).

Climate change adaptation in water governance requires principally asking fundamental questions about the propensity to attach a price tag to everything, including common assets such as water. This strikes at the heart of development trajectories and how "progress," "growth," and "advancement" have been defined and roadmapped, especially at a time when climate and development concerns are being increasingly integrated and pose an urgent agenda.

REFERENCES

Ahlers, R., & Zwarteveen, M. (2009). The water question in feminism: Water control and gender inequities in a neo-liberal era. *Gender, Place & Culture, 16*(4), 409–426. doi:10.1080/09663690903003926

Bakker, K. (2012). Water security: Research challenges and opportunities. *Science, 337*(6097), 914–915. doi:10.1126/science.1226337

Bankoff, G., Hilhorst, D., & Frerks, G. (2004). *Mapping vulnerability: Disasters, development and people.* London, UK: Routledge.

Bradshaw, S. (2001). Reconstructing roles and relations: Women's participation in reconstruction in post-Mitch Nicaragua. *Gender & Development, 9*(3), 79–87. doi:10.1080/13552070127757

British Broadcasting Corporation. (2011, October 18). *Thai flooding: Floodwalls reinforced to protect Bangkok*. Retrieved from https://www.bbc.co.uk/news/world-asia-pacific-15350948

Buechler, S. (2009). Gender, water, and climate change in Sonora, Mexico: Implications for policies and programmes on agricultural income-generation. *Gender & Development, 17*(1), 51–66. doi:10.1080/13552070802696912

Carney, M. A. (2014). The biopolitics of "food insecurity": Towards a critical political ecology of the body in studies of women's transnational migration. *Journal of Political Ecology, 21*, 1–18.

Castree, N., & Braun, B. (Eds.). (2001). *Social nature: Theory, practice and politics*. Oxford, UK: Blackwell.

Dang, K. C. (2009). *Vietnam's craft villages and environment*. Policy paper of the project Policy Advocacy Campaign in Vietnam: Stakeholders, Wastewater Management and Air Pollution Treatment in Craft Villages in the Red River Delta of Vietnam, Center for Natural Resources and Environmental Studies, Vietnam National University, Hanoi, Vietnam.

Denton, F. (2002). Climate change vulnerability, impacts, and adaptation: Why does gender matter? *Gender and Development, 10*(2), 10–20.

Di Gregorio, M., Rambo, A. T., & Yanagisawa, M. (2003). Clean, green and beautiful: Environment and development under the renovation economy. In H. V. Luong (Ed.), *Postwar Vietnam: Dynamic and transforming society* (pp. 171–199). Oxford, UK: Rowman & Littlefield.

Eakin, H., & Luers, A. L. (2006). Assessing the vulnerability of social–environmental systems. *Annual Review of Environment and Resources, 31*(1), 365–394. doi:10.1146/annurev.energy.30.050504.144352

Elmhirst, R. (2011). Introducing new feminist political ecologies. *Geoforum, 42*(2), 129–132. doi:10.1016/j.geoforum.2011.01.006

Enarson, E. (1998). Through women's eyes: A gendered research agenda for disaster social science. *Disasters, 22*(2), 157–173. doi:10.1111/1467-7717.00083

English, L. (2010). Poststructualist feminism. In A. J. Mills, G. Durepos, & E. Wiebe (Eds.), *Encyclopedia of case study research* (pp. 711–716). Thousand Oaks, CA: Sage.

Fairhead, J., Leach, M., & Scoones, I. (2012). Green grabbing: A new appropriation of nature? *Journal of Peasant Studies, 39*(2), 237–261. doi:10.1080/03066150.2012.671770

Government moves to protect inner city. (2011, October 12). *Bangkok Post*. Retrieved from http://www.bangkokpost.com/news/local/260863/govt-moves-to-protect-inner-city

Hanson, A.-M. (2015). Women's ecological oral histories of recycling and development in coastal Yucatán. *Gender, Place and Culture, 4*, 467–483. doi:10.1080/0966369X.2015.1013445

Harcourt, W., & Nelson, I. L. (2015). *Practicing feminist political ecologies: Moving beyond the "green economy."* London, UK: Zed Books.

Harding, S. (2008). *Sciences from below: Feminisms, postcolonialities, and modernities*. Durham, NC: Duke University Press.

Harris, L. M. (2006). Irrigation, gender, and social geographies of the changing waterscapes of southeastern Anatolia. *Environment and Planning D: Society and Space, 24*(2), 187–213. doi:10.1068/d03k

Harris, L. M. (2009). Gender and emergent water governance: Comparative overview of neoliberalized natures and gender dimensions of privatization, devolution and marketization. *Gender, Place & Culture, 16*(4), 387–408. doi:10.1080/09663690903003918

Harris, L. M. (2015). Hegemonic waters and rethinking natures otherwise. In W. Harcourt & I. L. Nelson (Eds.), *Practicing feminist political ecologies: Moving beyond the "green economy"* (pp. 157–181). London, UK: Zed Books.

Harvey, D. (1996). *Justice, nature and the geography of difference*. Oxford, UK: Blackwell.

Hawkins, R., & Ojeda, D. (2011). Gender and environment: Critical tradition and new challenges. *Environment and Planning D: Society and Space, 29*(2), 237–253. doi:10.1068/d16810

Hue, L. T. V. (2015). *Final technical report of the Vietnam case study for IDRC Project Grant Number 106960-001: Adapting to climate change in peri-urban Southeast Asia*. Bangkok, Thailand: Asian Institute of Technology.

Leach, M. (2015). *Gender equality and sustainable development*. New York, NY: Routledge.

MacKinnon, I. (2011, October 14). Bangkok braced for devastating floods. *The Telegraph*. Retrieved from https://www.telegraph.co.uk/news/worldnews/asia/thailand/8827594/Bangkok-braced-for-devastating-floods.html

Ministry of Natural Resources and Environment. (2008). *National report on the environment in Vietnam's craft villages*. Hanoi, Vietnam: Author.

Moeckli, J., & Braun, B. (2001). Gendered natures: Feminism, politics, and social nature. In N. Castree & B. Braun (Eds.), *Social nature: Theory, practice and politics* (pp. 112–132). Oxford, UK: Blackwell.

Morales, M. C., & Harris, L. M. (2014). Using subjectivity and emotion to reconsider participatory natural resource management. *World Development, 64*, 703–712. doi:10.1016/j.worlddev.2014.06.032

Morrice, S. (2012). Heartache and Hurricane Katrina: Recognising the influence of emotion in post-disaster return decisions. *Area, 45*(1), 33–39. doi:10.1111/j.1475-4762.2012.01121.x

Neumayer, E., & Plümper, T. (2007). The gendered nature of natural disasters: The impact of catastrophic events on the gender gap in life expectancy. *Annals of the Association of American Geographers, 97*(3), 551–566. doi:10.1111/j.1467-8306.2007.00563.x

Nightingale, A. (2006). The nature of gender: Work, gender, and environment. *Environment and Planning D: Society and Space, 24*(2), 165–185. doi:10.1068/d01k

O'Rourke, D. (2002). Community-driven regulation: Toward an improved model of environmental regulation in Vietnam. In P. Evans (Ed.), *Livable cities? Urban struggles for livelihood and sustainability* (pp. 95–131). Berkeley, CA: University of California Press

Peet, R., Robbins, P., & Watts, M. (Eds.). (2011). *Global political ecology*. London, UK: Routledge.

Philippine Atmospheric Geophysical and Astronomical Services Administration. (2015). *El Niño Advisory No. 10*. Quezon City, Philippines: Author.

Rocheleau, D. E. (2015). A situated view of feminist political ecology from my networks, roots and territories. In W. Harcourt & I. L. Nelson (Eds.), *Practicing feminist political ecologies: Moving beyond the "green economy"* (pp. 29–66). London, UK: Zed Books.

Rocheleau, D. E., & Nirmal, P. (2015). Feminist political ecologies: Grounded, networked and rooted on Earth. In R. Baksh & W. Harcourt (Eds.), *The Oxford handbook of transnational feminist movements* (pp. 793–814). New York, NY: Oxford University Press.

Rocheleau, D. E., Thomas-Slayter, B. P., & Wangari, E. (1996). *Feminist political ecology: Global issues and local experiences*. London, UK: Routledge.

Sachs, C. (1997). *Women working in the environment*. Washington, DC: Taylor & Francis.

Sinh, B. (2004). Institutional challenges for sustainable development in Vietnam: The case of the coal mining sector. In M. Beresford & A. Tran Ngoc (Eds.), *Reaching for the dream: Challenges of sustainable development in Vietnam* (pp. 284–295). Singapore: ISEAS.

Taylor, M. (2015). *The political ecology of climate change adaptation: Livelihoods, agrarian change and the conflicts of development.* Oxon, UK: Routledge.

Thailand Integrated Water Resource Management. (2012). *2011 Thailand flood: Executive summary.* Retrieved from http://www.thaiwater.net/web/index.php/ourworks2554/379-2011flood-summary.html

Truelove, Y. (2011). (Re-)Conceptualizing water inequality in Delhi, India through a feminist political ecology framework. *Geoforum, 42*(2), 143–152. doi:10.1016/j.geoforum.2011.01.004

Tschakert, P., Tutu, R., & Alcaro, A. (2013). Embodied experiences of environmental and climatic changes in landscapes of everyday life in Ghana. *Emotion, Space and Society, 7,* 13–25. doi:10.1016/j.emospa.2011.11.001

Van Mon People's Committee. (2012). *Van Mon People's Committee report on socio-economic status in 2012 and key directions for 2013.* Ho Chi Minh City, Vietnam.

Wichterich, C. (2015). Contesting green growth, connecting care, commons and enough. In W. Harcourt & I. L. Nelson (Eds.), *Practising feminist political ecologies: Moving beyond the "green economy"* (pp. 67–100). London, UK: Zed Books.

Wisner, B., Blaikie, P., Cannon, T., & Davis, I. (2004). *At risk: Natural hazards, people's vulnerability and disasters.* London, UK: Routledge.

World Wide Fund. (2008). *Santa Rosa Watershed Management Project: Hydrology study* (Unpublished report). World Wide Fund, Switzerland.

4

Older People and Climate Change

VULNERABILITY AND RESILIENCE TO EXTREME WEATHER
IN ENGLAND

Katie Oven, Jonathan Wistow, and Sarah Curtis

CLIMATE CHANGE AND HEALTH AND SOCIAL CARE
SYSTEMS IN THE ENGLISH CONTEXT

Climate change in England, as in other areas of Europe, is increasing the frequency and intensity of certain types of extreme weather events, resulting in an increased risk of heat waves and flooding (Intergovernmental Panel on Climate Change, 2011). At the same time, population trends and projections for European countries including England show a relatively large and growing proportion of older people,[1] especially in the oldest age groups. The European region has the highest median age in the world, and by 2050 the proportion aged 65 years and older is expected to reach 27% (World Health Organization, 2012). England is typical of this trend, with those in the oldest age groups having higher levels of use of, and reliance on, health and social care services. It is therefore significant that the proportion of people aged 85 years or older in England is predicted to more than double between 2008 and 2033 (increasing from 2.2% to 4.6%; Oven et al., 2012).

The combined effects of climate change and an aging population are causing growing concern in Europe regarding the health and well-being of older people. In England, this

---

[1] There is no fixed definition of an older person, with definitions defined based on the prevailing demographic structure of a population. In England, people older than age 65 years are often considered to be in the "older" age group.

is reflected, for example, in the *UK Climate Change Risk Assessment 2017* (Kovats & Osborn, 2016), which identified increasing risks to population health from mortality and morbidity caused by high temperatures, and some growing risks to health (particularly mental health) from the impacts of flooding. The risk assessment noted that extremely cold weather also carries significant health risks. Though extreme cold is likely to be less frequent in the future, cold spells will continue to occur, with the population health benefits of reduced exposure to cold weather likely to be offset by the growth of the older population. The assessment also identified risks in health service delivery and social care systems due to heat waves, floods, and very cold conditions affecting built infrastructure and utility systems, including transportation and power supplies. This is reflected in the current guidance for agencies responsible for health care and public health functions in England (Department for Environment and Rural Affairs, 2014; Public Health England, 2015a, 2015b).

Though England is not representative of Europe as a whole, several aspects are broadly typical of trends throughout the region. For example, England shares with many other countries in Western Europe a similar pattern of climate change and resulting health hazards, demographic trends producing a population with a relatively large and growing proportion of older people, and health and social care systems that are well established.

In this chapter, we explore how complexity and nexus thinking can help frame the challenges of climate change and population aging. We report on findings from a research project in England that illustrates key features of complex systems. The research demonstrates the importance of building resilience to extreme weather in systems of health and health care for older people. To do so, we argue that it is necessary to understand the challenges posed by complex systems and processes. Drawing on our empirical findings, we show how both local and broader scale factors affect the system and how personal experience also depends on individual social and cultural characteristics of older people. We conclude with a discussion about the wider international relevance of the key findings reported and their policy implications.

THEORIZING VULNERABILITY AND RESILIENCE: COMPLEX SYSTEMS AND NEXUS THINKING

International literature highlights the usefulness of viewing the emergency management system in terms of the typical features of complex, networked systems. This perspective is relevant globally. For example, research on emergency responses in the United States emphasizes a growing need to understand emergency management as a collaborative network or an "aggregation of structural arrangements" (Kapucu & Garayev, 2016, p. 933) that comprises both horizontal and vertical dimensions. *Horizontal dimensions* relate to connections that operate locally between different sectors that make up a system in a particular area, whereas *vertical dimensions* refer to the links to parts of the system that are organized or administered at a "higher level" through regional and national systems or in some cases through global agencies. Similarly, researchers comparing experiences of extreme events in England and the Netherlands (Noordegraaf & Newman, 2011) emphasize how multiple spheres of social action (e.g., political, social, administrative) come into play during extreme events and how various agents involved relate to social structures in the particular context where the event takes place.

Our research in English communities emphasizes the need to consider both formal and informal elements in these networks and the importance of strengthening connections between them to avoid discontinuities between different parts of the system (Wistow, Dominelli, Oven, Dunn, & Curtis, 2015). In addition, though the literature is motivated by the risks that extreme events pose and the particular vulnerabilities of some older people, efforts to improve resilience often involve identifying and enhancing the effective use of individual and collective assets, which include the knowledge and capacity of "vulnerable" older people (Howard, Blakemore, & Bevis, 2017; Rotegard, Moore, Fagermoen, & Ruland, 2010).

Complexity Theory

Ideas about resilience can also be applied to care systems, with research increasingly drawing from complexity theory to help conceptualize these systems (Curtis, Fair, Wistow, Val, & Oven, 2017). Complexity theory stresses the emergent properties of complex systems and the impossibility of precise prediction of events using linear models that assume future conditions can be predicted from previous experience. Complexity theory also highlights that the relationships within networks are highly contingent on local conditions (Herrick, 2016). Because these complex networks vary from location to location, it is necessary to draw on local knowledge and actors when planning for and enhancing resilience to extreme weather (Wistow et al., 2015). Though we acknowledge the emergent nature of complex systems, we argue that one may recognize certain typical features of complex systems that are universally applicable to different settings (Curtis, Oven, Wistow, Dunn, & Dominelli, 2018; Curtis & Riva, 2010a, 2010b; Gatrell, 2005).

Complex systems also tend to include features such as capacity for self-organization; networks of many different actors with imperfect knowledge of each other; linkages that combine openness and connectivity across the system with partial closure and isolation of different actors; potential for co-evolution, involving the different elements of the system; and path dependency (i.e., contemporary and future behavior that may be influenced by previous experience and practice). A deeper understanding of these attributes and their relevance to planning for extreme events can help local communities and agencies prepare for and build resilience to the kinds of uncertain futures anticipated under conditions of climate change (Curtis et al., 2018).

Nexus Thinking

A related stream of thought has identified the "nexus" as an important framework for planning for critical events, which may include extreme or unusual events. The nexus construct helps conceptualize a resource network across formal and informal health and social care systems that includes social, organizational, and built infrastructures (Curtis et al., 2017; Pelling, 2010; Zaidi & Pelling, 2013). Nexus thinking emphasizes the interconnections, tensions, and trade-offs between sectors that have traditionally been managed separately. As a result, it is promoted internationally as a tool for achieving sustainable development and integrated management across sectors, systems, and scales. By underscoring the interdependencies between sectors, nexus thinking offers ways to operationalize shared agendas, often drawing on "bottom-up ways of knowing" (Leck, Conway, Bradshaw, & Rees, 2015, p. 453), and it enables more equitable and just outcomes (Stringer et al., 2014).

In summary, both complex systems and nexus thinking highlight the importance of the interrelationships among systems (e.g., the built, institutional, and social systems responsible for health and social care delivery, climate change adaptation, and emergency response); the potential value of local self-organization, which recognizes and values local knowledge; and the support required from other parts of the system (e.g., from national and local government). We demonstrate below how these theoretical ideas offer a potentially useful and practical framework to support the development of more robust preparedness and adaption strategies to make health and social care more resilient to extreme weather in the context of climate change.

THE BIOPICCC PROJECT: APPLIED RESEARCH USING COMPLEXITY AND NEXUS FRAMEWORKS

The kinds of theoretical models discussed above were applied in the English context from 2009 to 2012 in a project titled Built Infrastructure for Older People's Care in Conditions of Climate Change (BIOPICCC).[2] The project sought to find ways to ensure the continuity of health care for older people during extreme weather events, particularly heat waves, very cold weather, and flooding. The crucial nexus for this project was therefore the linkage between key *resource elements* (social, institutional, and physical infrastructures that deliver health and social care services, crossing the formal and informal sectors), *consumer elements* (older people dependent on continuous access to these services), and *environmental elements* (processes associated with climate change). Figure 4.1 provides a simplified representation of this nexus.

---

[2] The authors were part of the BIOPICCC research team that included social scientists, natural scientists, and engineers.

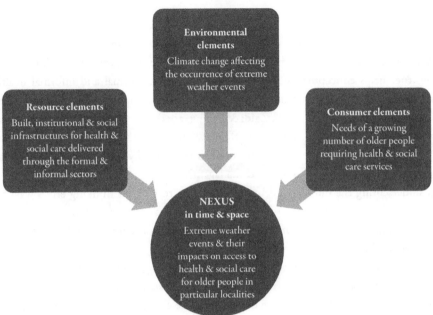

FIGURE 4.1 A simplified diagram of the "nexus" of health and social care access for older people during extreme weather events.

The research team began this project by drawing together key knowledge about the geographical distribution of different elements shown in Figure 4.1. Doing so enabled the team to identify localities in England where it would be informative to explore how the nexus of linkages operated during extreme weather events. Moreover, it also helped determine how to strengthen the system in the face of future extreme weather events.

The research team started this process by mapping local areas throughout England and predicting trends in future risks of extreme weather and in projected growth of the older population. In addition to age, the team mapped some known aspects of vulnerability, including socioeconomic deprivation measured using quantitative indicators of local area conditions such as the Index of Multiple Deprivation.[3] This exercise enabled the research team to identify areas of England where a particularly marked change in the risk nexus could be expected. These were places likely to experience relatively large increases in the occurrence of extreme weather hazards and in the growth of vulnerable populations in the oldest age groups (Oven et al., 2012). The researchers noted, for example, that the places where there was a change in risk of extreme events such as heat waves were not always the areas that were already experiencing relatively high prevailing temperatures,

---

[3] The Index of Multiple Deprivation is based on seven domains of deprivation: income; employment; health deprivation and disability; education, skills, and training; barriers to housing and services; living environment; and crime (Communities and Local Government, 2010).

and the places that currently had the largest proportions of older people were not always those experiencing the most rapid increases in population aging. The research team focused on local areas where environmental and demographic conditions were changing most quickly and where, as a result, local communities and key actors would have had less opportunity to adapt to changing conditions.

Having selected two localities, one in northern and one in southern England,[4] in which researchers would carry out the investigation, BIOPICCC then progressed to a second stage in which appropriate stakeholders from the different nexus elements were identified and convened in focus groups. In the first instance, this involved participants from the formal sector, including various institutional agencies (i.e., the resource elements) and experts concerned with monitoring the environmental elements of the nexus across the whole study area. The focus groups convened in local urban centers with representatives from local informal sector organizations (i.e., consumer elements) providing for older people. Partly on the basis of knowledge generated in this first round of discussions, BIOPICCC followed up with a series of focus group discussions and semistructured interviews in more dispersed localities identified as (or likely in the future to be) places with particularly high risks of environmental elements affecting the consumer elements. More than 35 people were consulted at the strategic level, including representatives from the local authority, National Health Services, and the community and voluntary sector (CVS); in addition, BIOPICCC consulted 19 frontline staff representing the local authority, statutory services, CVS and the parish council, among others. This led the research to local communities where older residents had been most severely affected by floods, prolonged cold and snow, or heat waves, often in more isolated rural parts of the study area. A total of 35 older people with different health and social care needs were interviewed. Participants valued the BIOPICCC meetings as opportunities to bring together people who did not normally have the chance to engage around this issue, to draw on local knowledge and experience from past events, and to share ideas about how to build resilience to possible future risks. For further detail on the research methodology, see Curtis and colleagues (2018).

In addition to dialog, the activity produced tangible outputs in the form of locality-specific organograms (Table 4.1) that summarize the different resource elements of the system at the wider level of the whole study area, as well as the local sites where the extreme event nexus was likely to have particular impact. The diagrams helped local participants grasp the cross-sectoral and multiscalar institutional and social structures made up of diverse actors necessary to build resilience in the health and social care system.

---

[4] To protect the confidentiality of research participants, the exact locations of the case study local authorities and communities are withheld.

TABLE 4.1

Organogram Summarizing the Diverse Types of Agencies Involved in Health and
Social Care Delivery, Climate Change Adaption, and Resilience Planning in England

Sector	Agencies
Local government	Adult social care
	Emergency planning
	Climate change adaptation
	Coordinating bodies (e.g., local resilience forums, health and well-being boards)
National Health Services (NHS)	Primary care trust (e.g., general practitioners)
	Acute trust (hospital care; e.g., accident and emergency, NHS estates)
	Community trust
Informal sector	Community voluntary sector (e.g., Age UK, Older People's Forum, local service user groups)
Independent (for-profit) care providers	Private care companies
	Care homes
Emergency providers	Fire and rescue service
	Police
	Ambulance service
Other agencies	Utilities providers (e.g., gas and telecommunications companies)
	Transport providers (e.g., local bus companies, dial-a-ride services)
	Inspection and regulation (e.g., Environment Agency)

Source: Adapted from Curtis et al. (2018).

Participatory mapping also helped identify and locate the health and social care assets (including built infrastructure) that were of concern and likely to be at risk during extreme weather events (Figure 4.2). This material was developed to be incorporated into a toolkit that was later used by other groups in different areas of the country wanting to bring together different types of knowledge and expertise around this issue.[5]

OBSERVATIONS ABOUT COMPLEXITY AND THE NEXUS OF EXTREME WEATHER AFFECTING CARE FOR OLDER PEOPLE

Here, we summarize the findings from the BIOPICCC research relevant to Western Europe and other regions globally with aging populations and well-established and complex health care systems. Though the circumstances and experiences participants reported

---

[5] See https://www.dur.ac.uk/geography/research/researchprojects/biopiccc/toolkit.

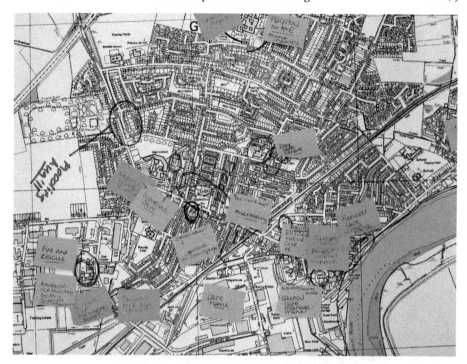

FIGURE 4.2 Participatory mapping exercise with frontline service providers. Participants worked together to map the parts of the health and social care system that older people were most likely to need to use continuously, which might also be disrupted during extreme weather events. This helped identify priorities for preparedness planning.

are specific to the settings and communities that participated in the project and cannot be generalized in detail, some more general points reinforce understanding from other areas of the international research literature. These points relate especially to three overarching themes: (1) the complex interaction between vulnerability and resilience; (2) the significance of path dependency and the potential for vertical and horizontal knowledge exchange to influence evolution across the system at a wider scale; and (3) the problems of gaps in connectivity and imperfect knowledge sharing between different elements in the system, resulting in system failure in extreme situations.

Interactions Between Vulnerability and Resilience

The findings from the BIOPICCC project emphasize the complex relationships between vulnerability and resilience and between resource elements and consumer elements in the system. Vulnerability is often associated with the interdependencies between the built, institutional, and social infrastructures that make up these elements. However, the diversity and dynamic nature of the linkages in the system mean that resilience is built partly on the potential—when one important linkage system fails—for another to emerge as an alternative connection that allows the system to continue functioning.

For example, health and social care agencies operate service delivery functions across fairly wide geographical catchments (especially in the rural and semirural settings studied). There is a strong interdependency between service delivery and the physical infrastructures—especially road transport systems—upon which they rely for connectivity. Health and social care often need to be delivered to older people's homes, and patients also need to attend clinics for outpatient care on a regular basis. If flooding or heavy snowfall interrupts transport systems for prolonged periods, these systems cease to function as normal, which presents risks for the older people involved. One solution adopted by provider agencies was for workloads to be reallocated so that carers deliver domiciliary care to older residents living close to them rather than visiting their normal clientele who might be farther away and difficult to reach if transport systems are disrupted. A local authority representative explained:

> So we've been encouraging people who . . . for example in times of heavy snowfall . . . if they don't work in the area in which they live and can't get to the place where they normally work that they should report to somewhere that's nearer . . . [and] contribute to providing some kind of community response to vulnerable adults in the local community.

Alternative infrastructures such as telephone support were also reported. For example, the charity AgeUK, which runs a day center in one of the case study local authorities, telephoned members during a period of severe cold weather to ensure continuity of contact. There are also examples of "exceptional" exchanges of assets between the informal and formal sectors in the study area. Local farmers offered use of their four-wheel-drive vehicles better suited to the extreme conditions. Per tradition in rural settings, a local public house (a traditional bar licensed to sell alcohol, often providing a convivial place to eat and drink and a natural focus for local communities) provided an informal rest center for older people at risk during a serious flood.

Though "emergency" arrangements of this type often work well in the initial stages of an extreme weather event, they usually involve provision of essential, short-term care rather than the full range of services normally available. Thus, further problems arise if the extreme weather episode is protracted. The BIOPICCC findings therefore demonstrate that local initiatives and assets may be very important as part of the "first response" to an emergency, but they cannot provide sustained continuity of care over a longer period.

Discussions with participants also highlighted that emergency planners, and health and social care providers, often view older people in poor health as a group of health care consumers especially likely to be vulnerable during extreme weather events. Reasons included the fact that some older people depended on continuous care at various health service facilities as well as in their own homes, their physical or mental frailty made it difficult to cope with extreme weather conditions, and being at risk of social isolation in their domestic settings.

At the same time, participants in the BIOPICCC research, especially older people, emphasized that though they are a vulnerable group, they may simultaneously demonstrate considerable resilience in the extreme weather nexus. Some described preparing for extreme events by stockpiling items such as basic food supplies and battery-powered flashlights. Others talked about their capacity for stoicism in the face of adversity.

Many of the older people interviewed also had strong local connections to family and neighbors (who were often also older people themselves) on whom they could rely for help during extreme weather. One older person explained, "It's pretty good in the village from that point of view. . . . I had people call, you know, that said did you want anything?" In one focus group discussion, participants reflected upon a local scheme set up by the community to help house-bound older people:

> "That was where you had [a sticker of] a hand, everybody had one and if you needed anything . . . you stuck it in your window and then you [scheme volunteers] knocked on the door and said "We're from [community scheme], what do you need?"

There was also mention of the growing cohort of "silver surfers," older people who were more adept and inclined to use modern technologies including the internet to meet their needs for services, information, and communication during emergencies. As one older person explained, "I'm a silver surfer and so if I'm confined to barracks in bad weather I'll get online and get [the supermarkets] to deliver." Every group of older people discussed the reciprocity across social networks that helped them access essential supplies and feel emotionally supported.

Path Dependency and Evolution Through Knowledge Exchange

The BIOPICCC research considered past experience to be an important source of resilience, helping actors in the system evolve and build added strength and adaptability into the systems upon which they rely. Some older people interviewed exhibited the phenomenon of *post-traumatic growth*, a process whereby surviving a crisis makes a person psychologically stronger in the face of future challenges, which has been noted in the wider literature (Gelkopf, Berger, Bleich, & Silver, 2012; Villagran, Reyes, Wlodarczyk, & Paez, 2014).

Older people often commented that their own resilience was based partly on experience of challenging conditions. For example, they had lived through periods of conflict during World War II, which had helped them acquire coping skills during disruptive events. One older person explained, "I was called up [to serve in the war] and, erm . . . you just had to plod on, you know."

A participant in a focus group discussion with frontline service providers reflected on the floods in one of the case study local authorities: "The older people in the floods coped fantastically with it. They weren't perturbed by it because 'well, we did this in the Blitz.'"

Others reported experiencing housing conditions without all the domestic equipment and facilities that are now considered standard in British homes as children, enabling them to manage when infrastructures failed during extreme events. For example, having lived in housing with fewer appliances or more basic hygiene facilities, they could manage if power or water supplies were interrupted for a period of time. Some reported stocking supplies of essential food and other requirements to help cope with periods when they might be out of reach of normal retail outlets. Such older people view themselves as mentally more resilient to such hardships than younger people.

Similarly, the resource elements of the nexus demonstrated capacity to evolve and build resilience in ways that were often *path dependent*—that is, based on previous experience and accumulated local knowledge. This involved organizing at the community level to prepare to take special action during emergencies, collecting information to identify potentially vulnerable older people, and sharing the information across the local system to ensure their safety during extreme weather events. In one rural village, past experience motivated a community group to perform a local household survey to identify and connect vulnerable older people with individuals who could provide assistance. Some emergency planning was based on protocols for data sharing among the formal service providers. Other communities designated local caretakers who knew the older residents and encouraged older people to prepare effectively for extreme weather. Communities organized safe rest centers to be used during an emergency in places where older people had to be evacuated from their homes in the past. In addition, spontaneous self-organization occurred in the informal sector, reflecting the community spirit of local residents who took responsibility to check on neighbors who might need help.

The BIOPICCC research also demonstrated that local actors (i.e., older people, service providers, planners) are more willing to discuss extreme weather events in the context of their own experience. It proved unhelpful, for example, to preface discussions with justifications based on future predictions of climate change; this seemed disconnected from participants' lived experience and risked diverting into controversy about whether climate change is really taking place. As a result, most of the discussion involved "actual" instances of severe cold weather with prolonged periods of snow and ice, which occurred during two successive winters while the research was taking place, and recent flood events. One older person explained, "We are unlikely to meet anything we haven't met before." This reinforces the idea that in complex systems, adaptation is more likely to be driven by previous exposure to disruptive hazards than by potential future risks. For some older people, there was also the issue of priorities: "Somebody who is struggling just to keep mobile and warm and watered might have other things on their mind rather than worrying about the external weather."

Imperfect Knowledge and Gaps in System Connectivity as Vulnerability

Despite the efforts to build more effective communication across the system, vulnerabilities during extreme weather events arise because of the imperfect knowledge and lack of connection between different actors. For example, some individual older people were not aware of the need to, or were not able to, protect themselves during extreme weather. Older people suffering from dementia were thought to be among the groups most at risk, which highlighted the limits to individual capacity and responsibility for preparedness. Other groups include older people who live alone, who do not access services, and who are therefore not included in service records of those at risk. Some older people are seemingly unaware of widely published advice and warnings and are unconcerned about their potential vulnerability, either because they do not view themselves as vulnerable to extreme weather or because they are able to rely on family or friends for help. This reflects findings from other areas of England (Wolf, Adger, Lorenzoni, Abrahamson, & Raine, 2010).

Communication failures also exist among formal service providers and between the formal and informal sectors. In one case, a designated rest center established by the formal health service in the local authority was not used during an emergency because locals were not aware that it was available. In another case, the expertise about how to operate emergency pumping equipment of staff working at a regional center was not immediately available to local residents during a flood. Knowledge about local voluntary initiatives (e.g., sharing four-wheel-drive vehicles to travel over blocked roads) is not always disseminated to all potential users. Under normal circumstances, formal agencies are not allowed to share information about vulnerable individuals to protect confidentiality, which makes it more difficult to organize cross-agency systems for emergency checks during extreme weather events.

The previous examples demonstrate the importance of both vertical and horizontal connection and transmission of knowledge across the system within the local authority areas. This concept also applies to the vertical connections operating across the whole country. The BIOPICCC research indicates that national guidance information issued by Public Health England (a national organization tasked with public health policy for the country as a whole) was neither fully understood at local levels nor delivered to all frontline staff involved in care provision. The research also found that national policymakers responsible for extreme weather planning have a strong demand for information about the challenges faced at the local level. This is valuable because it illustrates how national advice might need to be designed to be adaptable for variable local conditions. It also creates the potential for local experience in some areas of the

country to be cascaded more widely to other areas, enabling people in those areas to benefit from experience in other places and adapt tools and methods to suit their own local
conditions (Curtis et al., 2018).

POLICY IMPLICATIONS

In this section, we reflect on the relevance of the findings from the BIOPICCC case
study for policy and practice by highlighting the following recommendations:

- Extreme weather events underscore the need for immediate planning. Framing
  discussions in this way is important because adaptation is more likely to be driven
  by previous exposure to disruptive hazards, which are seen to be connected to
  everyday lives, rather than by potential future hazards associated with climate
  change.
- There is a need to build good vertical as well as horizontal communication links
  across health and social care systems as part of preparedness planning for extreme weather events. The BIOPICCC toolkit provides a resource to assist with
  locally sensitive adaptation measures and offers wider co-benefits in coordi-
  nating both planning and service delivery across a "resource network."
- So-called "vulnerable" groups and local communities have considerable knowledge and capacity to build resilience through their own efforts. It is important,
  therefore, to consider the impact of extreme weather events from an end-user
  perspective. Robust national-level planning is essential to facilitate, support, and
  enhance coordination of such efforts.
- Preparing for extreme weather events is one of many issues competing for attention in health and social care systems. Many agencies in countries such as
  England are increasingly under pressure due to austerity measures to reduce
  resources and staff capacity at a time of increasing need and demand (Curtis
  et al., 2018; Wistow & Curtis, 2017). It is therefore important to engage with
  the potential economic (along with health and well-being) benefits of climate
  change adaptation, including ensuring "business continuity" of services across
  the resource network and mitigating the costs for society arising from impacts of
  extreme weather on population health.
- Though successful future adaptation is often based on the capacity to learn from
  past experience, it is also necessary to look forward to new developments that
  may transform the ways that complex systems operate during extreme weather
  events. For example, technological advances in informatics are creating the potential for systems to respond immediately to changing demands as they emerge
  and to evaluate how the systems are responding. An example is the development
  of syndromic surveillance methods, which are being used to monitor trends in
  health service activity in England in real time during extreme weather events

(Elliot et al., 2014). This illustrates how information is now being passed increasingly rapidly between and across different levels of the complex health care system. The rise in the use of social media to provide immediate information on the development of disasters has also been noted in the international literature (Allaire, 2016; Andrews, Gibson, Domdouzis, & Akhgar, 2016; Callaghan, 2016). Furthermore, the coming generations of older people will be more familiar with new technologies that may allow individuals to access important information and maintain essential contact even when confined to their homes during extreme weather events.

CONCLUSION

Extreme weather events are occurring now and are likely to increase in the future, with significant impacts on systems that are essential for human well-being, such as health and social care. At the same time, the older population is increasing, with the number of people in the oldest age groups projected to increase in the future. The BIOPICCC research highlights the need to address these challenges and sets out an applied framework for doing so, which draws upon ideas from complex systems and nexus thinking, with the aim of ensuring "integrated management across sectors, systems and scales" (Leck et al., 2015, p. 446). In doing so, we highlight the relationships between vulnerability and resilience, the ways that knowledge exchange operates across agencies and communities to build resilience on the basis of past experience, and the barriers and communication failures that can present obstacles to effective response to extreme events.

ACKNOWLEDGMENTS

The authors gratefully acknowledge the help provided by our partners with the research presented in this chapter and funding from the Engineering and Physical Sciences Research Council UK, grant No. G060843.

REFERENCES

Allaire, M. C. (2016). Disaster loss and social media: Can online information increase flood resilience? *Water Resources Research, 52*, 7408–7423.

Andrews, S., Gibson, H., Dondouzis, K., & Akhgar, B. (2016). Creating corroborated crisis reports from social media data through formal concept analysis. *Journal of Intelligent Information Systems, 47*, 287–312.

Callaghan, C. W. (2016). Disaster management, crowdsourced R&D and probabilistic innovation theory: Toward real time disaster response capability. *International Journal of Disaster Risk Reduction, 17*, 238–250.

Communities and Local Government. (2010). *The English indices of deprivation 2010: Neighbourhoods statistical release.* Retrieved from https://www.gov.uk/government/uploads/system/uploads/attachment_data/file/6871/1871208.pdf

Curtis, S., Fair, A., Wistow, J., Val, D., & Oven, K. J. (2017). Impact of extreme weather events and climate change for health and social care systems. *Journal of Environment and Health, 16*(Suppl. 1), 128.

Curtis, S., Oven, K. J., Wistow, J., Dunn, C. E., & Dominelli, L. (2018). Adaptation to extreme weather events in complex local health care systems: The example of older people's health and care services in England. *Environment and Planning C: Politics and Space, 36,* 67–91.

Curtis, S., & Riva, M. (2010a). Progress report: Health geographies I: Complexity theory and human health. *Progress in Human Geography, 34,* 215–223.

Curtis, S., & Riva, M. (2010b). Progress report: Health geographies II: Complexity and health care systems and policy. *Progress in Human Geography, 34,* 513–520.

Department for Environment and Rural Affairs. (2014). *The national flood emergency framework for England.* Retrieved from https://www.gov.uk/government/publications/the-national-flood-emergency-framework-for-england

Elliot, A. J., Bone, A., Morbey, R., Hughes, H. E., Harcourt, S., Smith, S., . . . Smith, G. (2014). Using real-time syndromic surveillance to assess the health impact of the 2013 heatwave in England. *Environmental Research, 135,* 31–36.

Gatrell, A. C. (2005). Complexity theory and geographies of health: A critical assessment. *Social Science & Medicine, 60,* 2661–2671.

Gelkopf, M., Berger, R., Bleich, A., & Silver, R. C. (2012). Protective factors and predictors of vulnerability to chronic stress: A comparative study of 4 communities after 7 years of continuous rocket fire. *Social Science & Medicine, 74,* 757–766.

Herrick, C. (2016). Global health, geographical contingency, and contingent geographies. *Annals of the American Association of Geographers, 106,* 672–687.

Howard, A., Blakemore, T., & Bevis, M. (2017). Older people as assets in disaster preparedness, response and recovery: Lessons from regional Australia. *Ageing & Society, 37,* 517–536.

Intergovernmental Panel on Climate Change, IPCC Working Groups I and II. (2011). *Managing the risks of extreme events and disasters to advance climate change adaptation: Summary for policy makers.* New York, NY: Cambridge University Press.

Kapucu, N., & Garayev, V. (2016). Structure and network performance: Horizontal and vertical networks in emergency management. *Administration & Society, 48,* 931–961.

Kovats, R. S., & Osborn, D. (2016). *UK climate change risk assessment 2017: Evidence report* (Chap. 5). Retrieved from https://www.theccc.org.uk/wp-content/uploads/2016/07/UK-CCRA-2017-Chapter-5-People-and-the-built-environment.pdf

Leck, H., Conway, D., Bradshaw, M., & Rees, J. (2015). Tracing the water–energy–food nexus: Description, theory and practice. *Geography Compass, 9,* 445–460.

Noordegraaf, M., & Newman, M. (2011). Managing in disorderly times: How cities deal with disaster and restore social order. *Public Management Review, 13,* 513–538.

Oven, K. J., Curtis, S. E., Reaney, S., Riva, M., Stewart, M. G., Ohlemuller, R., . . . Holden, R. (2012). Climate change and health and social care: Defining future hazard, vulnerability and risk for infrastructure systems supporting older people's health care in England. *Applied Geography, 33,* 16–24.

Pelling, M. (2010). *Adaptation to climate change: From resilience to transformation*. London, UK: Routledge.

Public Health England. (2015a). *Cold weather plan for England 2013*. Retrieved from https://www.gov.uk/government/collections/cold-weather-plan-for-england

Public Health England. (2015b). *Heatwave plan for England 2014*. Retrieved from https://www.gov.uk/government/publications/heatwave-plan-for-england

Rotegard, A. K., Moore, S. M., Fagermoen, M. S., & Ruland, C. M. (2010). Health assets: A concept analysis. *International Journal of Nursing Studies, 47*, 513–525.

Stringer, L., Quinn, C., Berman, R., Hue, L., Orchard, S., & Pezzuti, J. (2014). *Combining nexus and resilience thinking in a novel framework to enable more equitable and just outcomes*. Retrieved from http://www.cccep.ac.uk/wp-content/uploads/2015/10/WP-193-Stringer-et-al-2014.pdf

Villagran, L., Reyes, C., Wlodarczyk, A., & Paez, D. (2014). Coping community, collective posttraumatic growth and social well-being in context February 27 earthquake in Chile, 2010. *Terapia Psicologica, 32*, 243–254.

Wistow, J., & Curtis, S. (2017). Governance, state capacity and competing policy agendas in a neo-liberal context: A study of policy and planning for extreme weather events in England. *Public Management Review,* forthcoming.

Wistow, J., Dominelli, L., Oven, K. J., Dunn, C. E., & Curtis, S. (2015). The role of formal and informal networks in supporting older people's care during extreme weather events. *Policy and Politics, 43*, 119–135.

Wolf, J., Adger, W. N., Lorenzoni, I., Abrahamson, V., & Raine, R. (2010). Social capital, individual responses to heat waves and climate change adaptation: An empirical study of two UK cities. *Global Environmental Change—Human and Policy Dimensions, 20*, 44–52.

World Health Organization. (2012). *Strategy and action plan for healthy aging in Europe 2012–2050*. Retrieved from http://www.euro.who.int/__data/assets/pdf_file/0008/175544/RC62wd10Rev1-Eng.pdf?ua=1

Zaidi, R. Z., & Pelling, M. (2013). Institutionally configured risk: Assessing urban resilience and disaster risk reduction to heat wave risk in London. *Urban Studies, 52*(7), 1218–1233.

PART III

Land

5

Normalizing Discourses

URBAN FLOODING AND BLAMING THE VICTIM IN MODERN SANTA FE, ARGENTINA

April L. Colette

‿‿ _____

BACKGROUND: PLANNING ON DISCOURSES OF RISK

In March 2013, I accompanied Federico, a municipal engineer, around Santa Fe, Argentina's neighborhood of Candioti Sur. Candioti Sur is one of the city's oldest neighborhoods of some 10,000 people located in the east, adjacent to the port. In the late 19th century, Candioti Sur was the centerpiece of Santa Fe's urban improvement project, and it continues to be a critical space for infrastructure development and planning. The neighborhood stood out in many ways; its clean streets were organized in a grid pattern, and the Spanish- and Italian-style houses boasted large central courtyards. Many of them were gated. As we walked southwards toward the port, Federico pointed out that this particular part of the neighborhood was most at risk of flooding due to the Caseros Drain:

> Modern life reveals different ways of being. Each one is different because everybody's experience of risk is shaped in a different way. Maybe you have money, maybe you don't. Maybe you have stormwater drains and maybe you don't. These divisions make it so that people experience risk differently and they separate people. Here in Candioti Sur, we don't come into contact with the poor people from the city's peripheries.[1]

_____

[1] Interview on March 21, 2013.

87

I do not wish to romanticize Candioti Sur. Rather, I use it as an example that opens up a wider debate about how risk is shaped. Vast literatures have long tried to understand risk through investigations of its wider historical, social, environmental, political, and economic processes (Oliver-Smith, 1996, 1999; Wilkinson, 2010; Wisner, Blaikie, Cannon, & Davis, 2004). This chapter engages with the growing literature on *climate-related risk* and *vulnerability*—two terms that are often used interchangeably. Climate-related risk is associated with extreme climactic events, such as a flood or hurricane, that have direct and adverse effects on society. However, climate-related risk is not caused by biophysical events alone. It is produced by biophysical factors that work in conjunction with historical, social, political, and economic conditions. For example, the combination of poverty, poor infrastructure, and lack of planning when faced with a flood often results in a specific outcome: displacement. The biophysical hazard—the flood—is just one among multiple causes that put people at risk of displacement.

I define *risk* as the probability of a threat of damage, injury, or loss. Risk, in essence, is the combination of two elements: hazard and vulnerability. Following Hewitt's (1997) definition of a hazard as "something . . . to the extent that it threatens losses we wish to avoid" (p. 25), I argue that a hazard is not solely a biophysical agent. It is the possibility that a biophysical event will result in damage or harm. Using this understanding, a flood that does not harm anyone is therefore not a hazard. The other crucial element that defines risk is vulnerability or the predisposition to damage. Vulnerability is precisely what determines the impact of a particular hazard (Blaikie, Cannon, Davis, & Wisner, 1994). Both hazard and vulnerability are necessary to create risk. Without hazard, there is no risk. Without vulnerability, there is no risk.

As Federico noted, different people experience different risks in the same city—even while facing the same hazard (Blaikie et al., 1994; Ribot, 2010)—because of the complex relationship between climate and outcomes. Ribot (2010) contends, "Climate events or trends are transformed into differentiated outcomes via social structure" (p. 49). The world's poor and marginalized experience different risks because they are disproportionately vulnerable. The differences in outcomes after a hazard depend on "place-based social and political–economic circumstance" (p. 49)—not simply from a storm with gale force winds and heavy rainfall. People's ability to manage risk is shaped by existing conditions such as "social inequality; unequal access to resources; poverty; poor infrastructure; lack of representation; and inadequate systems of social security, early warning and planning" (p. 49). For instance, as this chapter demonstrates, the lack of planning or provision for drainage means that relatively minor storms can cause severe flooding—particularly for those living in neighborhoods lacking basic stormwater infrastructure.

Despite the rich theoretical work on the social production of risk, few studies delve into the nitty-gritty of how people understand and talk about risk. How risk is understood is fundamentally linked to where the burden of explanation is placed. This is a key point, for which I return to Hewitt (1997), who explains, "Whereas a hazards perspective tends to explain risk and disaster in terms of external agents and their impacts, vulnerability looks to the internal state of a society and what governs that" (pp. 27–28). Though climate change literature recognizes the interaction between hazard and vulnerability as fundamental in producing risk, risk remains largely understood as a physical phenomenon, and the solutions for risk reduction tend to focus on natural hazards—stopping short of addressing the historical, social, political, and economic factors that make people vulnerable in the first place.

Taking the case of Santa Fe, a city with a long history of flooding and infrastructure used to guard against flooding, this chapter aims to further integrate the hazard and vulnerability sides of the risk equation. Based on archival and ethnographic research in Santa Fe between 2011 and 2013 with a focus on one of four spatially separate neighborhoods, each with different social, historical, and political–economic contexts and different experiences of flooding and infrastructure development, I show that risk is produced both materially and discursively. I center my analytical focus on how infrastructure not only physically transforms the urban landscape but also produces and is produced by people's (both government and individuals) notions of what and who is at risk. The way people understand and talk about risk and infrastructure is rooted in a legacy of postcolonial planning and infrastructure development. This discourse shapes the construction of the material world, the social order of the city, and very much influences how government and individuals perceive and frame risk and, importantly, develop climate-related risk reduction solutions.

Infrastructure development and planning practices are linked to the *discourses* of modernization and improvement that produce and reproduce an unequal distribution of risk. Rose (1996, p. 331) argues that discourses shape the practices and strategies that address risk by "seeking to *act upon* the dynamics" of neighborhoods. They configure the territory upon which these strategies should act and "they extend to the *specification of the subjects* of government as individuals who are also, actually or potentially, the subjects of allegiance to a particular set of community values, beliefs and commitments" (p. 331). These discourses are embodied in the ways risk is framed in terms of neighborhood features, infrastructure, cleanliness, and belonging.

Crucially, the discourses resulting in social inclusion and exclusion of subjects were not only deployed by the state but also co-constituted by the discourses of residents themselves as subjects of government (Rose, 1996). By routing residents' affective responses to the city's risky and safe spaces through a discursive field defined by high modern ideals, those who settled on low-lying land view risk as a normal outcome of their placement or their own actions. Because people believe the discourse of government, risk appears natural and risk subjects, rather than the state, appear responsible. Using Friedrich Engels' concept of false consciousness, I argue that the power of the discourse keeps risk subjects from recognizing and rejecting blame (Bourdieu, 1977; Kilminster, 1979). As a result of blaming the victim, the poor end up in a discursive realm shaped by the location of infrastructure, and their vulnerability is normalized so that their risk is made less visible and more acceptable.

This chapter explores (1) the history of the development of Candioti Sur as a site of modernity and progress; (2) one crucial piece of infrastructure—the Caseros Ditch, now the Caseros Drain—that led to the formation of a sacrifice zone in the southern sector of the neighborhood; (3) how the city, in attempting to solve the drainage problems associated with Caseros Ditch, actually increased flood risk for residents; and (4) the normalization of risk.

A MODERN CITY WITH IDEAL, MODERN SUBJECTS

Infrastructure development and planning organized Santa Fe around risk. These government practices played a key role in the way risk was understood and in the development of strategies for its management, particularly in terms of the people and places that were classified and categorized as "at risk" versus those that were not (Rose, 1996). Since the 19th century, Santa Fe's planners apportioned risk unevenly among citizens, and society placed different demands on the land (Bankoff, 2002, 2003; Cannon, 1994; Hewitt, 1983, 1995; Wisner, 1993). Higher ground, for instance, was reserved for the middle and upper classes, whereas low-lying (riskier) land was left for the lower classes—a common practice throughout the world. Furthermore, the government carved out different spaces in the city by servicing some neighborhoods with infrastructure and allowing the middle class to settle there, while consciously allowing the poor to settle on land not serviced by infrastructure and/or exposed to flood risk, such as floodplains, riverbeds, or stormwater channels, until that land was deemed "developable" by flows of capital. In other words, they placed people vis-à-vis the riskiness of space and provided infrastructure in the interest of those who were already less at risk.

In the late 1800s, Santa Fe's government began an urban improvement project with the goal to unfetter the city from its colonial past and create a new city based on modernity and progress. The first step toward this goal was to carve out a new space where the government could employ European design and planning principles. City officials enlisted the help of British engineers who "saw what they knew"—problems facing similar postcolonial cities—and proposed plans that were effectively futures for the elite who occupied them (McFarlane, 2008). They determined that the northeastern edge of Santa Fe was the most logical site for the new neighborhood for two strategic reasons: its elevation and its location between three important modes of transportation (the port to the south, the Santa Fe River to the east, and a new boulevard to the north). In 1910, the city government named the neighborhood Candioti Sur in homage to Pablo Marcial Candioti, the elite land owner who donated the land to the city. In line with the modernization paradigms of the time, the city commissioned major urban infrastructure and services, including large public parks and gardens, paved streets, bridges, street lamps, and sewers—infrastructure critical to the reduction of risk for which some neighborhoods in Santa Fe are still fighting a century later.

FIGURE 5.1 Lake Plaza in 1907.
Source: Dalla Fontana (2003).

Lake Plaza and the Problem of Drainage

Infrastructure projects, particularly drainage, quickly became associated with the ability to "cleanse" city spaces (Felbinger, 1996, p. 11, cited in Graham & Marvin, 2001). One such infrastructure project was the Lake Plaza (Plaza del Lago). Situated at the heart of the neighborhood adjacent to the boulevard, the site for the plaza was originally a brickyard with a large treading pit for brickmaking. Each time it rained, the mud pit transformed into a vast lagoon, which the urban bourgeoisies found problematic, claiming that the mud pit was a "disease-ridden" cesspool that was "detrimental" to their health (Dalla Fontana, 2003, p. 28). When they demanded the government take action, the city converted the mud pit turned lagoon into a proper lake with French-style gardens and a grotto around it. They called it Lake Plaza (Figure 5.1).

Initially content with the solution, the middle- and upper-class residents embraced Lake Plaza and used it for recreational purposes, noting that it offered all the "perks distinguished society could want" (Dalla Fontana, 2003, p. 28). Yet a larger urban problem soon emerged: the lack of drainage infrastructure. Constructed of impervious surfaces without adequate drainage infrastructure, Lake Plaza overflowed and impeded residents from using its "perks." The standing water attracted mosquitoes, and soon the lake was again considered "disease-ridden." Lake Plaza went from being the pride to the bane of the neighborhood. The mayor thus ordered the infilling of the lake and the leveling off of the land around it, which remains prone to flooding to this day.

Discourse and the Making of the Middle Class

In the 19th century, Santa Fe's government agencies deployed a discourse that included language such as "moral," "immoral," "hygienic," and "dirty" to define neighborhoods and divide their subjects. Fed by the concern among the urban bourgeoisies over disease and health issues, city administrators planned Candioti Sur as a clean, orderly, and, most important, a "moral" space (Scott, 1998). As such, the government invested in the development of Candioti Sur, a neighborhood on high ground, for the formation of "ideal subjects" while at the same time blamed those who settled on low-lying land at risk of flooding for having made bad decisions of their own, thereby creating risk subjects (Rose, 1996). Heavily engineered infrastructure projects, such as the Colgante Bridge, the railroad, and the port, were premised on the discursive construction of Candioti Sur as the "fruitful terrain where fertile seed of the republic was planted" (Dalla Fontana, 2003, p. 30). This discourse took material form through three interconnected functions: place marketing, land ownership, and education.

Place Marketing

At the turn of the 20th century, waves of European immigrants flooded Santa Fe, lured by the employment opportunities in the railroad industry. As the center of modernity, Santa Fe became the headquarters of the French Railway Company (Empresa de Ferrocarriles Franceses), which by no coincidence was established in Candioti Sur. In fact, the railroad played an integral role in the development of the neighborhood as well as in the everyday lives of the Italian, French, and Spanish immigrants (Dalla Fontana, 2003). The railroad not only maintained central operations in Candioti Sur but also invested in its workers through skills training in metallurgy, mechanics, and carpentry (Vittori, 1997). It also provided workers with access to credit, which facilitated the purchase of land. Capitalizing on the opportunity, the state actively marketed Candioti Sur as the ideal location for the development of a middle class.

The purpose of the place marketing of Candioti Sur was to emancipate the "good" working—and soon-to-be middle-class—people from the "risks of immorality" (Graham & Marvin, 2001, p. 44). Using discourse rooted in the idea that people own their own labor, state agencies marketed Candioti Sur as an "opportunity for speculators to make money; laborers to become landowners" and "one block from the boulevard for laborers and the wealthy" (*Nueva Epoca* newspaper, 1909, cited in Dalla Fontana, 2003, p. 31). The state agencies promoted the well-ventilated "hygienic housing" to emphasize the differences between the organized and "moral" spaces of Candioti Sur and the dirty, disorganized, and disease-ridden spaces of the western periphery (Vittori, 1997). This demonstrates how the state mobilized discourse to construct a social order in the city. By discursively constructing Candioti Sur as morally superior to the unsanitary and impure westernmost neighborhoods, state agencies placed the visible burden of risk and the invisible burden of marginality onto specific spaces in the city.

Land Ownership

The state also encouraged citizenship through discourse. One state agency linked owning land in Candioti Sur with the moral basis of citizenship, using discourse such as "Here there are no voters without houses" (Dalla Fontana, 2003, p. 31). By encouraging land ownership principally among skilled European immigrants, state agencies excluded low-income people from locating in Candioti Sur (Dalla Fontana, 2003, p. 34).

Residents today still use this type of exclusionary discourse. Nacho, one of my informants from Candioti Sur, made sure I was aware of just how "different" Candioti Sur was compared to the rest of Santa Fe: "The other neighborhoods in your study have nothing to do with Candioti Sur. Due to cultural and educational reasons, we are very different."[2]

Education: The Foundation for Ideal, Modern Subjecthood

Nacho was not exaggerating. Education was a crucial factor that set Candioti Sur apart. It was part of becoming a modern city "whereby the few who know-how and own-how maintain domination over the many who do not know-how or own-how" (Luke, 2010, p. 68). As part of the overall logic of the urban improvement project, once people owned land, the next step was to educate them. Hence, education played an integral role in both creating modern Santa Fe and producing "ideal" subjects with the capacity for personal empowerment.

The ideal subjects were not necessarily European immigrants themselves, as the railroad already provided them with additional educational opportunities. Rather, they were their children, who, once educated, would go on to become government experts as well as members of the upper middle class. Horacio, another informant, told me,

> The first generation wanted their children to be better off than they were. They— and the school teachers—pushed their children to study. So the neighborhood went from being a neighborhood of working class to a neighborhood of "qualified professionals"—those that went on to get college degrees.[3]

---

[2] Interview on January 22, 2013.

[3] Interview on January 28, 2013.

According to Gramsci (1971), one of the most important functions of a state is "to raise the great mass of the population to a particular cultural and moral level, a level (or type) which corresponds to the needs of the productive forces for development, and hence to the interests of the ruling class" (p. 258). In the early 1900s, the neighborhood school founders considered it their moral duty to educate the children of Candioti Sur in institutions of modernity and progress (Dalla Fontana, 2003). One such institution was the School of Art and Trade, whose founding mission was, in fact, "to facilitate the instruction and improvement of the proletariat of the neighborhood" (Dalla Fontana, 2003, p. 30). Education reinforced the discourses of place marketing and land ownership, which together formed the foundation for ideal, modern subjecthood—what I call the *Candioti Class*.

The Candioti Class and the Relational Politics of Amiguismo

The Candioti Class became elite social markers of modernity. This newly established class was entrepreneurial, and because its members had access to different forms of capital, they were able to build influential relationships with government officials. In contrast to the poor western neighborhoods where residents' livelihoods were dependent on what politicians and government officials could give them, the power relations of the Candioti Class allowed them to *become* the politicians and government officials. As I was repeatedly told by my informants, Candioti Sur has many well-off residents, and many of them are politicians. Indeed, the last four mayors of Santa Fe came from Candioti neighborhoods.[4] When I asked Federico what made it different from other neighborhoods, he said, "It was a neighborhood where people worked towards excellence. The first residents went in search of businessmen, who had public recognition and economic power—and likewise, privilege—to serve as councilmembers for the municipal government."[5]

The strategy of inserting economic strongmen into the government involved multiple processes at different scales. At the neighborhood level, residents elected the local shop owners and business elites as their neighborhood representatives with the hope that they could transfer their economic prowess into political progress. Their economic resources provided them the bargaining power to make more credible commitments to the city, which in turn gave them social and political capital (Theesfeld, 2011). Their social, political, and economic capital together determined the degree to which the city government would be responsive to their demands. Leveraging their capital allowed

---

[4] Former Peronist Party Mayors Marcelo Álvarez (1999–2003) and Ezequiel Martin Balbarrey (2003–2007) both came from Candioti Sur and still reside in the neighborhood. Former Radical Party Mayor Mario Barletta (2007–2011) and incumbent Mayor Jose Corral (2011–present) came from Candioti Norte, the neighborhood to the immediate north.

[5] Interview on January 17, 2013.

them to strengthen their positions at both the neighborhood level and within the larger urban political system, bypass bureaucratic red tape, and respond to the neighborhood's problems. This, my informants told me, was called *amiguismo*, which roughly translates to an old boys' network. Through amiguismo, the Candioti Class actively constructed and maintained key positions in the government. Their higher levels of education provided them with privileged access to information and knowledge, thereby furthering their social and political connections.

Amiguismo is based on a relational politics whereby the positionality of the players and the consequential alignment of their social, political, and economic capital become the foundation to simultaneously "fix the problems" of the neighborhood and of government.[6] In amiguismo, the Candioti Class have considerable capacity to make demands on government in terms of their own interests. Amiguismo allowed them particular leverage in relation to the identification and management of risk. As Rose (1996) notes, the "novel intellectual techniques of risk identification, risk assessment and risk management bring into existence a whole new set of professional obligations" in which it is imperative for experts to "reduce the risk they may pose to others—their children, members of 'the general public'" (p. 349). For instance, in the early 1900s, the Candioti Class sought to mitigate the risk of crossing the north–south railroad tracks. Through the self-reinforcing process of amiguismo, they were able to wield their privilege to construct a footbridge over the railroad lines (Dalla Fontana, 2003, p. 55).

SACRIFICIAL LAND AND SACRIFICIAL SUBJECTS

Critical scholarship on risk emphasizes the historic, social, political, and economic characteristics that render people vulnerable (Bankoff, 2003; Blaikie et al., 1994; Pelling, 2003; Ribot, 2014). Much of that literature as well as local discourse illustrate how the elite's access to economic resources and political connections results in them getting what they want: the ear of those in power. Those in power are, in turn, responsive to the demands of the elite. Up to this point, the case of Candioti Sur fits that narrative. But not all of Candioti Sur was created equal.

In this section, I examine why, despite their status as ideal, modern subjects and the benefit of amiguismo, the Candioti Class failed to get the government to respond to their demands to reduce flood risk—even when that risk was recast as health-related. The lack of government response, which had dire consequences during the floods of 1982 and 1983, stemmed from the very intentional production of a "sacrifice zone" in the south of Candioti Sur (Lerner, 2010). Lerner argues that "low-income and minority populations, living adjacent to heavy industry and military bases, are required to make disproportionate health and economic sacrifices that more affluent people can avoid" (p. 3).

---

[6] Interview on January 10, 2013.

Borrowing the term from Lerner, I argue that the government consciously made the southern sector of Candioti Sur a sacrifice zone, thereby spatially diverting risk onto a land and a people it deemed undeserving of state investment.

The Caseros Ditch

The spatial and social division of the neighborhood hinged on one particular infrastructure: the Caseros Ditch. Only when there was an influx of capital—from mega infrastructure projects funded by the central government—did the city government take interest in the land to the south of the Caseros Ditch, known as El Chilcal.[7] Indeed, central government-funded improvement projects not only prompted the city's revaluation of El Chilcal but also triggered local investment of capital in it. The government labeled poor people who inhabited El Chilcal as "encroachers"; therefore, they mattered little in urban political processes. The political elites surely did not need their votes, nor did they care that the poor people occupied the sacrifice zone until they saw the profitability from capital being drawn to large-scale infrastructure projects around El Chilcal (Mitchell, 2014). The label of "encroachers" was less about their poverty and more a designation of these inhabitants as sacrificial subjects who served to soak up the unequal distribution of risk placed on the land so that the Candioti Class did not have to deal with it. This is akin to Rose's (1996) point that government produces risk subjects "in terms of an ethic of activity which establishes new divisions between those who are considered to be competent citizens and those who are not" (p. 337). That ethic of activity is produced not only through territorialized government practices but also crucially through the autonomous practices of risk subjects themselves. As Ribot (2014) states,

> Individuals internalize the explanations of risk as if it were produced by their behavior and not by broader social and political–economic forces. . . . By blaming themselves for the risk, risk subjects take on the burden of self-protection rather than seeking social protection. This is a causal link that dampens government accountability and demand for response. (p. 690)

Despite the host of urban infrastructure and services allocated to Candioti Sur, there was one crucial type of infrastructure missing: stormwater drains. This posed an indirect flood risk, and the presence of standing floodwater in turn posed a direct health risk (Dalla Fontana, 2003). This risk, however, did not affect everyone equally. The gentle north-to-south slope of the neighborhood led toward the port. But it was not just physical geography that determined which areas of Candioti Sur were risky. Risk was

---

[7] Named after an indigenous plant.

FIGURE 5.2 Aerial view of Caseros Ditch dividing El Chilcal from Candioti Sur, circa 1930.
Source: Dalla Fontana (2003).

produced by a complex set of socionatural relations whereby both the state and private industry were implicated.

In 1910, when the port was established to the south of Candioti Sur, the Port Authority did everything it could to ensure its success. The location of the port had already changed twice since Santa Fe's founding. Its re-establishment to the south of the neighborhood was particularly important due to the proximity to the urban core. However, the lack of stormwater drains in Candioti Sur complicated its drainage situation. Thus, the Port Authority, sanctioned by the state, dug a canal—the Caseros Ditch—to divert pluvial and industrial run-off away from the port (Figure 5.2). It ran parallel to the east–west railroad lines and divided Candioti Sur into two sectors: the residential north and the industrial south. Indeed, the Caseros Ditch was a spatial signifier that divided the neighborhood into the not-so-risky higher land where the Candioti Class resided and the risky low-lying land where those who would be sacrificed for the port lived. Because it was important for the city to maintain good relations with the Port Authority, the main economic driver of Santa Fe, it was both politically and economically advantageous to sacrifice the southern sector, shifting flood risk there.

The Poor: Carrying the Burden of Risk

Caseros Ditch sealed the fate of El Chilcal as a sacrificial zone. It became a place for development of private industries that could easily exploit the land and dump their run-off. Over time, El Chilcal became populated by unskilled day laborers. Their employment with the port was erratic, and they did not have the income to buy property or fit into the modern social space of the Candioti Class, so they rented low-cost ir-regular parcels of land in El Chilcal on which they built wood shacks with thatched roofs. There, exposed to the mix of sewage and industrial run-off that spilled over Caseros Ditch when it rained, their shacks stood out against the backdrop of the Candioti Class's European-style houses. The unsightly flows of sludge and foul smells emanating from the ditch were enough for the Candioti Class to make complaints. On the basis of a health and sanitation risk, the Candioti Class demanded that the city enclose the ditch. As a first step, the state took disciplinary action—not against the Port Authority that constructed the ditch but, rather, against the poor who settled in El Chilcal.

In 1913, the city government labeled the settlement of El Chilcal an "encroachment" and prohibited the construction of wood shacks in the entire eastern half of Santa Fe. The city government gave residents of El Chilcal 8 months before it would raze their houses; however, this deadline passed without eviction. Residents of El Chilcal continued to oc-cupy the zone for another 40 years before they were removed (Dalla Fontana, 2003). Because El Chilcal was already considered a sacrifice zone, the state tolerated their occu-pation (Voyles, 2015).

Moreover, the poor inhabitants of El Chilcal served a purpose. They would never be ideal, modern subjects. Instead, they were the *sacrificial subjects* of Candioti Sur—sacrificed so that neither the Candioti Class nor the port would carry the burden of risk. Because they lived in a constant state of precarity, they were already the least able to buffer themselves against flood risk. There was also a kind of congruence between what was deemed "good" for the poor who were allowed to occupy El Chilcal and what was considered "good" for the Candioti Class. In this sense, there developed a simultaneous "effectiveness for the regulator and happiness for the regulated" (Rose, 1998, p. 122). This relation between the poor and the Candioti Class results in a framing whereby the poor's precarity is treated as a "normal" condition and obscures the government's own role in producing vulnerabilities that could have been avoided through more rigorous land-use and zoning policies and a broader scope in infrastruc-ture development.

The Mid-Century Infusion of Public Funds for Infrastructure Development

Because the city considered El Chilcal a sacrifice zone, city officials had little incentive to clean it up or evict its residents. But the impulse came in the 1950s when there was a nationwide focus on large-scale infrastructure projects. For Santa Fe, that meant a reno-vation of the port.

Where capital is successfully drawn into large infrastructure, it often flows into smaller projects (Mitchell, 2014). The infusion of public funds for infrastructure projects led to a revaluation of El Chilcal. The central government-funded infrastructure projects that were being carried out around El Chilcal rendered it "colonizable by capital" and claimable for residential development (Ranganathan, 2015, p. 14). The city sold the land of El Chilcal to a private developer that built chalet-style houses, touted as a "beautiful residential development"—a necessary step to finance El Chilcal's infrastructure needs ("Un Nuevo y Hermoso Barrio," 1957). It meant that after 55 years of demands, the time had come to enclose Caseros Ditch to add cohesion to the neighborhood (Dalla Fontana, 2003).

In 1968, at the height of El Chilcal's transformation, the city culverted Caseros Ditch into a closed-conduit storm drain—the Caseros Drain. But, in keeping with the historic precedents of building and rebuilding infrastructure in Candioti Sur, it failed to permanently solve the drainage problems. The new Caseros Drain resulted in increased risk for residents. Compounding drainage problems, the middle class was increasingly urbanizing the southern sector of Candioti Sur, creating more impervious surfaces and stormwater flows into the closed-conduit drain. Not built to sufficient capacity, Caseros Drain flooded houses and businesses within a four-block radius after every heavy rain. The risk to the Candiotti Class was no longer a health-related problem; it was one of the city's failed infrastructural fixes.

Slipshod Drainage Infrastructure: The City's Failed Fixes

Caseros Drain remains a sore subject—one that has plagued the neighborhood for more than a century. My neighborhood informants repeatedly complained about the Caseros Drain. Federico mentioned how the culverted Caseros Drain was an example of the poor construction of infrastructure in the city: "Here in Candioti Sur we have all the necessary infrastructure—things that other people in the city don't have. But it doesn't make it any less risky for us if they [state experts] keep doing things *a media*."[8] *A media* is a colloquial expression used to describe something that is done slipshod, carelessly, or halfway. Residents of Candioti Sur believe that one of the greatest errors of government is constructing short-term *a media* infrastructural solutions. Federico continued, "Of course you can't prevent rain, but you can prevent a risky situation as a function of drainage . . . but not if they do a poor job on the infrastructure!"[9] Whereas rain and the rivers pose a direct risk of flooding, slipshod infrastructural solutions pose an indirect risk, which is infuriating to residents. Importantly, infrastructures are not "separated and autonomous"; they are linked to humans as well as to nature and "co-evolve closely in their interrelationships with urban development and with urban space" (Graham & Marvin, 2001, p. 8).

Residents' critical view of the slipshod drainage infrastructure goes hand-in-hand with the city's failed attempts at fixing Caseros Ditch. Their criticism intensified after

---

[8] Interview on January 18, 2013.
[9] Interview on January 29, 2013.

the flood of 1983, the worst flood Candioti Sur had ever experienced. Elena, one of my informants, explained,

> The biggest flood here was in 1983. The Paraná [River] reached 7.35 meters high then went down to 7.10 meters, and water came through the grates of the storm drains. From Alberdi [Street] to the Caseros Drain was full of water. It was a meter high! People used canoes to get around. They also built wooden footbridges just to get from one side of the Caseros Drain to the other.[10]

Relief came to the flood-prone area around Caseros Drain 15 years after this flood. In 1998, the city installed a major trunk drain with two drainage pipes with sufficient carrying capacity. This infrastructure has reduced but, as residents know, will never eliminate the risk of flooding in the area.

OTHERING AND THE NORMALIZATION OF RISK

Writing on pollution and taboo, Mary Douglas (1966) argued that

> ideas about separating, purifying, demarcating and punishing transgressions have as their main function to impose system on an inherently untidy experience. It is only by exaggerating the difference between within and without, above and below, male and female, with and against, that a semblance of order is created. (p. 5)

Douglas's work has contributed to a body of literature about symbolic boundary maintenance to establish certain norms as good and necessary and others as bad. According to Kingfisher (2007), efforts to differentiate, exclude, and "other," through which the "inside," "normal," and "safe" are produced, "occur on an ongoing basis via the mundane interactions which constitute the day-to-day reproduction of institutional arrangements" and social order in the city (p. 195).

Likewise, there are spaces and times whereby those efforts to other are intensified, such as in the low-lying, peripheral neighborhoods, when the rivers rise, or during a prolonged period of heavy rains.[11] The ways that people in Santa Fe define and differentiate themselves in relation to other people and places are products not only of the social order that is created through city planning and infrastructure development but also of the *discourses*

---

[10] Interview on January 10, 2013.

[11] More than 90% of my informants believe that Santa Fe's climate is changing from subtropical to tropical due to an increase in humidity during the past 20 years. They also believe there is a connection between the changing climate and the intensity of rainstorms in recent years, which echoes the scientific evidence that shows that as temperatures get warmer, the atmosphere will store more water, resulting in an increase in the amount and intensity of rain.

of risk. Instrumental to that discursive production of risk are, as Rose (1996) states, the "self-governing properties of the subjects of government themselves in a whole variety of locales and localities" (p. 352). That is, the discourse of residents themselves determines, in part, who is included and who is excluded.

Residents repeatedly told me that those who inhabit certain places in the city that consistently get flooded are "used to" getting flooded. For them, flooding is "normal," and flood risk, as Bankoff (2003) posits, "has become an integral part of the daily human experience" (p. 153). If flooding is normal for certain people, the question becomes one of how the normalization of flood risk is socially produced. I argue that the normalization of risk is an artifact of two interlinked factors: the physical planning of the city and its related infrastructure and discourses on risk—both of which are related to how risk is framed. In other words, the normalization of risk is both a physical process (through which notions and locations of risk are constructed by physically separating people and places through infrastructure) and a discursive process (by socially eschewing those labeled "unsafe" who do not fit the precepts of social order or ideal, modern subjecthood to the margins of society).

Today, the city of Santa Fe is almost completely enclosed by infrastructure. Embankments with elevated highways and pumping stations line the perimeter of the city. Their purpose is the same as that of their predecessors—to control the rivers. Where these infrastructures are placed was not based on what Porter (1995) calls "mechanical objectivity" or "knowledge based completely on explicit rules" particularly with regard to scientific matters (p. 7). Though modern Santa Fe was built through techno-scientific processes, its infrastructure aligns with a more abstract vision that reflects the kind of social order the city's architects and engineers aimed to create at the turn of the 20th century. The unequal distribution of risk (i.e., the division between east and west) underlied the planning for a desired social order. The colonial core and northeastern neighborhoods comprise the highest elevations of the city and as such were planned for the middle and upper classes. Embankments made of concrete blocks and geotextile blankets protect those residents, notably the Candioti Class, whereas the embankments along the poor western periphery are mostly earthen, prone to erosion, and do not have as successful of a track record for flood protection as those in the east. Indeed, Santa Fe's city planning reflects the social hierarchies that shape who benefits from infrastructure and who does not, clearly marking the physical parameters of risk.

In addition, Santa Fe' city planning also influences the ways risk is discursively produced. It has created a normative grid to compare people and places with the norms and aspirations of the Candioti Class. For instance, being located "inside" the ring of embankments or on the higher land in the east of the city is equated with wealth, education, and order. In contrast, settling outside the ring or on the low-lying land at the peripheries is considered by the Candioti Class and other middle- and upper-class residents as befitting of those whose lifestyles or labor has *conditioned* them to get flooded—hence the distinction between what Rose (1996) calls the "affiliated" and the "marginalized." Making the distinction clear, Rose asserts,

> To remain affiliated one must . . . have become integrated within all the practices of everyday life, sustained by a heterogeneous array of "civilized" images and devices for lifestyle promotion. . . . But the marginal are those who cannot be considered affiliated to such sanctioned and civilized cultural communities. Either they are not considered as affiliated to *any* collectivity by virtue of their incapacity to manage themselves as subjects or they are considered affiliated to some kind of "anti-community" whose morality, lifestyle or comportment is considered a threat or a reproach to public contentment and political order. (p. 340)

One morning while talking about the natural cycles of the Paraná River, I asked Federico whether the river still poses a flood risk. His response reveals just how the Candioti Class differentiate themselves, in terms of risk, from other people and places in the city:

> No, here [Candioti Sur] there isn't much of a risk anymore. They closed the defenses and fixed Caseros Ditch. So, no. The people at risk are those who live on the riverbanks or the islanders.[12] They are at risk of flooding from the rise in the river, but the floods also benefit them because it brings them fish. Anyway, those people are *used to* living with risk.[13]

A pattern quickly emerged from my interviews with residents from all neighborhoods. They do not view flooding as a problem for people who live on the riverbanks or islands. Rather, flooding is considered "beneficial" for them because it contributes to their livelihoods. Flooding is something this group of people is used to, and risk is something they embody. Former Mayor of Santa Fe, Mario Barletta, even told me, "Risk for the people of the island zone is culturally accepted."[14] The common problematic vision is apparent: The people on riverbanks and islanders live in a waterworld; they are a rugged brood with a kind of primitive mentality whereby they clearly "prefer" to live with flood risk rather than have greater security living on higher, drier ground or within the limits of the embankments. The following newspaper article about the islanders also reflects this view ("Convivir con el Agua," 1984):

---

[12] Santa Fe is surrounded by small islands, some of which are inhabited by fishermen.
[13] Interview on August 15, 2012.
[14] Interview on March 11, 2013.

They are islanders. A handful of men, women and children who daily awaken on a piece of land surrounded by water, who are nourished by the river, who develop with a landscape that sometimes turns against them. And that is when *they prefer to stay* [italics added] and resist. Because they *are used to* [italics added] the roughness of a life stripped down to the most basic, which may be a roof that shelters them or a good plate of food that nourishes them. Life on the island is different. And it is not difficult only when the river rises. It is always difficult.

The way that this passage, among countless others, describes the islanders—*used to* the roughness of life, as if they were conditioned for economic hardship and flooding—is a clear example of how the normalization of risk is discursively produced. Local discourse produces a perception whereby the islanders embody risk as a "constant feature" of daily life (Bankoff, 2003, p. 153). Horacio described the islanders similarly, stating,

At best, it's like an extreme sport. They construct their houses knowing that the water is going to take them away. After the water recedes, they return and reconstruct their houses in the same place. Why? That's life. They can be at the point of dying thousands of times, but they still go back and do it.[15]

On April 29, 2003, when the Salado River covered one-third of the city, residents expected the people located on the riverbanks on the other side of the embankment to be the hardest hit. These were the inhabitants of Varadero Sarsotti, a piece of low-lying land to the south of the city. During past floods, because of their increased exposure, the people in Varadero Sarsotti suffered from flooding more than the residents "inside" the ring of embankments. Horacio told me, "Since they live on the banks of the river, *they've gotten used to* [italics added] floods. They have their community, they have their families . . . and they have more risk. But that's how they live."[16]

In a historic turn of events, the 2003 flood left them dry. Varadero Sarsotti remained untouched by the floodwaters because the very infrastructure that was meant to keep the water out of Santa Fe instead kept it in. For the residents of the urban core, it was ironic and disappointing. They were supposed to be better protected than the people on the riverbanks. This is a prime example of reality running counter to the dominant local discourses of risk. Nonetheless, residents chalked it up to a rare event—for the normalization of risk is a form of praxis through which the ideal, modern subjects constitute themselves.

---

[15] Interview on August 16, 2012.
[16] Interview on August 16, 2012.

RETHINKING POLICY INTERVENTIONS

The risk reduction paradigm in Santa Fe—and many other areas of the world—has trained our attention to technocratic approaches to risk reduction, particularly with regard to climate hazards. Such approaches rely on a reduction of physical exposure, thereby eclipsing the predisposition to damage that resides within society. Though technocratic approaches to risk reduction have received increasing criticism, "faith in simple technological fixes is still pervasive" (Wisner et al., 2004, p. 24). Part of the reason behind the confidence in these approaches is that they are touted for being rational, value-free, and apolitical, and the engineers and architects who develop them are regarded as devoid of political corruption and championed as the bringers of order and rationality to the city (Graham & Marvin, 2001). Politicians, too, use technocratic approaches as a select set of solutions that are visible to them—or those they can make visible (e.g., through discourse) for their political purposes. They use the visibility of infrastructure because they can articulate and extend the terms of a more materialist politics attuned to the sheer power and necessity of infrastructure through the creation of order, modernity, mobility, and security.

However, the focus on technocratic approaches to risk reduction is also part of the problem: Technocratic approaches occlude social and political causality on the vulnerability side of risk. This needs to be addressed rather than avoided. The first step is to recognize the framing of risk. How risk is framed will shape how it is understood and talked about. Moreover, it will affect the design and implementation of solutions—adaptive (and potentially maladaptive) measures—that can reduce or deepen vulnerability. Importantly, framing also leads to the attribution of responsibility and ultimately blame. When social, political, or economic causes are occluded, those responsible and able to respond are often the ones shielded from responsibility, and blame is instead transferred to the victims for putting themselves at risk. Bringing attention to framing is a critical process to confront human-induced climate change and variability without occluding the social and political causality on the vulnerability side of risk.

Policy interventions that aim to address the framing of risk must go beyond strengthening building codes, zoning, and land use regulations. They must be designed around the processes that shape risk and "the actors and organizations with authority and power to make decisions that can change these processes" (Ribot, 2010, p. 66). Crucially, such interventions must tackle long-term planning, particularly with regard to low-probability climactic events. Climate change does not happen overnight. Preparing for it requires iterative processes to reshape policies and practice that may affect people 20 years from now. Decision-makers in Santa Fe and other areas of the world do not typically make such forward-thinking decisions with regard to risk—not only due to questions of finance and electoral cycles but also because people are often more concerned with immediate risks. This is most evident in the technocratic approaches to risk. The fact that infrastructure (and structures) continues to be built on land at high risk of flooding demonstrates that people still believe infrastructure will protect them even if their actual past experience has proven otherwise.

The way we view risk must change, and the role of government in making this change is critical. With regard to infrastructure and flood risk, climate change needs to be part of the agenda and not made to be a discursively different beast that will only affect certain groups of people in the far off future. Governments' social, economic, and environmental policies can no longer be undertaken in isolation from climate change policy. This means that all policies should incorporate an integrative view of risk (hazard and vulnerability) and include the voice of local populations in their view of risk, their understanding of who is at risk, the problems that at-risk groups face, and possible solutions (Ribot, 2010). Reframing risk in such a way that citizens and governments better understand both sides of the risk equation will help shape the development and deployment of more equitable and effective policy interventions.

CONCLUSION: THE INVISIBLE POWER OF DISCOURSE

This chapter has shown how infrastructure development and planning practices, both materially and discursively, shape the unequal distribution of flood risk. Through material practices, the state carved out different spaces in Santa Fe by servicing some neighborhoods, such as Candioti Sur, with infrastructure and encouraging the budding middle and upper classes to settle there, while consciously allowing the poor to settle on land not serviced by infrastructure and exposed to flood risk until that land was deemed "developable" by flows of capital. In addition to the state producing such social inclusion and exclusion, residents contributed to a discourse that not only blames victims but also makes victims turn toward blaming themselves for choosing to live in risky areas (Rose, 1996). This case highlights the invisible power of discourse in cultivating a false consciousness among Santa Fe's population, resulting in the normalization—and therefore the nonquestioning—of risk.

Reflecting on the material and discursive production of risk in historical planning practices is useful for tracing causality and theorizing contemporary vulnerability. Past planning and infrastructure decisions and discourses shaped contemporary risks. Yet, the discursive production of risk is a key practice not only of government but also of its subjects. With an awareness of how citizens as subjects of government are implicit in the discursive production of risk, we can more effectively fight vulnerability and its underlying material inequities by bringing attention to the illusion of neutrality and objectivism in infrastructure development and planning practices (Gramsci, 1971; Kilminster, 1979). Because people internalize discourse, how government and its citizens identify what and who is at risk has important implications for the logics of inclusion and exclusion as well as for the allocation of responsibility and the taking on of response. In this way, discourse actively shapes the construction of the material and social world by projecting framings of risk that shape vulnerability and belonging in the contemporary city.

REFERENCES

Bankoff, G. (2002). Discoursing disasters: Paradigms of risk and coping. *Trialog, 73*(II), 3–7.

Bankoff, G. (2003). *Cultures of disaster society and natural hazards in the Philippines.* London, UK: Routledge Curzon.

Blaikie, P., Cannon, T., Davis, I., & Wisner, B. (1994). *At risk: Natural hazards, people's vulnerability, and disasters.* London, UK: Routledge.

Bourdieu, P. (1977). *Outline of a theory of practice.* Cambridge, UK: Cambridge University Press.

Cannon, T. (1994). Vulnerability analysis and the explanation of "natural" disasters. In A. Varley (Ed.), *Disasters, development and environment* (pp. 96–105). Chichester, UK: Wiley.

Convivir con el agua. (1984, May 12). *El Litoral.*

Dalla Fontana, M. A. (2003). *Memorias del Barrio Candioti Sur* (2nd ed.). Santa Fe, Argentina: Imprenta Capelietti de Raúl A. Capeletti.

Felbinger, N. (1996). Introduction. In *Architecture in Cities: Present and Future* (pp. 1–12). Barcelona, Spain: Centre de Cultura Contemporània de Barcelona.

Graham, S., & Marvin, S. (2001). *Splintering urbanism: Networked infrastructures, technological mobilities and the urban condition.* London, UK: Routledge.

Gramsci, A. (1971). *The Antonio Gramsci reader: Selected writings 1916–1935* (D. Forgacs, Ed.). New York, NY: New York University Press.

Hewitt, K. (1983). The idea of calamity in a technocratic age. In K. Hewitt (Ed.), *Interpretations of calamity from the viewpoint of human ecology* (pp. 3–32). Boston, MA: Allen & Unwin.

Hewitt, K. (1995). Sustainable disasters? Perspectives and power in the discourse of calamity. In J. Crush (Ed.), *Power of development* (pp. 115–128). London, UK: Routledge.

Hewitt, K. (1997). *Regions of risk: A geographical introduction to disasters.* New York, NY: Routledge.

Kilminster, R. (1979). *Praxis and method: A sociological dialogue with Lukács, Gramsci and the early Frankfurt School.* London, UK: Routledge & Kegan Paul.

Lerner, S. (2010). *Sacrifice zones: The front lines of toxic chemical exposure in the United States.* Cambridge, MA: MIT Press.

Luke, T. W. (2010). Power loss or blackout: The electricity network collapse of August 2003 in North America. In S. Graham (Ed.), *Disrupted cities: When infrastructure fails* (pp. 1–26). New York, NY: Routledge.

McFarlane, C. (2008). Governing the contaminated city: Infrastructure and sanitation in colonial and post-colonial Bombay. *International Journal of Urban and Regional Research, 32,* 415–435.

Mitchell, T. (2014). The life of infrastructure. *Comparative Studies of South Asia, Africa and the Middle East, 34*(3), 437–439.

Oliver-Smith, A. (1996). Anthropological research on hazards and disasters. *Annual Review of Anthropology, 25,* 303–328.

Oliver-Smith, A. (1999). "What is a disaster?": Anthropological perspectives on a persistent question. In A. Oliver-Smith & S. M. Hoffman (Eds.), *The angry earth: Disaster in anthropological perspective* (pp. 18–33). New York, NY: Routledge.

Pelling, M. (2003). *The vulnerability of cities: Natural disasters and social resilience.* London, UK: Earthscan.

Porter, T. M. (1995). *Trust in numbers: The pursuit of objectivity in science and public life.* Princeton, NJ: Princeton University Press.

Ranganathan, M. (2015). Storm drains as assemblages: The political ecology of flood risk in post-colonial Bangalore. *Antipode, 47*, 1300–1320.

Ribot, J. C. (2010). Vulnerability does not just fall from the sky: Toward multi-scale pro-poor climate policy. In R. Mearns & A. Norton (Eds.), *Social dimensions of climate change: Equity and vulnerability in a warming world*. Washington, DC: The World Bank.

Ribot, J. (2014). Cause and response: Vulnerability and climate in the Anthropocene. *Journal of Peasant Studies, 41*(5), 667–705.

Rose, N. (1996). The death of the social? Re-figuring the territory of government. *Economy and Society, 25*(3), 327–356.

Rose, N. (1998). *Inventing ourselves: Psychology, power, and personhood*. Cambridge, UK: Cambridge University Press.

Scott, J. (1998). *Seeing like a state: How certain schemes to improve the human condition have failed*. New Haven, CT: Yale University Press.

Theesfeld, I. (2011). Perceived power resources in situations of collective action. *Water Alternatives, 4*(1), 86–103.

Un nuevo y hermoso barrio esta surgiendo en sitio cercano a La Avenida Leandro N. Alem. (1957, April 16). *El Litoral*.

Vittori, G. J. (1997). *Santa Fe en clave*. Santa Fe, Argentina: Centro de Publicaciones, Fundación Banco BICA.

Voyles, T. B. (2015). *Wastelanding: Legacies of uranium mining in Navajo country*. Minneapolis, MN: University of Minnesota Press.

Wilkinson, I. (2010). *Vulnerability in everyday life*. London, UK: Routledge.

Wisner, B. (1993). Disaster vulnerability: Scale, power and daily life. *GeoJournal, 30*(2), 127–140.

Wisner, B., Blaikie, P., Cannon, T., & Davis, I. (2004). *At risk: Natural hazards, people's vulnerability, and disasters* (2nd ed.). London, UK: Routledge.

6

Reclaiming Land

ADAPTATION ACTIVITIES AND GLOBAL ENVIRONMENTAL
CHANGE CHALLENGES WITHIN INDIGENOUS
COMMUNITIES

Shanondora Billiot and Jessica Parfait

Shanondora Billiot and Jessica Parfait

BACKGROUND

Global environmental changes (e.g., coastal erosion, repeated disasters, climate change) affect human health, food security, water supply, and physical infrastructure (World Health Organization, 2014). In addition, environmental changes are projected to have adverse impacts on marginalized populations through placing additional pressures on struggling social systems. Indigenous coastal communities, given their attachment to and dependence on the land, are especially vulnerable to environmental changes.

Coastal Louisiana experiences land loss at an average rate of 35 square miles per year (Tidewell, 2003). The land loss is attributed to environmental changes caused by dams, drilling, dredging, and destruction (Tidewell, 2003). Within Louisiana, the United Houma Nation (UHN), comprising approximately 17,000 people, resides in an area that is covered by approximately 90% water and marshland. The tribe depends on the land and water for aquatic agriculture and subsistence livelihood. The permanent loss of land will not just suspend the tribe's way of life, as is the case with disasters, but will ultimately alter its place identity to the land and have impacts on well-being and mental health.

Indigenous peoples have long inhabited their lands, making their living from the natural resources of the area through fishing, hunting, and agricultural means (Colomeda, 1999). Gracey and King (2009) assert that colonization of indigenous peoples removed their way of life, subjected them to live as outcasts of their societies, and forced changes in lifestyle (through urbanization and removal efforts) that resulted in dietary changes. These colonial influences continue to contribute to the higher prevalence of noncommunicable diseases associated with sedentary lifestyles as well as infectious diseases associated with poverty and marginalization. Experts assert that global environmental changes will exacerbate existing social, economic, and health conditions among marginalized populations such as indigenous peoples (Adger, 2006). Global environmental change poses the latest threat for indigenous peoples' health and social and economic well-being (Wildcat, 2009).

There is a dearth of research on environmental changes, especially among indigenous peoples in the United States (Ford, 2012). This chapter presents a case study on how environmental change exposure (e.g., observations, frequency, threats) and felt impact are related to the likelihood of adaptation activities among the UHN, indigenous peoples living in a physically vulnerable coastal area of the United States. Next, it connects these findings with themes within other indigenous communities experiencing environmental changes. The chapter concludes with a discussion of policies within tribal communities addressing issues of environmental change and how social workers and other change agents can be involved.

IMPACTS OF ENVIRONMENTAL CHANGES ON INDIGENOUS PEOPLES

Global environmental changes adversely affect indigenous peoples by (1) disrupting their connection to and dependence on the environment to sustain tradition, culture, and livelihoods; and (2) generating or worsening water and food insecurity (Colomeda, 1999).

Disruptions to Place and Environment

Disruptions to place cause stress through negative feelings associated with place or sense of loss (Cunsolo Willox et al., 2012; Cunsolo Willox, Harper, & Edge, 2013; Healey et al., 2011). It can affect physical, mental, and emotional health and well-being (Brubaker, Berner, Chavan, & Warren, 2011) and can lead to increased family stress, drug and alcohol usage, and suicidal ideation (Cunsolo Willox et al., 2013). These findings are consistent with notions of *place attachment*, wherein the transformation or loss of interaction with the environment manifests as trauma for those whose traditions, memories, and resources are dependent on the environment.

The theory of place attachment posits that identities can be formed from having "positively experienced bonds, sometimes occurring without awareness, that are developed over time from the behavioral, affective and cognitive ties between individuals and/or groups and their socio-physical environment" (Brown & Perkins, 1992, p. 284). Place can be tangible, as in a specific location, and is transformed by human interaction and vice versa where one's subjective meaning of place is altered by interacting with one's place or environment (Berdoulay, 1989).

In the current context, the discourse between place and subject can lead to formation of an identity based on that place (Burley, 2010). Coastal Louisiana residents view their loss of identity in relation to their knowledge of land loss with the coast (Burley, 2010). Through momentous shared life experiences with the land, residents identify with the loss of land as a loss of themselves (Burley, 2010). They cite their attachment to the coast and the impacts of coastal erosion; for example, residents who had a significant history with the coast developed an attachment to that place (Burley, 2010). Interactions happen among people because the interactions have meanings within a culture, and that culture exists in a specific place (Richardson, 1989). These experiences with a physical place led to developing social meanings of that place, and the meanings in turn connected with their identity. Therefore, the threat to coastal land posed a threat to their identity. In the following case study, it can be seen how place and identity are subjectively intertwined with a particular place and a particular lifestyle. Though there is no comparative research showing differences among indigenous and non-indigenous identity based on their relationship with land, it is known that indigenous people form identities based on place similar to that reported in the Burley study (Colomeda, 1999; Wildcat, 2009).

For many indigenous peoples, identity is formed and expressed through the environment, as evidenced by Chief Dardar's 2012 congressional testimony pleading for federal assistance in protecting his tribe's lands:

> Common wildlife located in our homeland that historically provided for our people included rabbits, ducks, deer, and other wild game as well as fur bearing animals such as the mink and muskrat. . . . Naturally growing plants include sage, roots, palmetto and other plants that we've gathered for our traditional medicine and basket weaving. From this land come many traditions we still practice today.

As with the participants in Burley's (2010) study, members of Chief Dardar's tribe are experiencing an identity crisis or pending loss of identity as they lose their land. Many indigenous scholars believe that disruptions or loss of land can lead to psychological distress and other mental health issues (Berry, Bowen, & Kjellstrom, 2010; Colomeda, 1999; Cunsolo Willox et al., 2012, 2013; Healey et al., 2011). Attachment is not contingent on the specific place but, rather, on a particular population under certain circumstances.

Water and Food Insecurity

Indigenous communities in the Arctic, Africa, Australia, and Latin America are experiencing warming temperatures and deforestation, which affect their food and water quality, access, and availability (Berrang-Ford et al., 2012; Healey et al., 2011;

Hofmeijer et al., 2013). In addition, changes in wildlife and vegetation patterns, subsistence agriculture, and forest health are also occurring (Cunsolo Willox et al., 2012, 2013; Doyle, Redsteer, & Eggers, 2013; Hofmeijer et al., 2013). These effects create both water and food insecurity (Brubaker et al., 2011; Hofmeijer et al., 2013).

During the past three generations, much of the world's population has seen drastic changes in its relationship to food. In addition to separating meanings of food from most cultures, mass-produced items and big agriculture contribute substantially to the amount of greenhouse gases in the atmosphere and use inordinate amounts of water and fossil fuels to accommodate mammoth infrastructures and transportation needs (Moran, 2010). Ironically, widespread food distribution contributes to increasing food shortages (Moran, 2010). Subsistence communities are affected the most from mass production and big agriculture. These communities maintain their connection to food, rely on ecosystems for nutritional and economic purposes, observe environmental changes, and experience decreased crop seasons due to climate change (Cunsolo Willox et al., 2012; Furgal & Seguin, 2006; Moran, 2010; Tam, Gough, Edwards, & Tsuji, 2013).

A CASE STUDY: UNITED HOUMA NATION

To understand how one particular tribal community is adapting to global environmental changes, it is necessary to first learn its history of repeated forced relocation, structural discrimination, and chronic exposure to disasters and changes in its environment.

Houma History

Anthropologists speculate that in approximately 1540, the Houma separated from Chakchiuma, located near the Yazoo River in present-day Mississippi (Swanton, 1911). This is believed to be the case because "uma" or "Houma" means "red" in Mobilian Jargon within the Muskogean languages used by the Chakchiuma (Swanton, 1911). The first written documentation of the Houma was by the French explorer Henri de Tonti in 1686, who met them while on an expedition to meet Robert La Salle at the mouth of the Mississippi River (Bureau of Indian Affairs [BIA], 1994; Swanton, 1911). Subsequent encounters with the French explorer Sieur de Bienville recorded that at approximately this time the Houma shared hunting grounds with the Bayougoula separated with a "large pole decorated with fish heads and bear bones" or the red stick (BIA, 1994). This "red stick" later gave name to the state capital of Louisiana, Baton Rouge.

There were approximately 29 known tribes in Louisiana during this time (Kniffen, Gregory, & Stokes, 1987). Dwindling numbers caused by the spread of disease and hostile European forces led smaller tribes to band together or be absorbed by larger tribes for protection. By 1739, Houma, Acolapissa, and Bayougoula were virtually one tribe collectively referred to as Houma (BIA, 1994). During this time, the English made pacts with some Indian tribes in the eastern colonies and lands to gather tribal members located in French territory to use as slaves. The Houma, Bayougoula, and many other tribes began moving southward to escape the headhunters (Kniffen et al., 1987). When smallpox hit New Orleans that summer, the collective Houma tribe moved to the entrance of Bayou Lafourche in Ascension Parish, settling on both sides of the river that became known as Houma's coast. Following a defeat to Great Britain in the Seven Years War, France gave up its French territories east of the Mississippi River with the exception of New Orleans (BIA, 1994).

While France and Britain were working out a treaty from the war, France secretly transferred New Orleans to Spain. Under Spanish rule, Native American slavery was decreed unlawful in 1769 but was not abolished in practice until 1808 (BIA, 1994). In 1800, the Spanish ceded Louisiana back to France with the Treaty of San Ildefonso (BIA, 1994), but soon afterward, in 1803, France sold it to the newly named United States of America for $15 million. Louisiana was declared a state in 1812, doubling the size of the young country. After the purchase, President Thomas Jefferson sent John Sibley, whom he appointed as Indian Agent, to gather information on the newly acquired territory. Sibly noted 60 Houma and claimed they moved to Lake Charles but "disappeared" in a few years; thus, he concluded that they "barely exist as a nation" (Swanton, 1911). However, there is little evidence Sibley himself actually visited the area. From this point onward, the United States considered Houma as an extinct historical group. However, in 1814, the Houma filed its first land claim with the U.S. government, only to be denied despite Article VI of the Louisiana Purchase Treaty, which stated that the U.S. government must uphold treaties between Indians and Spain (Duthu, 2001).

Records show that by 1840, the Houma and the Chitimacha had settled in the Terrebonne and Lafourche parishes (Fischer, 1968; Speck, 1943; Stanton, 1979; Swanton, 1911). Throughout the 1800s, Houma living in Terrebonne and Lafourche retained Indian identity, but the Muskogean language began to disappear as the French language became more dominant (Fischer, 1968; Speck, 1943; Stanton, 1979; Swanton, 1911). During this time, the Houma and other tribes started converting to Catholicism (Fischer, 1968; Speck, 1943; Stanton, 1979; Swanton, 1911).

In 1910, Houma counted its people as 900 women, men, and children; however, the U.S. census counted the population as 120 (BIA, 1994). There are many possible causes for this variation. Census takers were only interested in Indians who owned land and lived in communities that were easily accessible, unlike the marshland and swamps where many tribal members resided (BIA, 1994). In 1930, the U.S. count was 936 after changes were made to counting of races other than White or African American. There is strong evidence that from the 1930s to the present day, Houma existence has defined communities in the Terrebonne and Lafourche parishes (BIA, 1994).

One could argue that life among Houma communities was virtually unchanged from the late 1800s until two major social and economic events occurred in the United States: the civil rights era and the oilfield expansion in the 1970s. Resulting from pressure from the civil rights movement, the Department of the Interior's Bureau of Indian Affairs began the federal recognition process in June 1978. Similarly, the oil industry began drilling and exploring in the 1930s; however, it was not until the United States was unable to obtain oil from Middle Eastern countries that pressure mounted internally for oil production to increase "at home." Though "at home" is not literal for most oil and gas consumers, it is literally in the backyards of people along the Gulf Coast, especially for members of the UHN. These two events placed additional stress on an already marginalized people and helped shape who the Houma are today.

Oil Field Dredging and Navigation Canals

The oil field industry arrived in Louisiana in approximately 1928, and many participants believe the industry practices began the dramatic shift in loss of land: "Oil companies started drilling—opened canals and then didn't fill them, left them open. That started the erosion. First noticed it when they built the canal—Houma Navigation canal [around the late 1970s]" (survey comment, Billiot, 2017). Another participant reports, "It's saltwater intrusion you know and that's coming from the oilfield digging bayous and not concerned about what it would do to the land you know" (participant 1; Billiot, 2017).

After decades of exposure to salt water, the once small canals are much larger. One participant describes, "When the first oil company started digging [the] canal—and then today, what was a canal back then, that's a bayou now. It's a navigation bayou now" (participant 15; Billiot, 2017). One participant goes on to say that in the past, oil companies could dig wherever they wanted—"This island was 5 miles wide and 7 miles long before the oil field came in here" (participant 6; Billiot, 2017)—but that today, the companies would not be able to dig canals like they did in the past.

Federal Recognition

In 1985, the UHN filed a petition to the BIA for status of federal recognition. The UHN began the process in 1979 by gathering documents and information from locals for the application, when the BIA opened the recognition. Though that petition was denied, the bureau was cognizant of the social, political, and economic forces that prohibited it from granting recognition, stating, "Their way of life is limited by four factors, loss of land, legal pressures, identity and rise in apartheid-type discrimination" (BIA, 1994, p. 288). For Houma, living in an isolated and closed system due to discrimination, in part, contributed to the maintenance of their identity, but it also ultimately hindered their quest for federal recognition (Miller, 2004). For many U.S. indigenous people, federal policies interfere with and to some extent dictate how and where the expression of identity and sovereignty occurs.

Today, the UHN is a state-recognized tribe of approximately 17,000 tribal members residing within a six-parish service area encompassing 4,570 square miles. The six parishes—Terrebonne, Lafourche, Jefferson, St. Mary, St. Bernard, and Plaquemines—are located along the southeastern coast of Louisiana. The tribe is presented with the unique challenges of preserving and maintaining culture while the land is disappearing from underneath it.

Global Environmental Change Impacts on United Houma Nation

Coastal Louisiana experiences land loss at an average rate of 35 square miles per year (Couvillion, Beck, Schoolmaster, & Fischer, 2017). In fact, since 1932, Louisiana has lost the land size equivalent to the state of Delaware. By 2050, it is expected that Louisiana will further lose land approximately the size of the Baltimore and Washington, DC, area. The land loss is attributed to environmental changes caused by dams, drilling, dredging, and destruction (Galloway, Boesch, & Twilley, 2009; Lee & Blanchard, 2012; Moorehead & Brinson, 1995; Reed & Wilson, 2004). Indigenous coastal communities such as the UHN, given their attachment to and dependence on the land, are especially vulnerable to environmental changes (Ford, 2012). The most vulnerable parishes (counties) are where the majority of indigenous peoples reside in Louisiana.

The health of the environment affects the health of the people. Participants experienced a loss of medicines and social support as a result of land loss. This has resulted in a loss of cultural knowledge being maintained and passed onto new generations. Such health deterioration has followed a cyclical process. As the salt water encroaches on the land, it changes the salt content of the land and water and its ecosystem. The living creatures in the water and on land are no longer able to survive in the new saltier environment. For the UHN, this means that the harvest decreases and the medicines from roots and plants disappear. As the harvest decreases, people move away from the community. Some participants shared how in the past their families would get together multiple times a week, whereas they now only see each other on holidays, thus reducing their social support. In addition, as newer generations move away, the older generation is less able to pass on its cultural knowledge.

Adaptation to Global Environmental Changes

There are four types of climate change adaptation research (Smit & Wandel, 2006). The first analyzes climate change models based on different projections of anthropogenic activities contributing to greenhouse gas emissions (Smit & Wandel, 2006). The second rates different adaptation options based on cost-effectiveness and country-level commitment to addressing climate change. The third analyzes the relative adaptive capacity of a country, region, or community using vulnerability as the rationale for developing adaptation strategies (Smit & Wandel, 2006). The fourth type of adaptation research—community-based adaptation—is focused on practical application of adaptation activities. It uses participatory methods to empower community members to develop adaptation priorities and activities. The aim is to document perceptual experiences of climate change and empower communities to develop or implement adaptations at the local level (Boyle & Dowlatabadi, 2011; Smit & Wandel, 2006).

This case study falls under the fourth type of adaptation research and explores what factors lead to adaptation activities among tribal members. Adaptation research has focused on country-level adaptation in the form of laws and national policies. Less is known, however, about how individuals participate in adapting or responding to climate change. In addition, environmental changes place additional pressure on marginalized populations, such as indigenous peoples (Billiot, 2017). This section discusses the methods and findings of adaptation activities that study participants profess to have done and would do if the mechanisms were available. With the lack of federal assistance and culturally relevant action from the state, adaptation activities will fall to the UHN government and its communities to adapt and respond to persistent environmental changes.

A study recently conducted using a convenience sample of UHN members explored factors that contribute to the likelihood of adaptation activities among participants (Billiot, 2017). This study found four factors related to adaptation activities: experiencing discrimination, strong ethnic identity, higher exposure to environmental changes, and felt impact of environmental changes.

Discrimination and Ethnic Identity Affect Adaptive Capacity

In November 2015, the state of Louisiana announced that it was funded through the U.S. Department of Housing and Urban Development to begin relocating residents of the island known as Isle de Jean Charles due to the extreme land loss (approximately 98%) that had occurred during the past 60 years (State of Louisiana, 2018). Based on a cost–benefit analysis, the state decided that it would no longer take measures to protect the land and that the community would not be habitable in a few decades. Approximately 25 families remaining on the island are UHN, and most enrolled UHN members can trace their ancestry to the island. Louisiana developed a model to remove residents with neither unanimous consensus nor coordination with the UHN tribal council. Despite meetings between the governor's office and the UHN tribal council in which government officials promised transparency and cooperation with the UHN, efforts are still proceeding to remove residents without notice or approval from the UHN.

This is not the first time a government has tried to remove the UHN. As mentioned previously, the governments of France, Spain, and the United States all developed laws to remove Houma people from their lands; removal by the Louisiana state government is just the latest effort. The UHN has endured a significant history of removal laws and other remnants of institutional discrimination. For example, Jim Crow laws prohibited UHN members in Terrebonne Parish from attending public schools until 1963, nearly a decade after *Brown vs. Board of Education*. Houma children attended missionary schools, termed *Indian schools*, up to the seventh grade until staged integration occurred from

1963 to 1968 (Ng-A-Fook, 2007). Those in seventh grade could attend public schools in 1963, followed by eighth grade in 1964, and so on until UHN members could graduate public high schools in 1968. Discrimination is a pervasive contemporary trauma in the collective memory of UHN members (Billiot, 2017). The sociopolitical processes that created institutional discrimination served to limit participants' adaptive capacity to maintain traditional activities and respond to persistent changes to their environment.

When asked how likely they were to participate in community-level adaptation activities, UHN study participants stated they were more likely to participate in informal activities compared to more formalized activities. Some informal activities were speaking with other UHN members, such as friends or elected UHN council members, and attending meetings with other UHN members, such as tribal council meetings or those after the BP oil spill. Formal activities they were less likely to do were responding to an environmental impact statement or writing a letter to the editor. In interviews, participants stated they did not feel welcome in those spaces initiated by the government or the city of Houma because they were UHN members. Past experiences of overt discrimination seemed to dissuade some participants from attending and then using their voice at regular town hall meetings on coastal erosion. In an interview, when asked whether there could be any UHN effort to organize an adaptation effort, one participant said, "None of the shrimpers on this bayou wanted to do it, because—first thing they said: 'Well, I don't have enough education'" (participant 14; Billiot, 2017). Yet, those who experienced more discrimination were more likely to participate in adaptation activities. This suggests that their past experiences of discrimination have simultaneously motivated and discouraged participation, further suggesting that when they do speak out, they do so because of their experiences but only in realms in which they feel most accepted.

High Exposure and Felt Impact to Environmental Changes Lead to Adaptation Activities

Members of the UHN live near physically vulnerable areas. Those who experienced greater exposure to environmental changes and those who felt more threatened by these changes were more likely to participate in adaptation activities. Members discussed the slow and sometimes damaging response from the state government. For example, one state-run levee protection project was given, through a no-bid contract, to the local state representative's company. The company was allowed to purchase land across the street from the levee location, dig a hole deeper and wider than the Twin Towers memorial in New York City, and transport the dirt across the street. The hole quickly filled with water because there was marshland on the other side of the property. The reason stated for digging the hole across the street from the levee locations was that it would have cost the company more money to transport the soil from a location farther away, even though this would have caused less damage (participant 9; Billiot, 2017). The state's actions to protect the land from erosion have been perplexing to residents for more than 30 years.

In addition, a common sentiment among the UHN members was a sense of being responsible themselves for the damage and the repair of the land. Several participants expressed that denying the UHN federal recognition as a sovereign tribal nation affected many members' notion of basic human rights to safety, equal protection, and well-being.

Despite having recorded contact with French explorers dating back to 1686, the Houma have yet to receive federal recognition from the U.S. government. Consequently, the tribe lacks the sovereignty to protect its lands, receives no funding, and is not recognized as "Indian" by the same government that persecuted it as such merely four decades ago. Recognizing the need to reclaim human rights and responsibility for the land, many UHN tribal leaders have been grappling with how to organize and respond to environmental and human threats within their scope of legal power. However, U.S. tribal communities that do have federal recognition have greater authority to develop policies to protect their lands.

POLICY INTERVENTIONS FOR U.S. TRIBAL COMMUNITIES

Within the United States, there are more than 560 federally recognized tribes and an estimated 200 more that are non-federally recognized; therefore, not all tribes, including the UHN, have a dedicated land base governed by tribal governments. In addition, a tribe's right to govern itself and manage its property (i.e., tribal sovereignty) is contingent on the acknowledgment of government-to-government relationships between the tribe and the federal government (Hicks, 2007). Therefore, tribal polices regarding adaptation to climate change are limited in scope because they can only be enforced at the tribal government level, if at all.

In contrast to the UHN, several federally recognized tribal governments have developed formal climate change policies (Durglo, 2013; Hansen, 2013). For example, Swinomish Tribe, in Washington state, passed the first climate change proclamation among U.S. indigenous peoples in 2007. The proclamation recognizes that effects of climate change have potential impacts for the tribe and that it is the responsibility of the Swinomish Senate to provide for the well-being of the community and natural resources. A few of the adaptation projects focus on coastal protection of specific tidal areas, dike maintenance, wildfire risk mitigation and management, and local emergency planning (Swinomish, 2010).

Other tribes concerned with climate change impacts such as wildfires, deforestation, drought, and water security have developed plans to address natural resource management. For example, the Mescalero Apache in New Mexico built solar-powered water pumps as an alternative water supply source (Hansen, 2013). Nez Perce in Idaho developed an afforestation project that provides carbon sequestration credits to the carbon markets. Confederated Salish and Kootenai Tribes of the Flathead Reservation in Montana enacted a climate change strategic plan that prioritizes climate change and traditional ecological knowledge through scientific research (Durglo, 2013; Hansen, 2013).

The plan focuses on preservation of forestry, land, fish, wildlife, water and air quality, infrastructure, culture, and people. For example, action plans that focus on humans include providing education with the Tribal Health Department, expanding community gardens, and monitoring vector-borne diseases (Durglo, 2013). Other tribes, such as Navajo Nation and the Eastern Band of Cherokee Indians, hold adaptation-planning workshops that address water and forest management issues associated with climate change.

These and many other tribal nations throughout the United States and the world have recognized the importance of developing plans, organizing their communities, and responding to environmental changes despite the lack of response from the governments in which they are nested. If UHN were a federally recognized tribe, it would have the sovereignty to be able to develop adaptation activities and a legal voice to prevent future projects that could further threaten its lands.

CONCLUSION

Many indigenous communities are documenting their observations and experiences of environmental changes, stating their beliefs on the anthropogenic causes of these changes, and attempting to organize their communities to adapt to the new reality of their physical vulnerability. However, to make systemic changes within tribal communities, social change agents must recognize and empower the importance of the community's voice in developing policies and adaptations regarding lands adjacent to and inside of tribal lands.

International climate change protocols set global standards but have weak binding authority to hold nation states accountable for producing emissions above set goals. High-emission countries such as the United States have not enacted comprehensive climate change policies. In addition, the current U.S. administration has pulled out of international agreements to address climate change and has rolled back previous administrations' efforts.

In the absence of federal laws that meet international standards, meaningful climate change mitigation seems distant, and so many U.S. states have enacted their own climate change adaptation measures. Likewise, tribal governments are following states' lead by also developing action plans and policies, which seek to reduce the disparate burden of climate change impacts on indigenous peoples. Funding is needed to support local-level and informal adaptation activities that could motivate individual and community participation. Such interventions could involve elders and cultural bearers to teach newer generations their traditional knowledge. These informal interventions could strengthen their ethnic identity and stimulate intergenerational knowledge transmission that incorporates traditional knowledge and modern technologies that adapt to today's reality. In addition, it is incumbent on social change makers to advocate for adaptation policies that incorporate traditional local knowledge.

REFERENCES

Adger, W. N. (2006). Vulnerability. *Global Environmental Change, 16*, 268–281.

Berdoulay, V. (1989). Place, meaning, discourse in French Language Geography. In J. D. Agnew & J. S. Duncan (Eds.), *The power of place* (pp. 56–71). Winchester, MA: Unwin Hyman.

Berrang-Ford, L., Dingle, K., Ford, J. D., Lee, C., Lwasa, S., Namanya, D. B., . . . Edge, V. (2012). Vulnerability of indigenous health to climate change: A case study of Uganda's Batwa Pygmies. *Social Science & Medicine, 75*(6), 1067–1077.

Berry, H., Bowen, K., & Kjellstrom, T. (2010). Climate change and mental health: A causal pathways framework. *International Journal of Public Health, 55*(2), 123–132. doi:10.1007/s00038-009-0112-0

Billiot, S. (2017). *How do environmental changes and shared cultural experiences impact health of indigenous peoples of South Louisiana?* (Doctoral dissertation). Washington University in St. Louis, St. Louis, MO.

Boyle, M., & Dowlatabadi, H. (2011). Anticipatory adaptation in marginalized communities within developed countries. In J. Ford & L. Berrang-Ford (Eds.), *Climate change adaptation in developed nations* (pp. 461–476). New York, NY: Springer.

Brown, B., & Perkins, D. (1992). Disruptions to place attachment. In I. Altman (Ed.), *Place attachment* (pp. 279–304). New York, NY: Plenum.

Brubaker, M., Berner, J., Chavan, R., & Warren, J. (2011). Climate change and health effects in northwest Alaska. *Global Health Action, 4*, 1–5. doi:10.3402/gha.v4i0.8445

Bureau of Indian Affairs. (1994). *United Houma Nation petition for federal recognition.* Retrieved from https://www.bia.gov/as-ia/ofa/056-uhouma-la

Burley, D. (2010). *Losing ground: Identity and land loss in coastal Louisiana.* Oxford, MS: University Press of Mississippi.

Colomeda, L. (1999). *Keepers of the central fire.* Sudbury, MA: Jones & Bartlett.

Couvillion, B. R., Beck, H., Schoolmaster, D., & Fischer, M. (2017). *Land area change in coastal Louisiana (1932 to 2016)* (No. 3381). Reston, VA: US Geological Survey. Retrieved from https://pubs.er.usgs.gov/publication/sim3381

Cunsolo Willox, A., Harper, S. L., & Edge, V. L. (2013). Storytelling in a digital age: Digital storytelling as an emerging narrative method for preserving and promoting indigenous oral wisdom. *Qualitative Research, 13*(2), 127–147. doi:10.1177/1468794112446105

Cunsolo Willox, A., Harper, S. L., Ford, J. D., Landman, K., Houle, K., & Edge, V. L. (2012). "From this place and of this place": Climate change, sense of place, and health in Nunatsiavut, Canada. *Social Science & Medicine, 75*(3), 538–547. doi:10.1016/j.socscimed.2012.03.043

Doyle, J., Redsteer, M., & Eggers, M. (2013). Exploring effects of climate change on Northern Plains American Indian health. *Climatic Change, 120*(3), 643–655. doi:10.1007/s10584-013-0799-z

Durglo, J. (2013). *Climate change strategic plan for Confederated Salish and Kootenai Tribes of the Flathead Reservation.* Durham, NC: National Institute of Environmental Health Sciences. Retrieved from https://www.cakex.org/documents/confederated-salish-and-kootenai-tribes-climate-change-strategic-plan

Duthu, N. B. (2001). The Houma of Louisiana: Politics, identity, and the legal status of "tribe." *European Review of Native American Studies, 15*(2), 37–40.

Fischer, A. M. (1968). History and current status of the Houma Indians. *Midcontinent American Studies Journal, 6*(2), 149–163.

Ford, J. D. (2012). Indigenous health and climate change. *American Journal of Public Health, 102*(7), 1260–1266. doi:10.2105/ajph.2012.300752

Furgal, C., & Seguin, J. (2006). Climate change, health, and vulnerability in Canadian Northern Aboriginal communities. *Environmental Health Perspectives, 114*(12), 1964–1970. doi:10.1289/ehp.8433

Galloway, G., Boesch, D., & Twilley, R. (2009, Winter). Restoring and protecting coastal Louisiana. *Science and Technology, 25*(2). Retrieved from http://issues.org/25-2/galloway

Gracey, M., & King, M. (2009). Indigenous health part 1: Determinants and disease patterns. *The Lancet, 374*(9683), 65–75.

Hansen, T. (2013, October 15). Eight tribes that are way ahead of the climate-adaptation curve. *Indian Country Today Media Network*. Retrieved from http://indiancountrytodaymedianetwork.com/2013/10/15/8-tribes-are-way-ahead-climate-adaptation-curve-151763

Healey, G. K., Magner, K. M., Ritter, R., Kamookak, R., Aningmiuq, A., Issaluk, B., . . . Moffit, P. (2011). Community perspectives on the impact of climate change on health in Nunavut, Canada. *Arctic, 64*(1), 89–97.

Hicks, S. (2007). Intergovernmental relationships: Expressions of tribal sovereignty. In M. Jorgensen (Ed.), *Rebuilding native nations. Strategies for governance and development* (pp. 99–115). Tucson, AZ: University of Arizona Press.

Hofmeijer, I., Ford, J. D., Berrang-Ford, L., Zavaleta, C., Carcamo, C., Llanos, E., . . . Namanya, D. (2013). Community vulnerability to the health effects of climate change among indigenous populations in the Peruvian Amazon: A case study from Panaillo and Nuevo Progreso. *Mitigation and Adaptation Strategies for Global Change, 18*(7), 957–978.

Kniffen, F., Gregory, H., & Stokes, G. (1987). *The historic Indian tribes of Louisiana: From 1542 to the present.* Baton Rouge, LA: Louisiana State University Press.

Lee, M., & Blanchard, T. (2012). Community attachment and negative affective states in the context of the BP Deepwater Horizon disaster. *American Behavioral Scientist, 56*(24), 24–47.

Miller, E. (2004). *Forgotten tribes: Unrecognized Indians and the Federal acknowledgement process.* Lincoln, NE: University of Nebraska Press.

Moorehead, K., & Brinson, M. (1995). Response of wetlands to rising sea level in the lower coastal plain of North Carolina. *Ecological Society of America, 5*(1), 261–271.

Moran, E. (2010). *Environmental social science: Human–environmental interactions and sustainability.* West Sussex, UK: Wiley-Blackwell.

Ng-A-Fook, N. (2007). *An indigenous curriculum of place: The United Houma Nation's contentious relationship with Louisiana's educational institutions.* Bern, Switzerland: Lang.

Richardson, F. C. (1989). Freedom and commitment in modern psychology. *Integrative & Eclectic Psychotherapy, 8*(4), 303–319.

Reed, D., & Wilson, L. (2004). Coast 2050: A new approach to restoration of Louisiana wetlands. *Physical Geography, 25*(1), 4–21.

Smit, B., & Wandel, J. (2006). Adaptation, adaptive capacity and vulnerability. *Global Environmental Change, 16*(3), 282–292. doi:10.1016/j.gloenvcha.2006.03.008

Speck, F. G. (1943). A social reconnaissance of the Creole Houma Indian trappers of the Louisiana bayous. *American Indigena, 3*, 134–146.

Stanton, M. E. (1979). Southern Louisiana survivors: The Houma Indians. In W. L. Williams (Ed.), *Southeastern Indians since the removal era* (pp. 90–109). Athens, GA: University of Georgia Press.

State of Louisiana. (2018). *Isle de Jean Charles Resettlement Project.* Retrieved from http:// isledejeancharles.la.gov

Swanton, J. (1911). *Indian tribes of the lower Mississippi Valley and adjacent coast of the Gulf of Mexico.* Washington, DC: Government Printing Office.

Swinomish. (2010). *Swinomish Climate Change Initiative: Climate adaptation action plan.* Retrieved from http://www.swinomish-nsn.gov/climate_change/Docs/SITC_CC_ AdaptationActionPlan_complete.pdf

Tam, B. Y., Gough, W. A., Edwards, V., & Tsuji, L. J. S. (2013). The impact of climate change on the well-being and lifestyle of a First Nation community in the western James Bay region. *Canadian Geographer, 57*(4), 441–456. doi:10.1111/j.1541-0064.2013.12033.x

Tidewell, M. (2003). *Bayou farewell.* New York, NY: Vintage.

Wildcat, D. (2009). *Red alert! Indigenous call for action.* Golden, CO: Fulcrum.

World Health Organization. (2014). *Climate change and human health—Risks and responses: Summary.* Retrieved from http://www.who.int/globalchange/summary/en/index1. html

7

Urban Development, Vulnerabilities, and Disasters in Indonesia's Coastal Land Reclamations

DOES SOCIAL JUSTICE MATTER?

Rita Padawangi

BACKGROUND

Despite numerous scholarly discussions on the adverse impact of urban development on environmental sustainability, environmental degradation from industrialization, urbanization, and other encroachments on natural areas continues to occur globally. Urban development also influences the vulnerabilities of the populations whose livelihoods are dependent on the parts of the environment and environmental resources that are affected. Common characteristics of such development include industrial pollution, deforestation, and overbuilt surfaces that lead to flooding. When they reach the scale beyond a society's capacity to cope, the environmental degradation can result in disaster.

Disaster mitigation projects are likely to follow existing urban development trajectories, subjected to the norms and ideologies that are behind the existing course of development. Therefore, mitigation projects and strategies to remedy the environmental impacts of urban development are unlikely to challenge the existing development discourses that cause environmental degradation in the first place. For disaster mitigation projects to alleviate social injustices brought about by environmental degradation, attention must be paid to social justice in the broader scope of urban development.

Therefore, it is crucial that proposed solutions understand the unjust distribution of development-induced environmental degradations and disasters; otherwise, they risk perpetuating—rather than alleviating—social injustices. For example, members of communities relocated from environmentally degraded areas may be unable to rebuild their livelihoods in their new homes. Moreover, urban flood mitigation projects with large, specific funding criteria may involve more large-scale development that further alters the natural landscape.

In this chapter, I address the following questions: Does social justice matter in urban development discourse? If so, to whom does social justice matter, and what are the implications for urban development? Embedded in these related questions is the wider question of environmental impact, which is inseparable from urban development.

To address these questions, I present two case studies from Indonesia: the land reclamation projects in the North Bay of Jakarta and in the Benoa Bay of Bali. The development plans of artificial islands as reclaimed land in the capital city Jakarta and the island of Bali are representative of wider development pressures with considerable environmental impacts. To construct my argument, I rely on data collected between 2013 and 2016 through observations of and interviews with civil society actors who are engaged in resistance movements against these projects.[1]

SOCIAL JUSTICE, SPATIAL JUSTICE, AND ENVIRONMENTAL JUSTICE

Social justice scholarship is a form of critical inquiry into the ways in which social structures shape outcomes, with a normative perspective on benefits and detriments that are experienced by the actors within those social structures. As a continuation of Marxist urbanism, *social justice* scholarship is linked to the analysis of the impacts of capitalist urban development on different economic classes in the city (Harvey, 1973). Therefore, in analyzing social justice in the city, it is important to consider segregations of economic classes as manifestations of capitalism in the urban landscape. Related are other forms of segregation, such as racial and ethnic segregation, with adverse economic impacts on marginalized groups. *Spatial justice* represents a specific reference to the spatial dimension of justice and distribution of spatial resources (Dikeç, 2001; Soja, 2010), but it is not limited to distributional justice. Spatial justice also encompasses *procedural justice*, through which attention is given to the struggles of marginalized groups to achieve social justice (Soja, 2010).

Environmental justice focuses on the unequal impacts of environmental degradation on various political, economic, and social classes (Dobson, 1998; Walker & Bulkeley, 2006). In addition to having a strong spatial aspect through the specific geographical locations of environmental issues experienced by the affected populations, environmental justice scholarship has been linked to resistance groups and social movements

---

[1] Some of the interviews and observations were conducted by me during the research project Governing Compound Disasters in Urbanizing Asia. Interviews of fishermen in Jakarta and Bali were obtained from WatchDoc (a documentary filmmaker based in Jakarta); these were conducted during the Ekspedisi Indonesia Biru (Blue Indonesia Expedition) in 2015.

that address these injustices. Both principles and outcomes of justice are included within environmental justice, reflected in attention paid toward intergenerational and intragenerational justice among different groups involved in the exploitation and conservation of resources (Blaikie & Muldavin, 2014). An editorial in the journal *Geoforum* ("Globalizing Environmental Justice?" 2014) states,

> Environmental justice thus may provide a powerful lens through which to make sense of struggles over environments and natural resources worldwide, providing a link between Northern literature on environmental justice and research on southern environmentalisms, and between the "environmentalism of the poor," liberation ecology and global political ecology. (p. 151)

Environmental justice literature, despite being focused on place-specific struggles, has historically connected practice and theory, and it potentially feeds into global social mobilization because environmental justice struggles globally have common core issues ("Globalizing Environmental Justice?" 2014; Schroeder, Martin, Wilson, & Sen, 2008; Walker & Bulkeley, 2006).

The main challenge in examining social justice in contemporary urban conditions, such as in Jakarta and Bali, is the situation in which social injustices are normalized as the requirement of progress through urban development. Such normalization occurs through gradual local and global processes that construct the sacrifices of some groups of society as the required collateral to achieve development—a "price to be paid." This "normalcy" may be the product of powerful institutions and their discourses of development-as-modernization, but in practice it may also be the product of popular democracy, in which the majority gives its support and credence to such a development discourse. In such a situation, achieving social justice requires breaking down existing norms, structures, and social relations—a problematic and uncomfortable process because it challenges accepted norms and wisdoms.

Questioning social justice in urban development and development-induced disaster, therefore, requires attention to the social struggles to change the trajectory—in other words, changing the course of the "normal." "Normalcy" reflects the situation socially constructed by institutions and actors in the city, which may vary across different geographies. Sen (2009) argues that institutions have "a critically important place in the enterprise of enhancing justice" (p. xii). The distribution of disaster impacts and development benefits need to be analyzed alongside the roles of different social actors in establishing and challenging the status quo. Though institutions are important in the context of Indonesia, the roles of the actors are key given the prevalence of a relational economy in which transactions are dependent on and affect various aspects of the actors' lives and social relationships—within and across social groups (Simone, 2009).

The legacy of environmental justice scholarship also applies action research that brings practice and theory into contact and conversation. In this chapter, I argue that action research is the only way to obtain a comprehensive understanding of existing social conditions, as urban development continues to evolve along with the constant struggles and negotiations.

LAND RECLAMATION IN JAKARTA AND BALI

Land reclamation has been a feature of development in many of Southeast Asia's major cities. Several capital cities in Southeast Asia have expanded land area through reclaiming the coast, including Phnom Penh, Cambodia; Metro Manila, Philippines; Jakarta, Indonesia; and Singapore. In Phnom Penh, the Diamond Island (Koh Pich) project is planned to cover 100 ha of land off the capital city's "coast" on the Mekong River. In the plan, the island will host more than 1,000 condominiums as well as "hundreds of villas, two international schools, a replica of the Arc de Triomphe, a near-clone of Singapore's Marina Bay Sands and one of the world's tallest buildings" (Horton, 2014).

Singapore, which inspired some of the buildings on Diamond Island, has been reclaiming land since 1822 "on swampy grounds in the area known today as South Boat Quay" (HistorySG, n.d.). This has resulted in an increase in the city-state's land area of approximately 23%, or 130 km^2. Covering 360 ha at the south side of the island, the Marina Bay reclamation was completed in 1992, a decade before major buildings were developed. However, it was not Singapore's last land reclamation project. In 2015, a major project on the east coast was begun to "build more houses, schools, parks and other community facilities for a growing population" and provide space and facilities for 200,000 people (Tan, 2015).

Land reclamation has spread in Indonesia since the country's decentralization policy was introduced in 2001, which provided city-level governments the authority to draft their own spatial plans. The autonomy to draft spatial plans has paved the way for more entrepreneurial approaches to urban development, particularly the opportunity to present themselves as competitive cities in the country and in the region (Susilo, 2015). Coastal areas have become opportunities for investment, as expanding land toward the sea makes more areas available for development.

Manado, the largest city in East Indonesia, became the first coastal city to reclaim land, starting with 114 ha in 1998 and potentially spreading to cover an additional 700 ha (Ikanubun, 2016). Implemented by a consortium of six private developers, the commercial boulevard on reclaimed land was the emblem of modern urban development that reflected Jakarta's commercial image in Manado (Susilo, 2015). Since then, more land reclamation has taken place in other coastal cities, though these projects were for public infrastructures such as port expansion in the city of Surabaya and airport expansion in the city of Semarang, rather than being private initiatives (Table 7.1).

Of all the reclamation projects listed in Table 7.1, those of Jakarta Bay and Bali's Benoa Bay have received the most media attention. Though these reclamation

TABLE 7.1

Reclamation Projects in Indonesia

Location	Area (ha)	Planned/In Process/Completed
South Aceh	6,305.82	Planned
Tangerang	7,500	Planned
Jakarta	5,155	In process
Semarang	204	Completed
Surabaya	600	Completed
Balikpapan	5,130	In process
Makassar	4,000	In process
Bali	700	Planned
Lombok	1,250	Planned
Palu	24.5	In process
Manado	114	Completed
Bitung	2,000	Planned
Kendari	17.5	Planned
Total (completed)	918	
Total (in process)	14,254.50	
Total (planned)	12,103.32	
Total (all)	27,275.82	

Source: KNTI (2016).

projects, amounting to 5,130 ha in Jakarta Bay and 700 ha in Bali, are not the largest, they have been the most contentious because of the contrast between the interests of private developers and local resistance against the projects, amid the role of the national and local governments in paving the way for reclamation.

Though the detailed spatial plans of reclamation projects are under the authority of the local governments, the national government must legalize all coastal reclamation plans before more detailed planning can take place. Jakarta's land reclamation relies on Presidential Decree 52/1995 signed by President Suharto before the Reform Era, and Benoa Bay reclamation relies on Presidential Regulation 51/2014 signed by President Susilo Bambang Yudhoyono near the end of his second term.

Jakarta's Coastal Reclamation

Jakarta has been an important port city for hundreds of years, including being one of the busiest trade ports and fisheries in the colonial era. Today, Jakarta is listed as a megacity of more than 10 million inhabitants that is threatened by sea level rise, along with Shanghai, Mumbai, Dhaka, Calcutta, Hanoi, and Hong Kong (Climate Central, 2015). As one of the consequences of climate change, sea level rise challenges the historical emergence of cities that are inseparable from water bodies as natural, social, and economic resources. These cities' historical evolution has been founded on their coastal location, but this location is now reworked as a threat in an era of climate change. Areas in Jakarta that have been identified by the government as prone to tidal floods are Kamal Muara, Pluit, Penjaringan, Kalibaru, Cilincing, and Marunda, which cover the coastal settlements from west to east (Pemprov DKI Jakarta, 2012). Coastal populations and ecosystems, particularly in the developing world, are prone to regular flooding and other impacts of climate change (Bijlsma et al., 1996; Nicholls, Hoozemans, & Marchand, 1999).

Developing the north coast marked a significant shift in Jakarta's city planning. The 1985 master plan of the city's metropolitan area designated the north coast a protected environmental zone not suitable for development. However, the signing of Presidential Decree 52/1995 redesignated it a Kawasan Andalan, or prime location with "strategic value from the perspective of the economy and the development of the city" (Keppres 52/1995, 1995). Though the presidential decree was issued in 1995, Jakarta's coastal reclamation has been documented at least since the 1960s with the development of a recreation park Taman Impian Jaya Ancol (Jaya Ancol Dreamland) on reclaimed land in 1966.

The Ministry of the Environment challenged land reclamation in 2003 as environmentally harmful, but the Supreme Court overruled it in 2011. The development of Jakarta's north coast intensified in 2010 when the government issued Master Plan 2010–2030, which featured extensive land reclamation. Echoing Presidential Decree 52/1995, the Master Plan viewed the north coast as a prime area for commercial activities, light industries, and selected prime economic activities (Padawangi, 2012b). The Master Plan also included two climate change mitigation plans: the Jakarta Urgent Flood Mitigation Project and the Jakarta Coastal Defense Strategy (JCDS). The JCDS included a proposed giant sea wall in Jakarta Bay, 6–8 km from the coastline, to protect Jakarta from sea level rise and to convert the mouth of the 13 rivers into a freshwater reservoir. The JCDS eventually evolved into the National Capital Integrated Coastal Development (NCICD) project in 2014.

Though climatologists list Jakarta as threatened by sea level rise (Climate Central, 2015), the NCICD master plan does not specifically refer to sea level rise as the reason for building the giant sea wall, which, if completed, will be the largest in the world. The document frames water as a threat and cites a prediction that North Jakarta will be 3 m under sea level by 2050 (Kementerian Koordinator Bidang Perekonomian Republik Indonesia, 2014):

> The same sea that is now a threat will be used in many ways to benefit the National Capital, and the country as a whole. Jakarta Bay provides room for a new city district that accommodates over 1.5 million people from all income classes and a National Tangerang-Bekasi Highway that connects the provinces [of] Jakarta, West-Java and Banten. The bay is also used to expand the port and strengthen the existing

fisheries, thus stimulating economic growth. The bay will be converted into a large *waduk* [retention lake]. It contributes to alleviate the urban floods and river floods which have affected the National Capital for so long, and will also serve as a sustainable source for drinking water for the citizens of Jakarta. (p. 11)

The NCICD master plan identifies land subsidence—rather than sea level rise—as the main threat of flooding. The same document claims North Jakarta is subsiding at the rate of 7 cm per year. Nevertheless, in the popular discourse, tidal floods and sea level rise enter the arguments to support the building of the giant sea wall (Ruqoyah & Mukti, 2014). Others in the media have also justified the giant sea wall, as well as land reclamation, as a means to reduce flooding (BeritaSatu, 2015). Land reclamation and the sea wall, then, become the means to protect the city from drowning.

Though the NCICD document makes it clear that the 1,250 ha of land reclamation is different from the 17 artificial islands that were in Jakarta's Master Plan 2010–2030, it makes a reference to these islands as current and planned land reclamations: "The development of the plan will mostly be complementary to the current and planned land reclamations. These are developed as mid- to high-end mixed-use urban villages" (Kementerian Koordinator Bidang Perekonomian Republik Indonesia, 2014, p. 53). Therefore, officially the reclamation of the 17 artificial islands, referred to in the document as "mid- to high-end mixed-use urban villages," is not part of the NCICD, nor the financing mechanism. At the same time, the NCICD's reliance on further land reclamation for its financing also serves as a justification for the 17 artificial islands (Figure 7.1) that were underway at the time of this writing in 2017. Another document issued by Bappenas (the National Planning Agency) in 2017 shows another possible scenario with 17 artificial islands as part of the sea wall itself, with dikes connecting the islands to form the sea wall.

The planned developments in Jakarta Bay reflect the 1960s vision of the "golden beach." Sentiments of both developers—starting with Ciputra in the 1960s and later, in 1992, with the Pantai Indah Kapuk project—and government officials, such as Basuki Tjahaja Purnama's argument for reclamation during his gubernatorial reign (2014–2017), reflect the aspiration to turn "waste" land into capital. These strategic values are also encapsulated in the landscape visualizations that depict a revitalization of a space that had been polluted for many years (Kompas, 2016a).

The developers' plans for the commercially marketed properties on the 17 islands are consistent with Jakarta's recent development trajectory of mixed-use, large-scale projects but are in contrast with the needs of poorer sections of the population. Jakarta's urbanized area expanded rapidly from the mid-1980s to 1997 through the development of new towns in the peripheries by large developers. The government allowed the private sector to handle the bulk of housing supply through the market mechanism, which contributed to the mushrooming of housing enclaves in the metropolitan area but largely failed to meet the housing needs of the poor (Kusno, 2013).

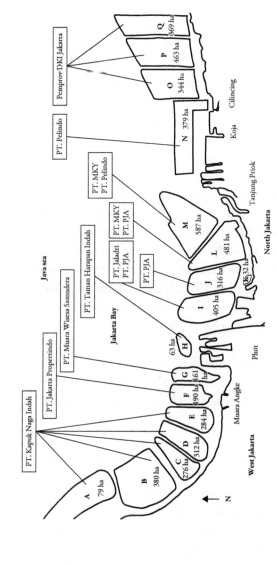

FIGURE 7.1 A schematic map of 17 artificial islands (Islets A–Q) in Jakarta's reclamation plan.
Source: Based on maps from Jakarta Provincial Government.

After recovering from the 1997 economic crisis, new mega projects within city boundaries and central locations reflect a "back to the city" phenomenon, in which mega developments feature upper- and middle-income housing in the city rather than in the outskirts as in the 1980s (Herlambang, 2010).

These plans and the images associated with the projects do not represent the current settlement and demography of North Jakarta. The administrative city of North Jakarta has a larger urban poor population than the other four administrative areas, with more than 48,000 poor households. Most occupy houses that are less than 50 square meters with insufficient basic infrastructure. The poor settlements of North Jakarta stand in contrast to the mega projects. Superblocks "set up their own space and time that do not quite match the temporal and spatial heterogeneity" of existing neighborhoods that have grown and accreted over time at much smaller scales (Kusno, 2013, p. xxi). The large developers in Jakarta also wield the political and economic power to set the terms of the debate (Winters, 1996). The government emphasized that the reclaimed islets, which cover 5,155 ha, will have 15% of the land allocated to public use functions. Maps of the islets, however, show that this allocated land for public use is mostly framed as green spaces rather than housing for the poor.

Furthermore, the reclaimed islands are positioned between the existing fisherfolk along the coast and the sea—the source of their livelihood. According to statistics from the city's Sea and Fisheries Office, there are 27,753 fisherfolk in Jakarta, comprising both long-term residents (considered "permanent") and more recent settlers (Figures 7.2 and 7.3). Some of these fisherfolk have been repeatedly relocated—when Ancol was reclaimed as a theme park in 1966 and when Muara Karang was reclaimed for the construction of a gas-powered electricity plant in 1979. As one poor female resident of Muara Angke explained in 2016 (audience member at DPRD DKI),

> My mother and father were fishermen. I was born in Ancol, Hailai was my birthplace. From Ancol I was moved to Muara Karang, and from Muara Karang to Muara Angke. And now in Muara Angke we will be moved again? We are not animals, sir, we are human beings.

Aided by the Jakarta Legal Aid Foundation, the fisherfolk of Muara Angke filed a lawsuit in 2015 against one of the artificial islands, named Islet G, in the reclamation projects. Citing the loss of income that would result from reclamation, the fisherfolk demanded that Islet G reclamation be canceled. Compared to the previous lawsuit by the Ministry of the Environment, the fisherfolk's lawsuit strategy focused on one artificial island and not the project as a whole. This strategy was chosen because of the focus on the economic impact on local communities rather than the project's large-scale environmental impact, though the environmental impact argument was still included in the lawsuit. Since then, lawsuits have been filed against three other artificial islands in the reclamation project—Islets F, I, and K—also assisted by the Jakarta Legal Aid Foundation. The fisherfolk secured a legal victory on May 31, 2016, that deemed Islet G illegal, but the

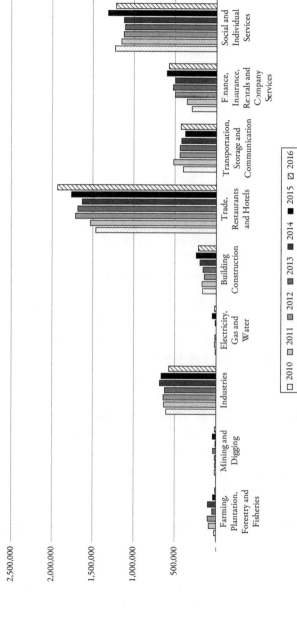

FIGURE 7.2 Selected professions in Jakarta, 2010–2016.

Source: Data from BPS 2016, February data cycle.

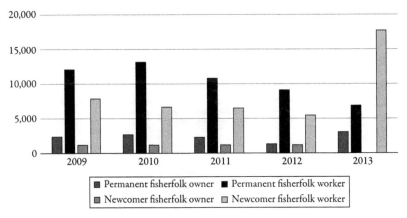

FIGURE 7.3 Fisherfolk population in Jakarta Province.
Source: Data from DKPKP Jakarta.

decision was overturned in the appeals court on October 20, 2016. Throughout the law-suit process, construction of Islet G continued despite a moratorium in place since a local parliament member was arrested for receiving a bribe from Islet G's developer in 2016.

Bali's Coastal Reclamation: The Case of Benoa Bay

The Benoa Bay reclamation project is relatively new compared to land reclamation in Jakarta. In June 2014, President Susilo Bambang Yudhoyono signed Presidential Regulation (Perpres) 51/2014 that revised Presidential Regulation 45/2011 on the Spatial Plan of Denpasar Urban Area, Badung, Gianyar, and Tabanan, Bali. Two reasons were cited to justify the revision: (1) the need to revitalize Benoa Bay based on "strategic national policies" and "internal dy-namics" of the area; and (2) the potential to develop economic activities along with social, cultural, and religious activities (Perpres 51/2014, 2014). The list of revisions set out plans for revitalization activities based on the reclamation of 700 ha of land in Benoa Bay. The Presidential Regulation also cited that this space might be used for "disaster mitigation."

Branded as the "Revitalization of Benoa Bay," the reclamation project was awarded to PT Tirta Wahana Bali International (TWBI), a subsidiary of Artha Graha Company in Jakarta. Signs of the project emerged at least 3 years before the Presidential Regulation, in 2011, when the tollway as a second link between Ngurah Rai Airport and the city of Denpasar was completed. The tollway has exits in the middle of the bay, leading nowhere, but the master plan by PT TWBI shows how these exits would link to the planned artifi-cial islands (Figure 7.4). PT TWBI announced interest in Benoa Bay at the end of 2012, whereas the Presidential Regulation was only issued in June 2014. Unlike the Jakarta Bay reclamation project, which was awarded to nine developers, the Benoa Bay reclamation project involves only one developer.

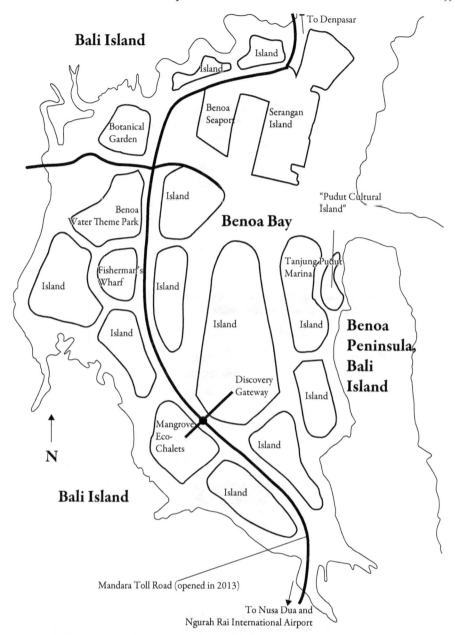

FIGURE 7.4 Benoa Bay reclamation plan access diagram.
Source: Based on information from Nusa Benoa (2016).

Bali's development trajectory is different from that of Jakarta because the island relies predominantly on tourism. Bali's terrain includes a significant share of land and workforce for farming, plantation, forestry, and fisheries. The share of the workforce

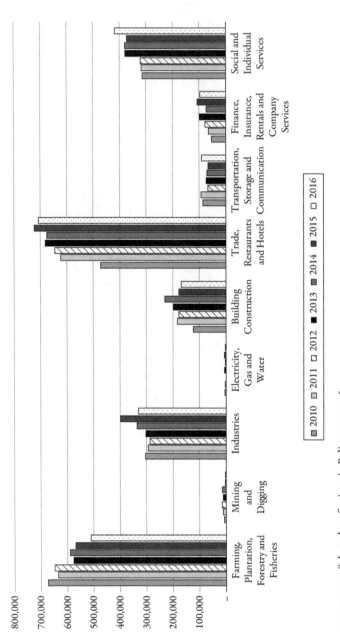

FIGURE 7.5 Selected professions in Bali, 2010–2016.
Source: Data from BPS 2016, February data cycle.

for agriculture, however, has been consistently decreasing (Figure 7.5). Between 2010 and 2016, the population working in the agricultural sector declined by 150,000. In contrast, the number of people employed in trade, restaurants, and hotels has been increasing. These changes in employment have their spatial concomitants in a reduction of irrigated rice fields and an expansion in settlement area (As-syakur, 2011). Most of the reduction of agricultural land has occurred in the vicinity of the city of Denpasar, and it has been attributed to tourism development (As-syakur, 2011; Sutawa, 2012).

Statistically, in the Benoa Bay area, farming and fishing are still significant. In 2013, there were almost 2,000 fisherfolk in the area, and farming remained the dominant profession (Suantika, 2015). Two fishermen explained,

> There are no other jobs here except fishing. It has been like that from the old days. Now the young ones get jobs in hotels, the beach. The elderly folks like me, we have been fishermen since long before, from my grandfather's, my grandmother's time. (Ketut Linggih, Fisherman, 2015)
>
> Then the local people here, will we be allowed to go there [to the water in the reclamation area]? If not, how will we work? No place to put our boats, if all of these area are reclaimed. It's going to be different. We are already kicked out. We would like to stay here, but that might be impossible. (Fisherman, 2015)

Benoa Bay has also opened up to tourism, with boat rentals and related services providing significant economic activity in the area. Local businessmen in the area have expressed skepticism regarding the impact of reclamation on their livelihoods, especially because their current business has slowed due to what they perceive as a saturated tourism market (WatchDoc, 2015).

Met with resistance on the ground, PT TWBI's marketing discourse was geared toward emphasizing the Balinese-ness of the project. The company's marketing used taglines such as "Development Based on People's Empowerment" and "Development Based on Balinese Culture" and featured short interview excerpts with local Balinese and experts who supported the idea of revitalizing Benoa Bay, which was described as already degraded with sedimentation and mud and losing its fisheries (TWBI website, 2016). This revitalization framing was further strengthened through the claim that it was geared "Towards Environmentally Friendly and Sustainable Cultural Tourism," and comparisons were drawn between the area of mangroves (1,400 ha) and water (1,400 ha) to be protected compared to the development area of just 400 ha.

Though the Benoa Bay Reclamation project in Bali is significantly smaller than that in Jakarta, the social movement against reclamation has been more organized. The announcement of the reclamation project, which planned to reclaim 700 ha with 23 million m³ of sea sand, was met with resistance from local groups. Upon learning about the project plan, hundreds of people, local nongovernmental organizations, villages, student bodies, youth organizations, artists, and musicians formed a civil society alliance called ForBALI (ForBALI, 2016). In addition to the social and economic arguments, the movement strongly believes that reclamation threatens Balinese identity, both ethnic and religious. A community representative at an environmental impact assessment public consultation on March 11, 2015, stated,

> First, we should see it together. Don't compare to, like you said just now, Singapore, which is already developed. Now, my question is, without what you showed to us, we have developed, Sir. Bali is still a touristic place. Maybe Singapore is still no comparison to Bali on tourist attraction. I am sure Bali is still sustained with its people who still hold tight to the traditions.

The maintenance of Bali's culture and traditions is inseparable from Bali's economic base because the tourist industry relies on it. According to data from the province's statistics bureau, Bali attracted more than 5 million international tourists in 2016, almost 1 million more than in 2015. It is the most popular tourist destination in Indonesia. Street demonstrations against reclamation usually feature traditional clothes and dances (Figure 7.6). Furthermore, popular local music bands have been involved in writing songs and staging concerts to critique reclamation and the national government, as well as to raise funds for the anti-reclamation movement.

FIGURE 7.6 A demonstration by ForBALI featuring cultural attributes such as a black-and-white sarong and an effigy of Batara Kala (the destructive god) in the form of a backhoe, August 2016. *Source*: ForBALI (2016).

SOCIAL JUSTICE IN THE RECLAMATION PLANS OF BOTH JAKARTA
AND BALI

Though it is clear from Table 7.2 that there are important differences between Jakarta and Bali, both sites are vulnerable to climate change impacts, particularly sea level rise. Jakarta and Bali are geographically exposed to coastlines and socioeconomically dependent on the coast. Regional sea levels are predicted to rise 0.91–1.18 m by 2100, and seawater is expected to inundate Jakarta's coast as well as reduce both Bali's and Java's rice fields, with one estimate suggesting that 182,556 ha of paddy land could be lost in Java and Bali by 2050 (Förster et al., 2011). In this scenario, land reclamation off the coast for the high-end property market would seemingly put the artificial islands on the front line of sea level rise, making them vulnerable to flooding. Flood risk on the north coast of Jakarta is already apparent, as the sinking city now regularly faces tidal floods.

Nevertheless, in the case of Jakarta, the NCICD claims that land reclamation by property developers is a necessity to reduce flood risk from the sea. In NCICD, concessions to construct artificial islands off the coast of Jakarta will be sold to private developers and the proceeds will contribute to financing the giant sea wall as the city's flood protection. In this way, the sea wall's financing mechanism officially uses land reclamation to generate the financial means to reduce flood risk while maintaining the development trajectory that intensifies large-scale, mixed-use mega projects in the city that amplify flood risk. Though the trend of mega projects has not been as rampant in Bali, high-end resorts have been mushrooming on the island to cater to the flourishing tourism industry, and agricultural land has been steadily decreasing as a result of development and groundwater depletion (As-syakur, 2011). Therefore, in both cases, private developers are dominant actors in the regime that is able to convert environmental threats into development opportunities.

The Centrality of Jakarta in Land Reclamation Projects

The development opportunities have unequal consequences for the existing population, highlighting the injustices of this pattern of development. The reclamation of 17 artificial islands in Jakarta Bay will provide housing in "mid- to high-end mixed-use urban villages" (Lembaga Bantuan Hukum Jakarta, 2016) of no relevance to the 27,735 fisherfolk living near Jakarta Bay and the more than 48,000 poor families in North Jakarta who will not be able to afford to purchase properties on the islands. Fisherfolk have also bemoaned the reduction of fisheries in Jakarta Bay, which they have attributed to decades of pollution as well as current construction activities of the reclaimed Islets (Lembaga Bantuan Hukum Jakarta, 2016).

The case of Jakarta's land reclamation illustrates how authorities reframe disaster risks as opportunities for further development. The case of Bali, however, sheds light on injustices both within a city or locality and among different geographical locations.

TABLE 7.2

Selected Characteristics of Reclamation Projects in Jakarta and Bali

Characteristic	Jakarta	Bali
Land area (ha)	66,152 (city/province) 640,071 (metropolitan region Jabodetabek)	578,000 (island/province)
Land reclamation plan (ha)	5,155	700
Share of public land from reclamation islets (ha)	773.25 (15%)	300 (42.86%)
Dominant use of reclamation islets	Housing (middle class and higher) Theme park Commercial Port	Housing (middle class and higher) Theme park Commercial Fisherman's wharf Botanical garden Mangrove
Population	10,075,300 (2014)	4,152,800 (2016)
Fisherfolk population	27,753	1,852
Land reclamation policy	Keppres 52/1995	Perpres 51/2014
Status of reclamation	In process	Planned
Climate change proneness	Sea level rise	Sea level rise
Environmental threats	Land subsidence (10× sea level rise) Seawater intrusion Flooding	Sedimentation of rivers and the bay
Environmental reasons in land reclamation	Revitalization of Jakarta Bay Combined with giant sea wall to protect against sea level rise	Revitalization of Benoa Bay
Number of developers	Nine (all Jakarta-based)	One (Jakarta-based)
Prior information to the people	No	No
Spatial planning	In process (draft to be signed by local parliament)	Planned

(*continued*)

TABLE 7.2   Continued

Characteristic	Jakarta	Bali
Resistance	Ministry of the Environment lawsuit (overturned, 2011)	Rejection of Environmental
	Fishermen's lawsuit on Islet G (overturned, 2016; appealing to the Supreme Court)	Impact Assessment (2015, 2016)
	Fishermen's lawsuit on Islet F (submitted, 2016)	Rejection from Parisada Hindu Dharma Council of Indonesia
	Fishermen's lawsuit on Islet I (submitted, 2016)	(October 2015) Street demonstrations
	Fishermen's lawsuit on Islet K (submitted, 2016)	(multiple, 2014–present)

It demonstrates how power holders and capital owners operate beyond particular territorial boundaries. This, then, leads us to consider the intersections between social and spatial (in)justice. The developer pursuing land reclamation in Benoa Bay, PT TWBI, is a subsidiary of a company based in Jakarta. Furthermore, the land reclamation was made official by a presidential regulation that was also enacted in Jakarta. These Jakarta-based actors—the developer and the national government—formed relationships with local actors, such as the local governor, experts, and members of civil society, in an attempt to legitimize the project. The Benoa Bay reclamation project highlights not only social inequalities in Bali but also social and political inequality between Bali and Jakarta, as development in Bali is inseparable from the dominant actors in the capital city.

That land reclamation in Jakarta is tangled with flood protection discourse reflects the legitimation of development through the exploitation of the city's most vulnerable. Though the entire city is prone to flood risks, the social and economic inequalities manifested in Jakarta's urban landscape result in flood impacts that disproportionately affect the poor. Not only does flooding more frequently affect areas in which the poor are concentrated but also the poor are less able to escape such floods (Padawangi, 2012a). However, the poor may also be more resilient to flooding through various community-based flood response mechanisms, grassroots flood warning systems, adaptations in residential structures, and knowledge about floods obtained from years of living in flood-prone areas (Padawangi & Douglass, 2015; Texier, 2008).

In the mainstream media, the poor are increasingly stigmatized as the cause of floods—through their characterization as irresponsible rubbish dumpers and as builders of waterway-choking settlements—and are portrayed as stubbornly refusing offers to be relocated to rental flats in the periphery (Kompas, 2016b; MetroTV, 2016). With the exception of two editions of *Tempo* magazine and *The Jakarta Post* ("Developer-Driven Reclamation," The Jakarta Post, 2016) that reported on the plight of fisherfolk and critically reported Jakarta land reclamation's profit-driven agenda, media reports often portray the financiers and developers building the giant sea wall as the ultimate protectors of Jakarta from flooding. Finally, the normalization of development has dampened the perceived need for social justice. The absence of participation from affected coastal communities in drafting the Jakarta Master Plan 2010–2030 and the NCICD Master Plan also reflects serious challenges in procedural justice. The defeat of the fisherfolk in the appeals court in October 2016 on the basis of "protecting investment certainty" of artificial islands has also perpetuated social injustices in Jakarta's urban development.

Anti-Reclamation Social Movements in Bali

The use of environmental rehabilitation discourse in legitimizing urban development is also apparent in the case of the Benoa Bay reclamation project in Bali. The developer, PT TWBI, branded the project as a "revitalization" program and not as a "reclamation" project. The claim by supporters of reclamation that Benoa Bay has been ruined because of oversedimentation from the river also echoes the claim that Jakarta Bay has been overpolluted, no longer suitable for fisheries, and therefore needs to be rehabilitated through reclamation. Though the Benoa Bay reclamation project involves nothing in terms of disaster mitigation, the environmental rehabilitation discourse it employs claims urgency for a sophisticated intervention on the bay. The argument for rehabilitation is also supported by the allocation of 42.6% of the proposed reclaimed land for green space and a fisherman's wharf.

The case of the Benoa Bay reclamation project and social movements against it in Bali features cross-class solidarity more significantly compared to Jakarta. In contrast to Jakarta, Bali still has a significant agrarian population clustered in traditional villages (Suantika, 2015), which can act as communities to voice their concerns. Though the fisherfolk who would be directly affected by land reclamation are poor, the social movement against reclamation is much wider and not just limited to those directly affected on site, with hundreds of organizations joining ForBALI. Supriatma (2016) noted that most of the participants in ForBALI are youths involved in *Sekeha Teruna Teruni* (STT), youth organizations that exist in each *banjar*, the smallest traditional organizational unit in Bali. STTs become nodes of mass mobilizations for the movement against reclamation, and the decision to conduct street demonstrations is made not only by ForBALI coordinators but also often by individual STT nodes (Supriatma, 2016). In addition to street demonstrations comprising thousands of protestors, the movement involves lobbying of local and national actors in the government, social media advocacy, performances of anti-reclamation songs, and expansion of ForBALI to establish chapters outside the island (Suardana, 2016; Supriatma, 2016).

ForBALI has been relatively successful in mobilizing against reclamation, not just because it is able to mobilize across different economic classes and geographies but also because it has influenced the public discourse on land reclamation as against Balinese culture, which also includes religion and identity. Subsequently, the developer started using Balinese cultural framings in its marketing and communication strategy. The developer's strategy responds to the arguments regarding tradition and culture that were posed during the first Environmental Impact Assessment socialization in March 2015, but the reclamation plans have not changed since then. The culture and tradition arguments also unite ForBALI because the land reclamation is viewed as violating the traditions of Bali. The movement received a boost when Parisada Hindu Dharma Indonesia, the Hindu Dharma Council of Indonesia, deemed in October 2015 that Benoa Bay was a sacred site. Despite the designation as a sacred site, reclamation plans have not been stopped.

SOCIAL JUSTICE, LAND RECLAMATION, AND FUTURE POSSIBILITIES

The cases of land reclamation in Jakarta and Bali demonstrate that national and local policymakers view the needs of development as more urgent than the challenges of climate change. Though previous research reveals how overdevelopment in Jakarta caused environmental degradation, particularly flooding and land subsidence, NCICD cited these as reasons to support further development in the form of land reclamation. Similarly, when Bali experienced decreasing agricultural land share and increasing sedimentation, the private developer cited these as reasons for further development. These land reclamation projects, supported by local and national policies, are marketed for groups that are wealthier than those whose livelihoods would be directly affected or groups who would potentially be displaced, such as the fisherfolk.

However, the argument that unites people and creates a social movement against land reclamation in these two cases is culture and tradition, not class interests as a Marxist social justice discourse would suggest. Still, the prominence of culture and tradition in the anti-reclamation movement in Bali is also inseparable from the entanglements between Balinese identity and the tourism industry as the engine that propels Bali to national and global prominence.

The cases of land reclamation in Jakarta and Bali and the social movements against them reveal at least two possible policy solutions in relation to urban development and climate change. First, social justice is a necessary concept to be embraced in the context of the climate change mitigation and adaptation agendas in rapidly urbanizing areas. In the case of Indonesia, normalized social injustices in urban development policies run deep enough to muddle the cause and impact of environmental degradation, which is reflected in the framing of the poor and traditional fisherfolk as part of the problem rather than the key to solving environmental problems. We see in the cases a failure to track the histories of injustices that would enable a temporal connection to be made between environmental and social conditions today and patterns of exploitation in the past. This then shifts "blame" from fisherfolk and the urban to decades of development that has prioritized the economic over the social and environmental, the rich over the poor, and outsiders over insiders (locals). Second, social justice can penetrate official policy through careful assessments of the social groups most adversely affected by development plans and environmental degradation, both climate change-induced and development-induced. Furthermore, social movements against land reclamation can be used to help identify particular groups being disproportionately affected; hence, a consideration of resistance voices is one way of identifying marginalized groups to analyze the distribution of environmental impacts. Engaged, participatory planning would consider such resistance groups not as problems to be assuaged or countered through the courts or by coercion but, rather, as means and mechanisms to help ensure that development is socially and environmentally just.

CONCLUSION

Does social justice matter in urban development discourse? The two cases of land reclamation projects and plans in Jakarta and Bali geared to the middle and upper classes demonstrate that social justice is rarely on the agenda of urban development. The aim of these projects is to establish new, visually beautiful enclaves of residential, commercial, and mixed-use buildings following established urban development norms. The environmental vulnerabilities of the sites, such as vulnerability to flooding in Jakarta, are formally responded to by framing the reclamation projects as "environmental rehabilitation." Nevertheless, those who are marginalized by this pattern of development and the discourse that informs it have attempted to resist through lawsuits and cross-sectoral social movements. Social justice arguments are more clearly manifested in the fisherfolk's lawsuit against reclamation islets to defend the rights of the fishermen as the most marginalized groups in the reclamation plan and project. Social justice is also reflected in Bali's movement against reclamation that criticized the ways in which the Balinese are sidelined in land reclamation projects.

If social justice does matter, to whom does it matter, and what are the implications for urban development? Though social movements seem to be embracing social justice in various ways, social justice is not a priority in the official discourses of land reclamation projects. As a result, vulnerabilities to environmental impacts of development continue to be distributed unequally, and dependence on specific actors rather than structural reform to promote social justice persists. The NCICD Master Plan and PT TWBI claim to pay attention to the affected population, particularly fisherfolk, but the discrepancy between the interests of the reclamation projects and those of the directly affected population has sparked public demands to be heard as well as for the public to be involved in the decision-making process. However, the limited access of these movements to official negotiations for policies and regulations has resulted in further disjuncture between the reclamation projects and the affected populations.

There are three implications of this disjuncture. First is the muddling of cause and response. The solutions to Jakarta's and Bali's environmental challenges are presented as lying in further development of the type that led to these problems in the first place. If anything, the poor living in these areas are viewed as part of the problem rather than part of the solution. Second, and notwithstanding the clear intersecting class interests of poor fisherfolk and other poor residents in the two sites, social movements have only been able to successfully mobilize around tropes of "culture and tradition." Finally, the normalization of development leaves little scope for alternatives. The mindset of development-as-modernization means that the cause and the solution inhabit the same policy space. This emphasizes how difficult it is to engineer (in policy terms) or engender (in social terms) approaches that can address climate change in ways that meet the demands of social and spatial justice.

POSTSCRIPT

The social movements against reclamation in Jakarta and Bali continued as this chapter was in the process of publication. In Jakarta, reclamation became one of the main policy differences among two gubernatorial candidates in the 2017 local election. The election resulted in the defeat of the incumbent who was in full support of the reclamation project (though reclamation was by no means the only reason of his defeat). On 26 September 2018, the current governor announced a "total halt" of the Jakarta Bay reclamation project as fulfillment of his campaign promise (Kompas, 2018). However, his administration only cancelled permits for 13 artificial islands, while letting the remaining four islands continue because—according to the governor—"[Islands] C, D, G, and N are already built, so it is impossible to cancel the permit" (Kompas, 2018). This partial cancellation of permits triggered criticisms from anti-reclamation activists as setting a bad precedent for future projects, as it gives the impression that artificial islands would eventually be legalized as long as the developer could build them regardless. Meanwhile, some fisherfolks who were in the original lawsuit against reclamation also withdrew their involvement and went fully in the other direction, to support reclamation (Jawapos, 2018), though many remain against it.

One month prior to the Jakarta Governor's announcement to halt reclamation, the Ministry of the Environment and Forestry announced the cancellation of the Environmental Impact Assessment for TWBI's location permit on 27 August 2018, for failure to secure support from the Balinese community (Tirto.id, 2018; CNN Indonesia, 2018). Though the Benoa Bay reclamation project is temporarily stopped, the status of Benoa Bay as a zone for economic development and revitalization still leaves possibilities for other developers to come in and propose reclamation. Hence, the social movement still continues to campaign for the cancellation of Perpres 51/2014.

ACKNOWLEDGMENTS

I thank WatchDoc, particularly Dandhy Dwi Laksono and Suparta Arz, who conducted Ekspedisi Indonesia Biru, which collected interviews in Bali and Jakarta. My fieldwork for this chapter was funded by the Singapore Ministry of Education AcRF Tier 2 grant for the project Governing Compound Disasters in Urbanizing Asia (MOE2014-T2-1-017).

REFERENCES

As-syakur, Abdul Rahman. (2011). Perubahan penggunaan lahan di provinsi Bali. *Ecotrophic, 6*(1), 1–7.

BeritaSatu. (2015, October 25). Reklamasi di Utara Jakarta Tidak Sebabkan Banjir. *BeritaSatu Megapolitan*. Retrieved November 8, 2016, from http://www.beritasatu.com/megapolitan/317178-reklamasi-di-utara-jakarta-tidak-sebabkan-banjir.html

Bijlsma, L., Ehler, C. N., Klein, R. J. T., Kulshrestha, S. M., McLean, R. F., Mimura, N., . . . Warrick, R. A. (1996). Coastal zones and small islands. In R. T. Watson, M. C. Zinyowera, & R. H. Moss (Eds.), *Impacts, adaptations and mitigation of climate change: Scientific–technical analyses* (pp. 289–324). Cambridge, UK: Cambridge University Press.

Blaikie, P., & Muldavin, J. (2014). Environmental justice? The story of two projects. *Geoforum, 54*, 226–229.

Climate Central. (2015). *New report and maps: Rising seas threaten land home to half a billion*. Retrieved November 7, 2016, from http://sealevel.climatecentral.org/news/global-mapping-choices

CNN Indonesia. (2018, August 28). Reklamasi Teluk Benoa Disetop Berkat Penolakan Warga Bali. Retrieved December 12, 2018, from https://www.cnnindonesia.com/nasional/20180828082316-20-325397/reklamasi-teluk-benoa-disetop-berkat-penolakan-warga-bali

Developer-driven reclamation leaves public behind. (2016, January 13). *The Jakarta Post*. Retrieved November 8, 2016, from http://www.thejakartapost.com/news/2016/01/13/developer-driven-reclamation-leaves-public-behind.html

Dikeç, M. (2001). Justice and the spatial imagination. *Environment and Planning, 33*, 1785–1805.

Dobson, A. (1998). *Justice and the environment: Conceptions of environmental sustainability and theories of distributive justice*. Oxford, UK: Clarendon.

ForBALI. (2016). *Tentang Kami*. Retrieved November 8, 2016, from https://www.forbali.org

Förster, H., Sterzel, T., Pape, A. C., Moneo-Lain, M., Niemeyer, I., Boer, R., & Kropp, J. P. (2011). Sea-level rise in Indonesia: On adaptation priorities in the agricultural sector. *Regional Environmental Change, 11*(4), 893–904.

Globalizing environmental justice?. (2014). *Geoforum, 54*, 151–157.

Harvey, D. (1973). *Social justice and the city*. Oxford, UK: Blackwell.

Herlambang, S. (2010). On city commercialization: A preliminary research. In *International Colloquium Series 2010: The strategy and concept for sustainable future of Jakarta*. Jakarta, Indonesia: Tarumanagara University.

HistorySG. (n.d.). *Singapore's first land reclamation project begins*. Singapore: National Library Board. Retrieved November 8, 2016, from http://eresources.nlb.gov.sg/history/events/feddcf2a-2074-4ae6-b272-dc0db80e2146

Horton, C. (2014, May 6). Giant development in Cambodia hinges on Chinese buyers. *The New York Times*. Retrieved November 8, 2016, from http://www.nytimes.com/2014/05/07/realestate/commercial/giant-development-in-cambodia-hinges-on-chinese-buyers.html

Ikanubun, Y. (2016, May 23). Bahowo, Benteng Terakhir mangrove dari Gempuran Reklamasi Manado. *Liputan6*. Retrieved November 8, 2016, from https://regional.liputan6.com/read/2513458/bahowo-benteng-terakhir-mangrove-dari-gempuran-reklamasi-manado

Jawapos. (2018, August 2). Reklamasi Dihentikan, Begini Nasib Nelayan Jakarta. Retrieved December 12, 2018, from https://www.jawapos.com/jpg-today/02/08/2018/reklamasi-dihentikan-begini-nasib-nelayan-jakarta

Kementerian Koordinator Bidang Perekonomian Republik Indonesia. (2014). *Master plan: National Capital Integrated Coastal Development*. Jakarta: Author.

Keppres 52/1995. (1995). *Keputusan Presiden No. 52 Tahun 1995 Tentang Reklamasi Pantai Utara Jakarta*. Jakarta: The President of the Republic of Indonesia.

KNTI. (2016). *Reclamation projects in Indonesia*. Menteng, Jakarta: Author.

Kompas. (2016a). *Perjalanan Panjang Reklamasi Jakarta*. Retrieved November 8, 2016, from https://www.academia.edu/29329052/PERJALANAN_PANJANG_REKLAMASI_JAKARTA_ReklamasiJakarta

Kompas. (2016b, April 28). *Dilema Ahok Setiap Lakukan Penggusuran*. Retrieved November 8, 2016, from http://megapolitan.kompas.com/read/2016/04/28/11353781/Dilema.Ahok.Setiap.Lakukan.Penggusuran

Kompas. (2018, September 27). 7 Fakta Seputar Penghentian Proyek Reklamasi di Teluk Jakarta. Retrieved December 12, 2018, from https://megapolitan.kompas.com/read/2018/09/27/07522331/7-fakta-seputar-penghentian-proyek-reklamasi-di-teluk-jakarta

Kusno, A. (2013). *After the new order: Space, politics, and Jakarta*. Honolulu, HI: University of Hawaii Press.

Lembaga Bantuan Hukum Jakarta. (2016). *Nelayan Muara Angke Antar Banding Reklamasi Pulau G. Gugatan*. Retrieved November 8, 2016, from http://www.bantuanhukum.or.id/web/tag/gugatan

MetroTV. (2016, September 29). Relokasi Warga Bukit Duri Tingkatkan Kualitas Hidup. Retrieved November 8, 2016, from http://news.metrotvnews.com/read/2016/09/29/590399/relokasi-warga-bukit-duri-tingkatkan-kualitas-hidup

Nicholls, R. J., Hoozemans, F. M. J., & Marchand, M. (1999). Increasing flood risk and wetland losses due to global sea-level rise: Regional and global analyses. *Global Environmental Change, 9*, S69–S87.

Nusa Benoa. (2016). *Revitalization of Benoa Bay*. Retrieved November 8, 2016, from http://www.nusabenoa.com

Padawangi, R. (2012a). The right to flood-free homes: Urban floods, spatial justice and social movements in Jakarta, Indonesia. In J. Widodo, J. Rosemann, L. B. Liang, & A. Gonzalez-Brun (Eds.), *Global visions: Risks and opportunities for the urban planet* (pp. 199–211). Singapore: National University of Singapore.

Padawangi, R. (2012b). Climate change and the north coast of Jakarta: Environmental justice and the social construction of space in urban poor communities. In W. G. Holt III (Ed.), *Research in urban sociology* (Vol. 12, pp. 321–339). Bingley, UK: Emerald.

Padawangi, R., & Douglass M. (2015). Water, water everywhere: Toward participatory solutions to chronic urban flooding in Jakarta. *Pacific Affairs, 88*(3), 517–550.

Parisada Hindu Dharma Indonesia. (2015, October 15). *Sastra Kuno Bali Sebut Teluk Benoa Kawasan Suci*. Retrieved November 8, 2016, from http://phdi.or.id/berita/ sastra-kuno-bali-sebut-teluk-benoa-kawasan-suci

Pemprov DKI Jakarta. (2012). *RPJPD Provinsi Daerah Khusus Ibukota Jakarta 2005–2025*. Jakarta: Author.

Perpres 51/2014. (2014). *Peraturan Presiden Republik Indonesia Nomor 51 Tahun 2014 Tentang Perubahan Atas Peraturan Presiden Nomor 45 Tahun 2011 Tentang Rencana Tata Ruang Kawasan Perkotaan Denpasar, Badung, Gianyar, dan Tabanan*. Jakarta: The President of the Republic of Indonesia.

Ruqoyah, S., & Mukti, F. G. (2014, June 12). Cegah Banjir, Proyek Reklamasi Pantai Jakarta Dibangun Tahun Depan. *Vivanews*. Retrieved November 8, 2016, from https://www.viva.co.id/ berita/metro/511907-cegah-banjir-proyek-reklamasi-pantai-jakarta-dibangun-tahun-depan

Schroeder, R., Martin, K., Wilson, B., & Sen, D. (2008). Third World environmental justice. *Society and Natural Resources, 21*(7), 547–555.

Sen, Amartya. (2009). *The idea of justice*. London, UK: Lane.

Simone, A. (2009). *On provisional publics and intersections: Remaking district life in North Jakarta*. Retrieved November 8, 2016, from https://rujak.org/ on-provisional-publics-and-intersections-remaking-district-life-in-north-jakarta/

Soja, E. W. (2010). *Seeking spatial justice*. Minneapolis, MN: University of Minnesota Press.

Suantika, W. G. (2015) *Resistensi Masyarakat Lokal Terhadap Kapitalisme Global*. Denpasar, Bali: Universitas Airlangga.

Suardana, W. G. (2016, August 3). *Orasi Wayan Gendo Suardana—Bali Tolak Reklamasi 3 August 2016* (Public speech). Retrieved November 8, 2016, from https://www.youtube.com/ watch?v=Y1WL8uipwTA

Susilo, C. R. (2015). *Public space transformation: The role of collective space in the boulevard commercial project of Manado, Indonesia* (Doctoral dissertation). Arenberg Doctoral School, University of Leuven, Leuven, Belgium.

Supriatma, M. (2016). Generasi Bali Tolak Reklamasi. *IndoProgress*. Retrieved from https:// indoprogress.com/2016/08/generasi-bali-tolak-reklamasi/

Sutawa, G. K. (2012). Issues on Bali tourism development and community empowerment to support sustainable tourism development. *Procedia Economics and Finance, 4*, 413–422.

Tan, T. (2015, September 27). S'pore's largest reclamation project. *The Straits Times*. Retrieved November 8, 2016, from https://www.straitstimes.com/singapore/ spores-largest-reclamation-project-begins

Texier, P. (2008). Floods in Jakarta: When the extreme reveals daily structural constraints and mismanagement. *Disaster Prevention and Management, 17*(3), 358–372.

Tirto.id (2018, August 27). Amdal Reklamasi Teluk Benoa Resmi Dibatalkan Kementerian KLHK. Retrieved December 12, 2018, from https://tirto.id/ amdal-reklamasi-teluk-benoa-resmi-dibatalkan-kementerian-klhk-cVjY

TWBI Website. (2006). Home page. Retrieved from http://twbi.co.id/

Walker, G. P., & Bulkeley, H. (2006). Geographies of environmental justice. *Geoforum, 37*(5), 655–659.

WatchDoc. (2015). *Kala Benoa*. Jakarta, Indonesia: WatchDoc.

Winters, J. A. (1996). *Power in motion: Capital mobility and the Indonesian state*. Ithaca, NY: Cornell University Press.

PART IV

Comparisons

8

Resilience to Climate Change in Uganda

POLICY IMPLICATIONS FOR TWO MARGINALIZED SOCIETIES

Shuaib Lwasa, James D. Ford, Lea Berrang-Ford, Didacus B. Namanya, the Indigenous Health Adaptation to Climate Change Research Team, Ambrose Buyinza, and Benon Nabaasa

---

BACKGROUND

Researchers and policymakers discuss resilience in human adaptation to climate change at a conceptual level; communities that rely on natural resources in those areas most affected deal with the here and now of climate change. It is not unusual for researchers and policymakers to ignore or underplay the accumulated wisdom and knowledge that come from living with climate change. This chapter focuses on two such communities in Uganda—the Karamajong pastoralists and the Batwa forest pygmies—that have demonstrably adapted to their environments. Despite their two distinct histories, these communities share similarities in how they have responded to climate risks.

Both communities face difficulties associated with the inequitable policies and programs put in place by both government and nongovernmental organizations (NGOs) to change their lifestyles, reflecting how researchers and policymakers have interpreted the climate change challenge. For example, pastoralism—a human activity in the arid and semi-arid African savannahs that has demonstrated resilience to the variable climate (Egeru, 2014; Kandagor, 2005)—is being undermined by recent land use changes associated with mining, conservation programs, and the promotion of field agriculture in a dry area. Moreover, government efforts to encourage pastoralists to adopt crop production to improve food security have been met with skepticism and, in some cases, resistance. The flurry of climate forecast information from meteorological services and NGOs is also not useful to the herders given the format in which this information is disseminated (Lwasa, Buyinza, & Nabaasa, 2017).

Changes to the Batwa forest pygmies' lives have been even more dramatic. Whereas the pastoralists are still in their ecological zone, the pygmies were removed from the forests in 1991 by the government to pave way for conservation of the mountain gorillas in the Bwindi Impenetrable Forest. Some have settled close to the forest, and others have settled in ecological zones that differ greatly from their previous environment. The settlements where they live are similar to the clustered family houses of their previous home in the forest. Conservation and tourism have affected their lifestyles, with many of them drawn into providing tourism-related services to diversify their livelihoods. The promotion of agriculture for food security and self-reliance is the other significant change that has affected the forest pygmies. As a result of being forced out of the forest, the pygmies have been exposed to various risks. For example, the Batwa fear that intermarriages with Bakiga are killing their culture and erasing their ethnic group. But the most significant risk is related to health from the increasing incidence of malaria (Hofmeijer et al., 2013). Our research shows that these communities have historically been resilient, but the current systems of health services are alienating the Batwa and accentuating health inequities.

These two communities may be differentiated by geography, demography, and social systems, but they share many common pressures transforming their lives. This chapter analyzes the experiences of lifestyle transitions and how historical resilience practices can inform adaptation to a changing climate. The aim of the chapter is to draw lessons from rather than compare the resilience of the two communities. We argue that such lessons can inform the design of adaptation and resilience programs in the face of climate change. Moreover, we argue that equity is a necessary principle in implementing resilience-building programs and therefore the attempt at unification of historically distinct cultural lifestyles presents inequities that have to be addressed. The chapter concludes by reviewing some of the specific resilience activities documented from the two communities.

FRAMING RESILIENCE OF KARAMOJONG PASTORALISTS AND BATWA FOREST PYGMIES

There is increasing interest in the study of the resilience of human systems (Bunce, Brown, & Rosendo, 2010; Lwasa, 2018; Motsholapheko, Kgathi, & Vanderpost, 2011; Muhonda, 2012; Rao, 2013; Rockström et al., 2009) to match the long-standing engagement with the concept in ecological studies. A *system* is a set of elements, organisms, and materials in the environment that interact through various mechanisms. In a social context, systems function as cultural customs, institutions, and structural elements that enable the "unit" to sustain productive capacity (Wallace, 2007). Systems usually operate within set realms or boundaries within which adjustments and fluctuations occur as external and internal changes occur to the units therein. When the system thresholds are interrupted, new thresholds force the system to adjust within limits unless the changes are so severe that new thresholds move the system to another status (Rockström et al., 2009). A system is considered resilient when its status changes in accordance to new thresholds—for example, a pastoral community adjusting livestock numbers to align new levels of biomass production. The transition may be temporary or permanent depending on the cycle of changes in the system. It is the ability of the system to move back to its "normal" status or maintain itself in the new "normal" that defines its resilience to external perturbations (Adger, 2006). The Resilience Alliance defines the resilience of a social–ecological system as "the ability to absorb disturbances, to be changed and then to re-organise and still have the same identity (retain the same basic structure and ways of functioning)" (as cited in Aerts et al., 2014; see also Standish et al., 2014, p. 4). This chapter employs the resilience framework to understand the social–ecological systems of pastoralism and forest pygmy lifestyles and how they have adjusted to changes in the system as influenced by climate change.

Climate Change Impacts in Uganda

Climate change is manifested in various forms in Uganda, with increasing extreme events of precipitation, drought, and shifting and uncertain seasons. In Karamoja and western Uganda, homes for the pastoralists and Batwa forest pygmies, respectively, climate change is experienced as extreme events and highly variable conditions (Lwasa et al., 2017; MacVicar et al., 2017; Morand et al., n.d.). Both communities have long been vulnerable to climate change but have always adapted to maintain their basic socioecological structures: reliance on pastures for the pastoralists and a hunter–gatherer lifestyle for the forest pygmies. For both systems, the basic structures are defined by reliance on natural resources for livelihood and daily requirements, with occasional migration when the socioecological system is disrupted.

However, since 2000, demographic transition, land use change, land appropriation, and public policies have been added to long-standing environmental variability, putting yet more pressure on the socioecological systems. Socioecological resilience is determined by risk, hazards, exposure, and vulnerability (Adger, 2006). When the hazards include climate risks—exposure determined by the geographical location of the socioecological systems—vulnerability can be viewed in different ways.

Vulnerability and Resilience Among Pastoralists and Forest Pygmies

Multiple conditions determine system resilience in the case of the two socioecological systems under consideration. For the Karamajong pastoralists, the balance of livestock numbers with the availability of water and pastures is critical. This in turn influences carrying capacity. Social institutions such as the elders' council mediate the availability of and access to the critical resources. For example, the pastoralist elders' council meets to discuss the seasonal herding decisions depending on the amount of rain. But, as in other socioecological systems, conflicts abound, and institutions have been developed to resolve them. Therefore, the vulnerability of such a system is a consequence of underlying institutional and structural processes that create the conditions rather than the characteristics. For example, concentrations of people and activities on safe sites are not a source of vulnerability; the unequal distribution of resources, the marginalization of segments of the population, and emerging activities such as mining and tourism that disrupt the pastoralist activities are the drivers of vulnerability (Hamza & Zetter, 1998).

For the Batwa forest pygmy hunter–gatherers, the variability in climate has long determined the amount of resources available in terms of food from both plants and animals. Forest pygmies have navigated the variation through migration and adapting to particular foods that are available across the forest and throughout the year during periods of food stress. A key aspect of their adaptation and resilience relates to health. Forest pygmies have historically adapted their health systems by accessing forest-based medicinal plants, adapting their language, and negotiating access to health resources. However, this community has become more vulnerable after its expulsion from the forest.

In keeping with the resilience framework, the vulnerability of the pastoralist and hunter–gatherer systems being exposed to stressors depends on their system's capacity to adjust (i.e., *adaptive capacity*) or to move to a less vulnerable condition. Vulnerability then becomes the difference between risks of the exposure and the adaptive measures (Smit & Wandel, 2006). Note that this measure of vulnerability aggregates various indicators to an index and is only useful when comparing vulnerability levels of different units of analysis at a meso or macro scale. Individual agent vulnerability is exposure to multiple stressors, all of which may be measured on different scales. Thus, for any assessment of the multiple stressors, a different method that could indicate the vulnerability of the unit of analysis would be required. Resilience is an even more complex condition to measure but is discussed in the context of this chapter as the ability for the socioecological systems to maintain their basic structures even after a disruption. The disruption is the variation in climatic conditions that leads to either drought or excessive rainfall in both systems. Among the pastoralists, the disruptions can lead to unusual destinations of migration and livestock health, whereas among the forest Pygmies, disruptions affect human health.

MATERIALS AND METHODS

This chapter is based on a compendium of methods used in the two socioecological systems to collect data and analyze the vulnerabilities and resilience. Longitudinal surveys of the Batwa forest pygmies were carried out during a period of 5 years from 2011 to 2016 and surveyed malaria, which has increased in the area because of the warming. A series of six longitudinal open-cohort census surveys were conducted in 3-month intervals. Given the relatively small Batwa population, each round of survey implementation aimed to capture a full census of Batwa households; 767 household and food security surveys were collected, with an average of 127 households participating in each survey administration. The surveys were complemented by focus group discussions, testing malaria using rapid diagnostic tests, and piloting the distribution of mosquito nets to understand the uptake and use of this preventive measure.

In the pastoralist socioecological system, extensive surveys, mapping, and geospatial tools were used to understand livestock herding, routes of migration, and when the decision to migrate is made. Cognizant of the complexity of mapping grazing lands in pastoralist communities, a mixed methods approach was applied that combined "actor" mapping, participatory geographic information systems (GIS) mapping, and focus group discussions that integrated participatory learning and action methods with geographic information technologies. Participants were trained on how to draw maps based on five thematic areas: grazing areas, seasonality, migratory routes, grazing areas related to conflicts, and water sources and livestock services. The same categories of representatives worked to map these thematic topics onto the base map that they generated first. The sketch maps were georeferenced in a GIS environment. In addition, a sample of kraal leaders were given global positioning system (GPS) devices for logging while grazing to gain insight into the patterns in the grazing fields. The method involved training and giving herders the GPS loggers to track their movements on a daily basis such that data could be downloaded and input into the GIS system for various analyses and visualization.

CLIMATE RISKS AND RESILIENCE

In this section, we discuss the climate risks and shocks that pastoralists and forest pygmies experience. This discussion is placed in the context of the resilience framework and how the two socioecological systems have built resilience to the shocks.

Pastoralist Socioecological Systems: Climate Trends and Risks in the Karamoja Region

The Karamoja region is a dry area, with some northeastern areas tending toward semi-aridity. It is inhabited by agro-pastoralists (Jie, Dodoth, Bokora, Matheniko, Pian, Pokot, and Tepeth) and sedentary ethnic groups such as the Labwor (Ethur), Nyangiya, Napore, Menning, and Ik (Teso) (Lwasa et al., 2017). The region covers an area of 30,000 km² and has seven districts: Amudat, Abim, Nakapiripirit, Moroto, Napak, Kotido, and Kaabong. The Karamoja region has a human population of approximately 1 million (Uganda Bureau of Statistics, 2009). The average annual rainfall in this region is 600 mm. The region is prone to frequent drought spells, with a greater than 60% probability of crop failure. Both Kaabong and Moroto exhibit similar monthly distribution of rainfall and temperature and can be assumed to represent the distributions in the Karamoja region. Between 1970 and 2012, the Kaabong and Moroto districts experienced a long rainfall season between April and November. The monthly rainfall data also exhibit similar characteristics. The resolution of the data set shows equal rainfall amounts for Kaabong and Moroto.

The Karamoja region's climate trends indicate the requirement for climate change studies at local scales where the impacts are felt. The data show gaps in the distribution of rainfall, with most of it occurring in short periods of time, not spread across the season, which results in floods and pasture shortages over the seasons. The mean monthly temperature in the region is higher than 28°C; maximum and minimum temperatures are higher in Moroto than those in Kaabong, implying a spatial distribution dependency of temperature. Topography, in addition to other factors, is known to influence local climate and weather conditions; hence, an in-depth analysis of the rainfall and temperature characteristics throughout this region may help explain the spatial variability. The monthly patterns are similar for the Karamoja region, where higher temperatures are experienced in January and February and the lowest temperatures occur between May and September.

The Office of the Prime Minister of Uganda (2012) defines drought as the prolonged shortage of water often caused by dry weather conditions. Cyclical weather patterns of rainfall failure in Uganda occur every 2 years, with severe drought episodes every 5 years (Byenkya, Mugerwa, Barasa, & Zziwa, 2014). The most drought-prone areas in Uganda are the districts in the cattle corridor, including the Karamoja region. Severe drought in the region results in human and livestock deaths from the reduced water table, diminishing water levels in the major lakes, and crop failure.

Pastoralists in the Karamoja region reported the 1980 drought as the most severe (Akwango, Obaa, Turyahabwe, Baguma, & Egeru, 2017; Jordaan, 2014). They experienced famine exacerbated by the national revolution and internal conflict in the country. To cope with drought, the pastoralists' main strategy is to migrate to regions with water and pasture. Pastoralism is the livelihood option best suited to the Karamoja region, given its erratic and poorly distributed rainfall patterns.

In addition to drought, other issues—diseases, cattle rustling and insecurity, inadequate veterinary services, limited access to markets, poor infrastructure development, and flooding—pose major risks to livestock production in the Karamoja region. Access to adequate veterinary services is a major challenge in such an economically low-potential area. In the early 1990s, a community animal health service delivery system was introduced in the region to control rinderpest. With the help of NGOs, local governments later adopted this strategy.

Failure of crops and reduced pastures are two of the major climate risks facing pastoralists (Kane & Eicher, 2004). Activities that reduce the risk of crop production (via use of improved seeds, early maturing varieties, improved land preparation, and other better agronomical practices) will reduce food and income risks faced by producers.

Forest Pygmy Socioecological Systems: Climate Trends and Risks in the Bwindi Impenetrable Forest

The Batwa forest pygmies live in a small area close to the Bwindi Impenetrable Forest with varied topography between 900 and 1500 m above sea level. The forest ecology and topography have a local influence on the climate, with rainstorms during the otherwise dry periods of June–August and December–February. During a 60-year period, this area has experienced an increase in average temperatures of 0.32°C, and rainfall totals have increasing by approximately 11% (McSweeney, Lizcano, New, & Lu, 2010).

Batwa forest pygmies report that rainfall used to occur on a daily basis during the normal wet season. In the surveys and focus group discussions, however, they noted that the intensity of rainfall in the area is changing, characterized by unusually heavy rainfall in the periods of March–May and October–December. The communities have observed that rain occurs when it should not and it is hot when it should not be. Such uncertainty makes it difficult for them to determine the appropriate time for planting, given their overreliance on small-scale subsistence agriculture to sustain their liveli-hood, a recent shift in their lifestyle. Programs for resettling the Batwa emphasized crop growing through small-scale agriculture on land purchased for them under the Bwindi Conservation Trust. The Batwa communities' reports of hotter and longer heat waves and long-term droughts correlate with the statistical analysis of the climate trend data, reinforcing earlier scientific predictions that areas of western Uganda will be adversely affected by climate change.

The climate risks to the Batwa can lead to food insecurity as their crops dry out or provide poor yields and also an increased prevalence of diseases (heavy rainfall can result in cases of cough, worms, and malaria) (Lewnard et al., 2014; Patterson et al., 2017). In addition, intense sunshine and heavy rainfall increase the likelihood of diseases (Donnelly et al., 2016; Lewnard et al., 2014). Such impacts reduce the productivity of the sedentary farming systems on which the Batwa now depend to secure own-account food security. To compound the problems of climate change, compared to their neighbors in Bakiga, the Batwa have limited access to land. Some Batwans provide labor services to the farms of Bakiga in exchange for food rather than a cash wage. The condition of Batwa people having less land than they need increases vulnerabilities and makes it difficult for the communities to be adaptive and resilient to climate change.

The Batwa communities have been relegated to living day-to-day and hand-to-mouth; it is the challenge of surviving that dominates their concerns, rather than worrying about the effects of climate change in the future. Communities are overwhelmed by the impacts of the changes in climate. The poor resilience and low coping capacity of the Batwa are due to the fact that since their eviction from the national park in 1991, they can no longer depend on the wide variety of foodstuffs in the forest but, rather, predominantly rely on semi-subsistence agriculture on the outskirts of Bwindi Impenetrable National Park. The Batwa from the Bwindi Impenetrable Forest were placed in camp-like settlements to the north and south of the forest, where nonprofit and religious organizations have continued to provide housing, education, and health services to the more than 800 Batwa people. Yet the continued policy regarding resettlement and pursuance of self-reliance is another driver of vulnerability for the Batwa.

LESSONS FROM RESILIENT COMMUNITIES

This section highlights lessons about resilience of the two communities. These lessons are understood as social, physical, and ecological measures undertaken by the communities as a response to the variable and changing climate.

Lesson from the Pastoralist Community

Pastoralism is a socioecological system that has demonstrated resilience for centuries. Moreover, pastoralists in the region have experienced variable climate over a long period during which they have "tested," validated, and enhanced adaptation measures that have built resilience. The most common resilience measures include migration to areas with more water and pasture that is done systematically after conflict resolution between elders of the regions where the pastoralists herd. The system of cultural and traditional negotiation is the basis for deciding on routes for migration and agreements with receiving communities to minimize and avoid conflicts where possible, which contributes to this long-term resilience. Receiving communities also have livestock, many are agriculturalists, and thus conflicts between livestock and crop systems would emerge quickly where no adaptive or compensatory measures are in place.

In the dry season, herders in the region experience higher mortality rates of livestock; reduction in milk yields; disease outbreaks; and emaciation of livestock, resulting in dismal prices on the market. These effects are a result of limited pastures, water shortages, long-distance livestock movement, and pests, among others. In the wet season, however, the quality of the animals improves in terms of growth, high milk yields, and reduced deaths from starvation and diseases. Unlike in the dry season, livestock and humans alike do not trek long distances in search of pastures and water because there is an abundance of both during the wet season. There is also easy access to veterinary services and close monitoring and supervision during the wet season because livestock and owners are more stationary.

In summary, during the wet season, there is an improvement in the survival rate of animals and reduced movement in search of water and pastures, whereas during the dry season there is a high death toll and long-distance movement in an attempt to survive. Key to resilience is the cultural system that enables intertribal negotiations to access water and pastures of neighboring communities. In search of resources, pastoralists migrate on a temporal basis, but the distances traveled from their homesteads differ widely. Migration is a key resilience measure for pastoralists; it requires viewing this resilience measure as context based. Therefore, any generic resilience measures must align with local conditions.

Livestock Migration Regimes

For pastoralist communities such as the Karamojong, migration is not only a lifestyle but also a means of survival in a harsh environment. In the Karamoja region, migrations take two forms: temporary short-term migrations and long-term migrations due to climate shocks such as long dry spells and drought. Temporary migration involves the group in question moving to a new location to access pasture and water for its livestock for a short time. This form of migration is triggered by abnormal seasonal changes, and the migrating groups return to their original base of livestock (kraals) when the rains begin again. Long-term migrations involve groups often moving hundreds of kilometers from their place of residence in search of pasture and water; they usually do not return or, if they do, return in small numbers when the climate shock subsides. Communities acknowledge that the latter form of migration was common in the past, when there was much vacant land to invade and occupy. The former type is a more recent development—a modification of the past to fit a changing environment.

The appropriation of land for agriculture, tourism, and mining in the region is changing the environment, which influences the migration of the different groups in the Karamoja region. The region's inhabitants migrate on a large scale to seek out pasture and water for their livestock. The migrations are determined by livestock numbers. As Table 8.1 illustrates, the numbers of livestock differ among pastoral communities.

Between 1950 and 2000, migrations in the Karamoja region were common and unaltered in distance, form, and nature. During this period, the region was still generally insecure; raids were rampant; and authority and order were still entirely in the hands of clan chiefs, opinion leaders, and kraal leaders. Migrations were thus constrained in the counties occupied by the aggressive, war-like groups.

Between 2000 and 2016, there were major shifts in the nature and number of migrations. The disarmament exercise of the Karimojongs in 2009 ushered in relative peace, greatly reducing migrations triggered by escape from raids. Increased government and NGO livestock veterinary and water services proliferated. This sparked migration both across districts and outside the country.

During a focus group discussion that mapped grazing areas from July to August 2016, community representatives reported reasons for this change: a shift from livestock to agriculture (for some pastoralists groups), construction of water dams in each county,

TABLE 8.1

District Veterinary Officer Livestock Estimates for 2014

District	Cattle	Goats	Sheep	Total Head
Kaabong	103,000	112,000	113,000	215,000
Kotido	280,000	300,000	380,000	960,000
Moroto	165,000	180,000	200,000	545,000
Nakapiripirit	143,137	174,687	136,921	454,744
Abim	20,000	54,354	12,236	86,591
Total livestock	711,137	821,041	842,157	2,374,335

Source: Data from the Food and Agriculture Organization/Global Information and Early Warning System (GIEW) livestock and market assessment mission in Karamoja region, 2014.

and the practice of zero grazing. However, the changes also created problems because restocking of livestock has resulted in very locale-specific increases, despite the general trend of reduction in numbers. Such increases have affected the carrying capacity of the grazing lands, effectively reducing pasture productivity, a problem compounded by mining and the deliberate policy of promoting agriculture in certain areas.

The lesson is that migration is important in resilience building. Migration is reinforced by traditional mechanisms for resolving tensions regarding water and pasture. Thus, the current emphasis on legal-based enforcement of migration with restrictions to nature reserves coupled with land alienation is counterproductive to resilience building. Another lesson is that the long-standing pastoral adaptation measures can and should inform resilience policies in the region.

Lessons from the Batwa Forest Pygmies

Since adopting their sedentary lifestyle after being forced out of the forest, the Batwa forest pygmies' critical concern is sustaining food security. Given their limited knowledge of crop farming, their adaptive capacity is low and thus climate change will continuously affect food systems beyond their threshold of tolerance (Berrang-Ford et al., 2012). With limited alternative sources of income, the Batwa depend on making cultural artifacts for tourism entertainment, which does not contribute much to livelihood sustainability. For those who are able to cultivate on the small pieces of land provided when they were resettled, the harvest is often just enough to meet daily home consumption. By the time the harvesting season phases out, the Batwa have accumulated no food stocks to sustain them through the "hunger season," as they refer to periods of shortage (Patterson et al., 2017). This is likely to affect Batwa communities because there will be insufficient food in the future when the climate change impacts are expected to devastate highly vulnerable populations.

The link between food security and health is well established among the Batwa. The more food insecure they are, the more vulnerable to diseases they are, especially malaria. Malaria is exacerbated by the variable climate and warming of the region, which is now loosely linked to an extension of the species range for *Anopheles* mosquitoes that carry the malaria parasite (Kulkarni et al., 2017; Lewnard et al., 2014; Pascual, Ahumada, Chaves, Rodo, & Bouma, 2006).

Land is a key basis for livelihood given the Batwa's reliance on semi-subsistence agriculture. Limited access to land is therefore a major constraint to agricultural activities, in turn leading to food insecurity in the area (Patterson et al., 2017). Alternative livelihoods such as tourism-based activities or manual labor for agriculture may not be sustainable. Provision of casual labor—for example, to the Bakiga—for wages is also not worthwhile because often they do not get paid, which implies a waste of their energy resources. The work per capita of the Batwa communities is also affected when they are idle, making many susceptible to alcoholism. This negatively impacts on the labor productivity among the individuals in Batwa communities and therefore implies that severe food insecurity will increase during such periods. Labor is essential to securing operational food systems, and the predicted changes in climate challenge labor capacity. The lesson here is that forest-based livelihoods were and are still a more resilient measure than the current agriculture-based lifestyle.

The Batwa forest pygmies suffer from high levels of poverty that pose challenges to ensuring food security and health. Because Batwa communities are isolated from the surrounding populations, they travel farther distances to access markets to buy food. Therefore, they incur greater transport costs, which deepens their poverty. However, NGOs are starting to give some support to Batwa communities in becoming food secure. Such NGO-supported activities include health, agriculture, and nutrition programs that aim to close the food security and health gaps among the Batwa. However, such programs lack continuity and emphasize adaptions that require different skills than those possessed by the previous generation. Though this approach may succeed in building resilience for future generations because they will likely not return to the forest, it leaves a gap for the adults and elderly Bawta on whom the new generation largely depends for food security. The lesson here is that access to forest for resources by older Batwa is an important resilience building measure.

As the climate continues to change, food security among the Batwa is increasingly at risk, as evidenced by its members eating fewer meals or skipping them altogether. Starvation and malnutrition are expected to increase. Rainy seasons will eventually lead to increased incidences of malaria and diarrhea. Such scenarios reduce individual ability to farm. Moreover, limited knowledge of the new area's variable climate jeopardizes food security. The lesson learned here is that more inclusive adaptive mechanisms are needed to respond to climate variability and enable Batwa communities to develop their own ways of ensuring food security through a diversity of methods.

Though the Batwa communities' poverty leads to less adaptive capacity to climate change, they have historically tested adaptive measures of migration, forest–hunter gathering, and traditional health systems that have built resilience. The emphasis on adapting to climate change in a new sedentary lifestyle requires rethinking because the experiences pose obstacles toward developing climate-sensitive agricultural activities within communities, providing poor conditions for agricultural production. This sedentary-focused resilience building results in communities being unable to establish and maintain efficient food systems by reducing food production, accessibility, and consumption. The lesson here is that a more robust resilience-building system is needed that incorporates positive aspects of the previous resilience measures through their history.

CLIMATE POLICY AND RESPONSES

Uganda developed a climate policy following its commitments to the Cancun Agreement in 2012. The national climate policy's goal is to ensure "a harmonised and coordinated approach towards climate-resilient and low-carbon development path for sustainable development" in the country (Ampaire et al., 2017, p. 82). Under this policy, "all stakeholders are to be mobilized to address climate change impacts through appropriate measures, while promoting sustainable development and green growth" (p. 81). The national climate policy considers adaptation the top priority for Uganda, whereas mitigation efforts are embraced by the policy as secondary in view of the country's development process and its current low levels of emissions. Given the multifaceted nature of climate change challenges in Uganda, policy priorities to mainstream climate change concerns in Uganda's development efforts cut across multiple sectors and address both adaptation and mitigation challenges. The climate policy is guided by principles of information sharing and research to better understand the impacts of climate change on particular groups and populations in Uganda and inform future actions for adaptation to climate change.

There are 14 objectives of the climate policy in Uganda, all of which are sector based with cross-sectoral linkages in implementation. The following objectives are important for this chapter: (1) to promote climate change adaptation strategies that enhance resilient, productive, and sustainable agricultural systems; (2) to promote value addition and improve food storage and management systems in order to ensure food security at all times, as a factor of resilience; (3) to strengthen adaptive mechanisms and enhance early warning systems and adequate preparedness for climate change-related diseases; and (4) to ensure disaster mitigation and adequate preparedness for climate change-induced risks, hazards, and disasters (Ampaire et al., 2017). Though the first two listed here concern agriculture and livestock, the objectives do not address livestock directly, making it less of a priority for implementation of adaptation, as observed in the case of Karamoja, where the emphasis has been on crop farming. This is not only a gap in the policy but also an indicator of how public policy affects people facing the brunt of climate change through action but also inaction.

The gap in livestock is further shown by the three priorities of the climate policy: agriculture, water, and health. For example, with regard to agriculture, the following measures are prioritized: supporting agricultural research; revising by-laws and ordinances; and implementing adaptation measures such as soil and water conservation practices, organic farming, forest restoration, preservation and promotion of indigenous species, and pest and disease control. The policy is beneficial for health among the forest pygmies in general but lacking with respect to indigenous health priorities and adaptations options. These priorities are selected because they could benefit from external funding with regard to the ongoing bi- and multilateral funding systems. With respect to adaptation costs, the allocation is approximately 1.2% of gross domestic product (GDP), whereas mitigation costs amount to 0.4% of GDP. Specifically, the total additional costs of adaptation represent U.S. $2.9 billion and the cost of mitigation U.S. $804 million over the next 15 years. Approximately 23% of all climate change resources are for the short term (1–5 years), 37% for the medium term (6–10 years), and 40% for the long term (11–15 years). Preliminary cost–benefit analyses of some adaptation measures have also been conducted. The benefits of implementing those with regard to agriculture, water, works and transport, energy, and disaster risk reduction outweigh the corresponding costs.

The implications of climate policy for the two communities discussed in this chapter will be far-reaching. There is a clear push to promote sedentary lifestyles among pastoralists as well as forest pygmies. This may be viewed as an adaptation measure to support food security and access to services, but it may also turn out to be a maladaptation, especially given that both communities have constraints that inhibit the complete change to crop farming, at least in the medium term. For example, the resettlement of the forest pygmies, who are less resilient to malaria, has led to increased malaria prevalence among the Batwa. As for pastoralists, the scope for successfully pursuing a sedentary lifestyle is constrained in such a water-stressed region that can barely support sustainable, productive cropping.

Policy implications for both socioecological systems are that care must be taken in emphasizing the impacts of climate change but also selection and prioritization of adaptations. The tendency to view development in such a way that all communities are expected to follow a similar transformation path is likewise problematic. "Unlearning" has to occur to learn how to plan for adaptation for equity and justice. Pastoralists will only produce food as long as the rains in their regions allow, but livestock is the system that has long been a basic structure on which both livelihoods and society are founded. Forest pygmies may not be able to return to the forest, but allowing them to access the forest for particular resources known to them and to build resilience is a policy that needs to be implemented. This would not be limited to guided periodic access. Likewise, it would not be limited to rules on what can and cannot be harvested. Thus, investments in adaptation for the two socioecological systems require elaborate planning and consideration of options, including how traditional resilient actions can complement innovations and new departures.

CONCLUSION

This chapter draws on the experiences of Karamojong pastoralists and the Batwa forest pygmies, and it argues that communities with long-standing traditional systems of adapting to climate change should inform any adaptation planning for climate change. These communities have faced and have been tested by varying climate risks for which adaptation measures have long been developed. The desire for development that enhances adaptation to be uniform without targeting regional differences is an issue that requires attention at the national level of implementation. There is evidence that NGOs and administrative districts in Uganda share a vision of a development path that is both unilinear and transformative of lifestyles and livelihoods. This approach to adaptation is potentially a process of pursuing maladaptation, as has been illustrated in this chapter. This will not deliver equitable development. Indeed, the same reasons outsiders consider these communities primitive will remain if their lifestyles are changed through adaptation and/or development. Thus, poor adaptation investment that forces the two communities to change lifestyles creates injustices. For climate change policy to deliver justice, the experiences and adaptations of the communities must be taken into account.

REFERENCES

Adger, W. N. (2006). Vulnerability. *Global Environmental Change, 16*, 268–281. doi:10.1016/j.gloenvcha.2006.02.006

Aerts, J. C., Botzen, W. W., Emanuel, K., Lin, N., de Moel, H., & Michel-Kerjan, E. O. (2014). Evaluating flood resilience strategies for coastal megacities. *Science, 344*, 473–475.

Akwango, D., Obaa, B., Turyahabwe, N., Baguma, Y., & Egeru, A. (2017). Quality and dissemination of information from a drought early warning system in Karamoja sub-region, Uganda. *Arid Environments, 145*, 69–80.

Ampaire, E. L., Jassogne, L., Providence, H., Acosta, M., Twyman, J., Winowiecki, L., & van Asten, P. (2017). Institutional challenges to climate change adaptation: A case study on policy action gaps in Uganda. *Environmental Science & Policy, 75*, 81–90.

Berrang-Ford, L., Dingle, K., Ford, J. D., Lee, C., Lwasa, S., Namanya, D. B., . . . Edge, V. (2012). Vulnerability of indigenous health to climate change: A case study of Uganda's Batwa Pygmies. *Social Science Medicine, 75*, 1067–1077.

Bunce, M., Brown, K., & Rosendo, S. (2010). Policy misfits, climate change and cross-scale vulnerability in coastal Africa: How development projects undermine resilience. *Environmental Science & Policy, 13*, 485–497. doi:10.1016/j.envsci.2010.06.003

Byenkya, G., Mugerwa, S., Barasa, S., & Zziwa, E. (2014). Land use and cover change in pastoral systems of Uganda: Implications on livestock management under drought induced pasture. *African Crop Science, 22*, 1013–1025.

Donnelly, B., Berrang-Ford, L., Labbé, J., Twesigomwe, S., Lwasa, S., Namanya, D. B., . . . Michel, P. (2016). *Plasmodium falciparum* malaria parasitaemia among indigenous Batwa and non-indigenous communities of Kanungu district, Uganda. *Malaria, 15*, 254.

Egeru, A. (2014). *Assessment of forage dynamics under variable climate in Karamoja sub-region of Uganda.* RUFORUM. Retrieved from http://repository.ruforum.org/documents/assessment-forage-dynamics-under-variable-climate-karamoja-sub-region-uganda

Hamza, M., & Zetter, R. (1998). Structural adjustment, urban systems, and disaster vulnerability in developing countries. *Cities, 15*, 291–299.

Hofmeijer, I., Ford, J., Berrang-Ford, L., Zavaleta, C., Carcamo, C., Llanos, E., . . . Namanya, D. (2013). Community vulnerability to the health effects of climate change among indigenous populations in the Peruvian Amazon: A case study from Panaillo and Nuevo Progreso. *Mitigation and Adaptation Strategies for Global Change, 18*(7), 957–978.

Jordaan, A. (2014). *Karamoja drought risk assessment: Is drought to blame for chronic food insecurity.* Albert Lea, MN: International Rescue Committee. doi:10.13140/RG.2.1.1195.6645

Kandagor, D. R. (2005). Rethinking pastoralism and African development: A case study of the Horn of Africa. Retrieved from https://www.codesria.org/IMG/pdf/kandagor.pdf

Kane, S., & Eicher, C. K. (2004). Foreign aid and the African farmer. Retrieved from http://ageconsearch.umn.edu/record/11602/files/sp04-13.pdf

Kulkarni, M. A., Garrod, G., Berrang-Ford, L., Ssewanyana, I., Harper, S. L., Baraheberwa, . . . Drakeley, C. (2017). Examination of antibody responses as a measure of exposure to malaria in the indigenous Batwa and their non-indigenous neighbors in southwestern Uganda. *American Journal of Tropical Medicine and Hygiene, 96*(2), 330–334. doi:10.4269/ajtmh.16-0559

Lewnard, J. A., Berrang-Ford, L., Lwasa, S., Namanya, D. B., Patterson, K. A., Donnelly, B., . . . Carcamo, C. P. (2014). Relative undernourishment and food insecurity associations with *Plasmodium falciparum* among Batwa pygmies in Uganda: Evidence from a cross-sectional survey. *American Journal of Tropical Medicine and Hygiene, 91*(1), 39–49.

Lwasa, S. (2018). Drought and flood risk, impacts and adaptation options for resilience in rural communities of Uganda. *International Journal of Applied Geospatial Research, 9*, 36–50. doi:10.4018/IJAGR.2018010103

Lwasa, S., Buyinza, A., & Nabaasa, B. (2017). Weather forecasts for pastoralism in a changing climate: Navigating the data space in north eastern Uganda. *Data Science Journal, 16*, 50. https://datascience.codata.org/articles/10.5334/dsj-2017-050

MacVicar, S., Berrang-Ford, L., Harper, S., Steele, V., Lwasa, S., Bambaiha, D.N., . . . Ross, N. (2017). How seasonality and weather affect perinatal health: Comparing the experiences of indigenous and non-indigenous mothers in Kanungu District, Uganda. *Social Science Medicine, 187*, 39–48. doi:10.1016/j.socscimed.2017.06.021

McSweeney, C., Lizcano, G., New, M., & Lu, X. (2010). The UNDP climate change country profiles: Improving the accessibility of observed and projected climate information for studies of climate change in developing countries. *American Meteorological Society, 91*, 157–166.

Morand, P., Kodio, A., Andrew, N., Sinaba, F., Lemoalle, J., & Béné, C. (n.d.). Vulnerability and adaptation of African rural populations to hydro-climate change: Experience from fishing communities in the inner Niger Delta (Mali). *Climate Change, 1–21*. doi:10.1007/s10584-012-0492-7

Motsholapheko, M. R., Kgathi, D. L., & Vanderpost, C. (2011). Rural livelihoods and household adaptation to extreme flooding in the Okavango Delta, Botswana. *Physics and Chemistry of the Earth Parts ABC, 36*(14–15), 984–995.

Muhonda, P. M. (2012). *Analysis of institutional mechanisms that support community response to impacts of floods and drought in the Middle-Zambezi River basin, Zimbabwe.* University of Zimbabwe Institutional Repository. Retrieved from http://ir.uz.ac.zw/handle/10646/793

The Office of the Prime Minister of Uganda. (2012). The 2010–2011 Integrated Rainfall Variability Impacts, Needs Assessment and Drought Risk Management Strategy. Retrieved from http://gfdrr.org/sites/gfdrr/files/UGANDA_PDNA_Report_2012.pdf

Pascual, M., Ahumada, J. A., Chaves, L. F., Rodo, X., & Bouma, M. (2006). Malaria resurgence in the East African highlands: Temperature trends revisited. *Proceedings of the National Academy of Sciences of the United States of America, 103*(15), 5829–5834.

Patterson, K., Berrang-Ford, L., Lwasa, S., Namanya, D. B., Ford, J., Twebaze, F., . . . Harper, S. L. (2017). Seasonal variation of food security among the Batwa of Kanungu, Uganda. *Public Health Nutrition, 20*, 1–11.

Rao, P. (2013). Building climate resilience in coastal ecosystems in India: Cases and trends in adaptation practices. In W. Leal Filho (Ed.), *Climate change and disaster risk management* (pp. 335–349). Berlin, Germany: Springer.

Rockström, J., Steffen, W., Noone, K., Persson, Å., Chapin, F. S., Lambin, E., . . . Foley, J. (2009). Planetary boundaries: Exploring the safe operating space for humanity. *Ecology and Society, 14*(2), 32.

Smit, B., & Wandel, J. (2006). Adaptation, adaptive capacity and vulnerability. *Global Environmental Change, 16*, 282–292. doi:10.1016/j.gloenvcha.2006.03.008

Standish, R. J., Hobbs, R. J., Mayfield, M. M., Bestelmeyer, B. T., Suding, K. N., Battaglia, L. L., . . . Cramer, V. A. (2014). Resilience in ecology: Abstraction, distraction, or where the action is? *Biological Conservation, 177*, 43–51.

Uganda Bureau of Statistics. (2009). *Uganda update on population and development.* Retrieved from http://www.ubos.org/?st=pagerelations2&id=17&p=related%20pages%202:Population

Wallace, K. J. (2007). Classification of ecosystem services: Problems and solutions. *Biological Conservation, 139*, 235–246. doi:10.1016/j.biocon.2007.07.015

9

Gender, Politics, and Water in Australia and Bangladesh

Margaret Alston

∽ ————————————————————————————————

BACKGROUND

Climate change and catastrophic weather events are increasing in intensity and frequency throughout the world, causing major disruption to environmental stability and agricultural production cycles—and hence to food and water security. Climate change leaves many people in local communities vulnerable by threatening regional security and national viability, destabilizing individual livelihoods, and compromising the well-being of industries and activities that depend on environmental resources. Critically, water insecurity caused by climate change is occurring at the same time as the global population expands toward 9 billion, exacerbating already intense pressure on the environment, food production, and access to safe water. This population growth will not be evenly spread and is predicted to be much higher in least developed countries (United Nations Population Fund, 2017), where extreme poverty levels are concentrated and resource access may be more complex.

Climate change has largely, and necessarily, been treated as a phenomenon threatening fragile environmental ecosystems; therefore, climate change research has tended to focus on scientific analysis and technological solutions (Tschakert et al., 2012). More limited attention has been paid to local-level social vulnerabilities caused by climate disasters or to the social impacts of these events (Alston, 2017). For example, despite warnings from feminist scholars that gender is a critical factor in vulnerability to climate change, policies have rarely taken up the challenge of gendered impacts (Alber, 2011; Alston & Whittenbury, 2012). Yet, in any disaster, gender is a critical factor shaping vulnerability, and as the frequency and intensity of climate change responses increase, an assessment of gendered vulnerability in disasters becomes critical. Furthermore, the barriers to adaptation and what fair and just social policies are required to address particular vulnerabilities are often overlooked (Hussey, 2014; Schlosberg, Collins, & Niemeyer, 2017). A major stumbling block to such policy attention is neoliberalism—the political ideology of choice in many countries—which leads governments to adopt a hands-off approach to state intervention and to rely on the primacy of the marketplace to resolve social disruption. This market-driven ideology creates significant roadblocks to the provision of social supports for those deeply affected by disasters, and this is particularly evident in developed nations. Though gendered patterns of vulnerability have long been recognized, they are exacerbated by climate change and indeed can be transformed under these critical circumstances, often in directions that further reduce gender equality.

In this chapter, I illustrate examples of local-level gendered vulnerability by focusing on water security in the context of climate disasters. I also confine my discussion of gendered impacts to those affecting women. In presenting this material, I draw on research projects conducted in Australia between 2014 and 2017 (Alston, Whittenbury, & Clarke, 2017; Clarke, Alston, Whittenbury, & Gosling, 2017) and Bangladesh between 2011 and 2014 (Alston, 2015; Alston, Whittenbury, & Haynes, 2014) that address social vulnerabilities resulting from climate change. With a critical focus on water access, I examine gendered adaptive responses adopted by local people to indicate that gender politics very much shapes adaptive capacity in response to climate events. In presenting these two case studies, I demonstrate gender adaptations in vastly different countries—one a high-income, developed country and the other less developed and marked by high levels of extreme poverty. Both are in the Global South and provide significantly contrasting cases. Levels of poverty, access to resources, the capacity of women to negotiate gender–power relations, their levels of autonomy, and their input to decision-making differentiate these cases. Though these factors shape gender negotiations, gender vulnerabilities are a feature of both.

The Australia study was conducted in an area of the country known as the Murray–Darling basin. This large region covers four states of Australia and is known as the food bowl of the country because of its significant contribution to food production and security. Water use in the basin is now problematic because there are concerns about declining river health and damage to fragile ecosystems caused by an overallocation of water for irrigation purposes, but also by long years of drought at the turn of the century. This concern for water security in the basin has led to policies aimed at reducing water use particularly for irrigation purposes with significant impacts on farm families and the communities that support them. It is important to note that farmers and their industry bodies have expressed strong support for these environmental measures. Nonetheless, this withdrawal of irrigation water has had a significant impact on many farm families, food production industries, and the communities that depend on these industries.

In comparison, the Bangladesh study was much broader in its geographical focus and was conducted across three diverse regions of the country, all subject to very different climate challenges. In most of these areas, water supplies have been threatened by drought, floods, cyclones, and other climate-related events leading to contamination of existing fresh water supplies or damage to fresh water infrastructure. In this very different case, I give examples of the ways women's lives have been reshaped by a need to access fresh water and to rebuild their livelihood strategies around damaged infrastructure.

CLIMATE CHANGE RISK, VULNERABILITY, AND ADAPTATION

Before discussing the studies, a brief analysis of climate change risk, vulnerability, and adaptation provides a framework for the research and demonstrates both the diversity of climate change impacts and the commonalities of gendered experiences.

Climate Risk Versus Climate Reality: Making Climate Change Personal

Given climate change skepticism, in Australia at least, from policymakers and commentators alike (Cox, 2015; "Deputy Prime Minister Barnaby Joyce," 2016), the reduced attention to the social impacts and a paucity of policy designed to address climate change come as no surprise. Even less surprising is that gendered consequences of climate change barely receive mention. Rather, under the neoliberal philosophy guiding policy developments in many countries, there is an unquestioned reliance on the market to shape outcomes. Unfortunately, the approach of challenging climate change knowledge and relying on a neoliberal market economy creates a dangerous negation of public responsibility for the uneven impacts of climate change and for actions that might defray them (Alston & Whittenbury, 2011). Furthermore, in Australia at least, where irrigation water access has been compromised, water has become commodified—treated as an economic asset with a high market value available for sale.

The climate change skepticism so dominant in Australia has a very unfortunate outcome for those critically affected, such as the farmers in the Murray–Darling basin, who come to view their experiences as a personal rather than a public crisis (Dunlap, 2010). The lengthy drought in Australia at the turn of the century, for example, was referred to by policymakers at the time as a "risk" to be managed at farm level rather than a natural disaster (Botterill & Fisher, 2003). This view places enormous stress on the affected people who try, and inevitably fail, to address climate challenges at farm or village levels, and this in turn engenders a strong sense of personal failure. By adopting this view, policymakers fail to address social vulnerabilities exacerbated by these events and are more likely to rely on market drivers to assist economic development in affected regions, thereby washing their hands of state responsibilities for the rights and needs of citizens.

Social Vulnerability and Transformative Adaptation

In climate change discussions, vulnerability refers to the susceptibility of ecosystems to harm and an inability to cope with adverse effects (International Panel on Climate Change [IPCC], 2001). *Social vulnerability* describes how well people are able to cope with a climate disaster and to adapt to critically changed circumstances (Adger & Kelly, 1999; Alston, 2017). The vulnerability of communities affected by climate change is a result of complex social inequalities reinforced by institutions, policies, customs, and culture (Tschakert et al., 2012). For example, the water crisis in the Murray–Darling basin area has a number of causes, including a historical overallocation of irrigation water licenses and an overlay of a lengthy climate-induced drought. Yet there are variable layers of vulnerability—and people experiencing similar circumstances may be affected differently. Poverty, gender inequalities, age, stage of life course, ethnicity, geographical location, and access to resources are critical factors that shape social vulnerability. In communities struggling with climate-related disasters, these factors frame the capacity to adapt.

At the community level, local people's lack of political influence and their inability to reach policymakers with their stories and experiences further influence social vulnerability. It is also affected by access to health and education services, transport and telecommunications infrastructure failures, how safe the community feels, ongoing community viability, exposure to climate-dependent economic resources/outcomes, and food and water security. At the individual level, vulnerability is further exacerbated by one's differential access to resources, health status, age, access to education, feelings of safety, level of influence over life choices, and feelings of social inclusion.

Without policies that address social vulnerabilities, adaptive capacity is undermined and people may adopt unsustainable coping strategies to climate-related disasters (Tschakert et al., 2012). Therefore, it is critical that such policies are developed with a clear understanding of vulnerabilities, with the intent of building resilience among those most critically affected. However, effective policies must be viewed by the communities as fair, just, and capable of producing transformative adaptation (Schlosberg et al., 2017). Such transformative adaptation requires attention not only to vulnerability but also to the human rights of the women and men affected (Mathies & Narhi, 2017; Pelling, 2011) and to actions that meet "a range of basic needs and processes necessary for citizens to construct a functioning life" (Schlosberg et al., 2017, p. 2).

THE RESEARCH

This chapter draws on two studies undertaken in Australia and Bangladesh to make some essential points about gendered vulnerability in relation to climate-related water security issues and the need for policies that address gender barriers, support women, and facilitate "a functioning life" (Schlosberg et al., 2017, p. 2). Australia is a highly developed country with a population of 24 million spread over the vast areas of this large island nation. It has a democratic system of government, with both of the large political parties adopting a neo-liberal approach to water policies in recent years. This approach has ensured that water has become commodified, with access heavily reliant on market conditions. The Australian case study focuses on research with Victorian dairy farmers in the Murray–Darling basin area affected by declining water for irrigation. The withdrawal of a significant amount of water from irrigation in the region has facilitated major structural and social adjustments in the basin. The study specifically addresses the gendered impacts of this development, which affects both livelihood strategies and industry in the area.

The research focuses on one such industry—the dairy industry—in the state of Victoria. Water policies and government schemes designed to improve water efficiency have reshaped this industry and geographical area. For example, up to one-third of Victorian dairy families have left the industry, with the number of families declining from more than 2,000 in 2007 to just more than 1,550 by 2012 (Dairy Australia, 2013). Those who have stayed either expanded their enterprises by purchasing neighboring farms and upgrading their infrastructure with the support of government water efficiency funding schemes or remained as they were but are now critically reliant on off-farm sources of income. In both cases, there are deep implications for gendered livelihood strategies, with women on larger farms being drawn more into the physical labor in the dairies, and those on smaller farms seeking work off-farm to support the family. The research was conducted in three affected communities, in which 90 interviews and focus groups were held. It provides a perspective on strategies adopted by people directly affected in the developed world when water security is threatened.

By contrast, Bangladesh is one of the countries most vulnerable to climate change. Home to 160 million people, two-thirds of this small delta country is less than 5 m above sea level, and the coastline is expected to retreat inland by as much as 10 km by 2100, resulting in a potential loss of 18% of the land mass (World Bank, 2000). Access to clean water is already compromised. The World Health Organization (2012) suggests that 20% of Bangladeshis who live in the Char and Hill areas will increasingly find it difficult to access clean water. As Pender (2008) notes,

> In terms of the impact of climate change few places in the world will experience the range of effects and the severity of changes that will occur in Bangladesh, which will include: average weather temperatures rising; more extreme hot and cold spells; rainfall being less when it is most needed for agriculture, yet more in the monsoon when it already causes floods; melting of glaciers in the source areas of Bangladesh's rivers altering the hydrological cycle; more powerful tornados and cyclones; and sea level rise displacing communities, turning freshwater saline and facilitating more powerful storm surges. (p. 27)

From 2011 to 2014, research was conducted in Bangladesh to assess the gendered impacts of climate change in nine rural villages in three different regions throughout the country (Alston, 2015; Alston et al., 2014). The sites chosen were subject to a diverse range of climate challenges, including intense flooding, cyclonic activity, riverbank erosion, and extreme drought conditions. In these nine communities, the research team conducted 29 focus groups, 23 interviews, and a follow-up quantitative survey of 617 respondents. In this chapter, I focus only on issues relating to household water security and discuss this in a gendered context. By comparing two vastly different countries and communities within those countries, experiencing multiple climate challenges and variable vulnerabilities, it is nonetheless possible to discern commonalities in gendered vulnerability and adaptation as they relate to women. In both cases, access to water is compromised: In Australia, livelihoods depend on irrigation water; in Bangladesh, they depend on access to potable water and water for agriculture in areas experiencing major climate events.

Murray–Darling Basin, Australia

The following information is drawn from the study of dairy communities in the Murray–Darling basin area of Australia (Clarke et al., 2017). In this large fertile area, access to irrigation water has been compromised by a lengthy decade-long, climate-related drought at the turn of the century; the historical overallocation of water licenses; and the withdrawal of a significant amount of water by the government from the area in the interest of protecting the environment. This has resulted in significant divisions within the basin communities between those who have water and those who do not, as well as inequalities in access to water, the development and consolidation of larger farms by those who have benefited, and the stagnation or static growth of farms and communities where water is less available. Thus, there are areas experiencing growth and development and others where their decline is evident in the numbers of empty farmhouses and shopfronts. The economic consequences of the mandated withdrawal of irrigation water and its transference back to the environment in the interests of protecting threatened iconic sites and wildlife are wide-ranging. Critically, consequences of the lengthy drought and the needs of the environment are understood and accepted by stakeholders, including dairy families. However, the manner in which these water policy changes have been implemented, the uncertainty surrounding decisions regarding water, the lack of trust among stakeholders, and the uneven outcomes have raised tensions across the basin. For example, despite the decline in the number of dairy farms, many of the remaining farms have expanded and increased their productivity. This has been facilitated by government grants to farmers in exchange for water savings, a scheme that has been successful in allowing some dairy farmers to upgrade their infrastructure and build their enterprise. Those who have not been successful or have not applied for grants have remained small and largely reliant on off-farm income. Economically, the production of milk in the basin faltered for a time and then increased as farm productivity improved. However, a significant decline in the price of milk received by farmers for their product in 2016 again destabilized the industry. These changes, and the uncertainty they engender, make it difficult for farm families to restructure their livelihood strategies with any certainty or to predict their futures.

Given the economic consequences of the reduction in the number of dairy farms, the social consequences are equally significant. Respondents report shrinking social networks as neighbors move away, leaving farmhouses abandoned. As people leave, community groups decline and fewer people are available for voluntary work. There are also fewer children in the communities. As a result, schools have lost teachers, and funding for school buses and other services is under threat. People report significant health impacts, particularly mental health issues. Thus, social vulnerability in the basin has been exacerbated by constant change, loss of family and friends, stress, and uncertainty.

It is clear that water policies have been implemented according to neoliberal principles, with market processes being the dominant rationale in the restructure and, thus, arguably the neoliberal principles underpinning policy have exacerbated climate vulnerability. A number of trends are emerging from this process of water rationalization in the basin area, including a consolidation of larger farms as small farms are swallowed up and larger, technologically advanced enterprises are emerging, many of which have benefited from government grants and water access. In less favored areas, smaller farms have tended to miss out on grants and to be in static growth, heavily reliant on off-farm income generation. In addition, across the dairy areas there are pockets of farms that have sold their water and dried off their farms, leaving a patchwork of dry areas among the irrigated farms. The adaptations have been uneven, and this has flowed on to the small communities dotted across the basin, leading to a decline in community cohesion and social capital in many and a loss of population.

Gender Challenges

The study reveals a number of gender challenges affecting women and men as a consequence of water policies and the social impacts in communities. For example, the loss of social networks, the decline in people available for volunteer work and indeed as hired workers on the newly expanded dairies, the loss of teachers, and the challenges of accessing services have particular gendered consequences and emerging gender vulnerabilities most evident in women's restructured work roles (Alston, Clarke, & Whittenbury, 2017). Though these community-based challenges are evident, in this chapter, I focus only on the gendered impacts of industry changes and the implications for women in dairy families. The research finds two significant gendered trends directly resulting from water policy changes (Alston et al., 2017). The first concerns women in expanded enterprises, who are contributing more labor in the dairies and in the hands-on work with the dairy herd given the economic uncertainty and the difficulties of finding hired labor to work on dairies. As one female dairy farmer noted,

> I do the most milking, [husband] helps me and we also have two others, we have [husband]'s mum that milks as well so I work with her predominantly and then we have people on the weekends to give her a spell; she wants to do it and she's [in her 70s] and she wants to stay in it as long as she can so that's not us telling her to. So, I milk with her mostly and do the bookwork, and when I'm needed I do whatever else he tells me to do, which might be drenching cows, calves, seeding— not very often I do seeding because the boys do that—it might be raking hay or mowing. . . . It's about two and a half hours per milking, just milking cows alone is 35 hours, so 35 hours of my week I'm just milking cows before I do anything else, before I do any bookwork, before I do anything on the farm, and I'm still doing stuff on the farm, so it's just a lot, and the kids, so just everything.

There is little doubt that women are adjusting their work roles to accommodate processes of restructuring. Yet it is significant that women's labor is often invisible, subsumed, and, in fact, romanticized. For example, as one male dairy farmer noted,

> Women, I think—they seem to have a natural empathy maternally with the cows, so they can tell if a cow is sick, they know what they look like, they think, "Yes, that cow looks sick." They are quieter on the whole, and I mean you get some fellows that aren't too bad, but overall we find women are better in the dairy. They don't tend to raise their voices they don't tend to yell.

Though this may be true, these views can render women's work largely invisible to people outside the enterprise and indeed to government or industry personnel. As a consequence, there are limited measures in place to support women's enhanced workload. For example, the need for child care was raised as the number one priority by most dairy families and community members, and yet there is almost none in place. Furthermore, there are few women in dairy industry leadership roles, so issues affecting women are rarely addressed in industry forums.

The second trend on smaller farms is women increasingly working off-farm to secure income for the family. Many report the stress associated with trying to keep income coming in and the family's basic needs met while also helping keep a business running. As one woman who worked as a partner on a dairy farm noted, despite her efforts, the stressful financial position did not disappear:

> I'm working off farm because it puts food on the table, and that is a good thing. That is a good thing. . . . But as far as running the farm's concerned it doesn't touch

the edges. Not even close, it wouldn't even touch a quarter of the interest. It might keep food on the table. And, it keeps me sane, because as much as it's interesting to talk about the water I couldn't do it all day every day.

These gendered changes in labor allocation and the implications for women create significant stresses. At the same time, women's lack of control over resource decisions leaves them feeling sidelined in business decisions, and despite their "doing the books" and knowing the farm's financial position, they are not always included in business decisions. As one female dairy farmer noted,

> We've just put in automation . . . and that's cost a lot of money and I was very dead against putting that in because of the season that we're facing and my concerns about the finances, but [husband's name] just pushed through and just ignored me, and I dug my heels in as far as I could and stalled and did whatever I could to not let it go ahead, but in the end he just did it, so now we have a loan to service as well on top of all the other things.

The research reveals significant gendered changes in the workload sharing in dairying usually revolving around livelihood decisions—decisions that also affect men. For women, these reshape their orientation to dairy farming, often in ways that are stressful and not entirely their choice. Thus, the study finds climate and environmental challenges and neoliberal water policy responses intersecting with gender power relations on farms. Policies are implemented, structural changes occur in response, individual farm enterprises must restructure to accommodate the changes, gender power relations and livelihood strategies are renegotiated in partnerships in which women may have less influence as a result of ownership issues, and women and men reorganize their work roles in response. In many instances, the water crisis and consequent restructuring require the need to act quickly, ostensibly reducing women's negotiating capacity. Women's vulnerability in these circumstances is shaped by their differential access to decisions concerning resources and their age, stage of life course, and health. Critically, this study finds that their vulnerability in these circumstances is particularly dependent on the level of influence they feel they have over their life choices.

Bangladesh

This section draws on research undertaken at sites across Bangladesh (Alston, 2015; Alston et al., 2014). It provides a contrast to the Australian study because of the country's less developed status, levels of poverty, and the greater vulnerability of Bangladeshis to the impacts of climate events. In this vulnerable country, the number of climate events (e.g., river erosion, cyclones, storm surges, drought, floods) affecting water security is increasing (World Health Organization, 2012). The significant consequences of these events include high mortality and morbidity, food and water insecurity, poor sanitation, displacement, family destabilization, infrastructure destroyed, difficulties accessing services and education, significant health impacts, interrupted education, and reliance on remittance income. Climate change has also had significant impacts on water security for Bangladeshi women.

Water Security Post-Disaster

Because much of the land in Bangladesh is low-lying, the impacts of climate events can be catastrophic. Early warning systems throughout the country have been dramatically improved but are not comprehensive. Thus, there may be minimal warnings of catastrophic weather events, as evidenced by one young woman's description of the impact of a flash flood on her family:

> After dinner when we went to bed, there was a possibility that the river may take away my house. Water comes, we raise the upper bed mattress, bed sheets, and other things so that they cannot get wet. We lift the bed and boxes. We ensure that the children do not fall into the water. We have to be careful about that. After the water lessens, our wooden furniture and the pillars of my cottage break from the flood. Soil makes the inside dirty and I need to clean them after a flood. I need to reconstruct my cottage. I need to clean everything. Someone in my family will be affected by diarrhea or cholera, it makes the clothes dirty. I need to clean them. That is what we have to do [after a flood].

As noted by a nongovernmental organization (NGO) key informant, these sudden disasters have a major impact on all family members:

> We work with communities who live there. Their houses are gone, their food security is gone, the water source is disturbed, children cannot go back to school, health is affected, and some of the areas where we [work], there's none of these services anyway, especially in the river islands called the Chars.

For women, the time-consuming task of cleaning up is made more difficult because access to fresh water is one of the highest priorities in the immediate post-disaster phase in any disaster. Women in Bangladesh have considerable difficulty finding fresh water sources given the water contamination common in post-disaster circumstances. Therefore, women often have to walk long distances to find safe water, as reported in a women's focus group:

We have to go to the nearest water source 5 miles away from here, to collect water. So if you want to drink a glass of water in the afternoon, you would only finally get it in the evening. Male or female, everyone is engaged in the act of going far to collect some water. That's not a choice either, we're forced [to do it]. It's a choice between that bad and this worst. Whichever is suitable. So, living in these kind of conditions is extremely hazardous.

In one village, a woman spoke about having to bring fresh water by boat after floods, a situation that motivated her to earn enough to install a tube well: "During the floods we had to bring [safe] water from across the river. We carried water by pitcher. Now we have a tube well bought with my own earnings."

According to a key NGO informant, reduced access to fresh water has led to the rationing of water in some villages, particularly when fresh water sources are a significant distance from home:

Women walk several kilometres to get a pitcher full of water. And they train their offspring, that's even more painful—they ration water. Because otherwise, on a single day, they have to go there again, walking [through contaminated] water, walking there and coming back. Because there is no system for them to be able to collect it in their dwelling . . . . they train their children to drink less. So, that risks their organs because there is no alternative, right? Otherwise they are forced to drink the same water that they defecate in.

Given the importance of this issue for participants in the qualitative interviews, the research team followed up with questions on a survey of 617 residents across the nine villages. Participants were asked about the impacts of water insecurity in post-disaster situations. More than two-thirds noted reduced access to drinking water after a disaster, and nearly half noted the increased time required to access fresh water. Despite this, only 15% of respondents noted that there had been changes in who collects water—for the most part, this remains the task of women (Table 9.1).

Other outcomes of limited access to fresh water following a disaster include time constraints and significant health impacts (e.g., skin diseases, gynecological problems) for women who walk long distances through contaminated water:

[The water causes] problems like itching, dandruff, allergy, skin diseases these have increased due to saline water. Cholera and dysentery are also affecting people. Women and children are facing the same problems. (Women's focus group)

Sometimes the tube well goes under the water. Once we drank the water during a flood, and faced serious misery—fever and coughs. (Older woman)

TABLE 9.1

Impact on Water Security

Water Security Issue	Women (%)	Men (%)	Total (%)
Reduced availability of drinking water	63	66	64.5
Increase in water availability	6	9	7.5
Salinity in dry season	54	56	55
Increased time to collect water	47	46	46
Need to find new source of drinking water	48	44.5	46
Change in who collects water	14	16	15

Sources: Data from a 2013 Bangladesh survey and from Alston et al. (2014).

Two other older women expanded on the health consequences of disasters:

> During floods we suffer from cholera, typhoid, dysentery. In the dry season there
> is dysentery and jaundice. . . . The diseases that are carried by water increase
> during flood.
>
> Heart failure, fever, diarrhea and other diseases [are present here]. We have
> to spend huge amounts of money for treatment. . . . My elder sister's daughter
> died. . . . Our legs become rotten, all of us suffer from skin diseases. We suffer from
> diarrhea and cholera.

Survey participants indicated the importance of water access to their quality of life;
more than one-third responded that water security was the most important factor

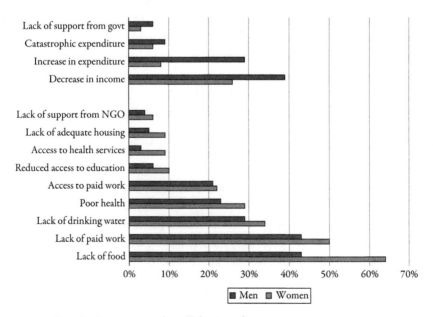

FIGURE 9.1 Negative impacts on quality of life arising from water insecurity.

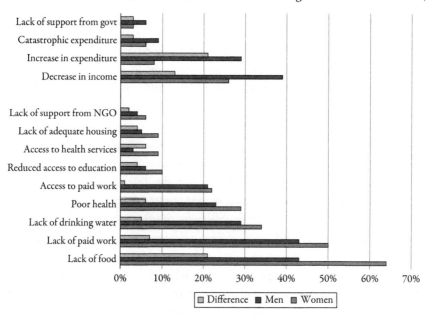

FIGURE 9.2 Gender differences in reported negative impacts.

negatively affecting their quality of life (Figures 9.1 and 9.2). When these responses are mapped, it becomes clear that men are more likely to view the economic or livelihood consequences of water access as most problematic, whereas women are more likely to address the social impacts (Table 9.2).

TABLE 9.2

Factors Negatively Affecting Quality of Life

Factor	Women (%)	Men (%)	Total (%)
Lack of food	64	43	53
Lack of drinking water	34	29	32
Lack of paid work	50	43	46
Access to paid work	22	21	21
Poor health	29	23	26
Access to health services	9	3	6
Lack of adequate housing	9	5	7
Reduced access to education	10	6	17
Decrease in income	26	39	33
Lack of support from NGO	6	4	5
Lack of support from government	3	6	5
Increase in expenditure	8	29	18
Catastrophic expenditure	6	9	7

NGO, nongovernmental organization.

COMPARING LONG-TERM IMPACTS IN AUSTRALIA AND BANGLADESH

The two case studies are, on the face of it, significantly different. The Australian study explores the effects of policy-induced water reduction in a high-income developed nation. Though many affected individuals suffer significant livelihood disadvantage, their lives are not necessarily threatened and they have access to resources that allow them choices. For the people of Bangladesh, however, water access is a much more immediate threat due to conditions of extreme poverty and reduced options. For the Australian participants, the need to increase family labor circumscribes their choices and places a significant burden on women's time. In contrast, the time constraints the women of Bangladesh face are far greater as a result of the life-threatening issue of fresh water access. These two studies demonstrate that disasters, whether climate-induced or policy-induced, have major gendered repercussions and often within uneven gender power relations.

In both countries, women appear to be at a disadvantage in gender negotiations because of their lack of power and lack of ownership of resources in their patriarchal family unit. Uneven power relations are reinforced by customs such as patrilineal inheritance practices such that agricultural land passes to males, leaving women disempowered in subsequent negotiations. Cultural prescriptions relating to work roles and responsibilities are also relevant, with women in both countries expected to take on caring roles and household tasks. In both cases, women have less power in gender negotiations when livelihoods are threatened, leading to inequitable gender relations and women needing to undertake enhanced work roles. In Australia, women on larger consolidated farms are drawn into greater roles in the dairies, and women on smaller farms take on more off-farm work. Arguably, these choices are imposed and may not have been their preferred choice. By contrast, in Bangladesh, women are required to walk considerable distances under difficult conditions to access safe water for their families when their usual water sources are compromised.

Drivers of Women's Vulnerability

Given the evident differences between the two study contexts, it would be natural to focus on how the experiences of women in Australia and Bangladesh are at odds or contrasting. In reality, however, for women in the two countries, many of the challenges they face cross cultures and feature in both case studies. Women are particularly vulnerable in disasters for a number of reasons. Chief among these are their responsibilities for care work. This takes much of their time and requires organization and additional household tasks. There are major gaps in service infrastructure that could assist in these tasks. For the women of Bangladesh, having to source fresh water adds a significant burden of time to their already busy lives. For the families in the Australia study, there are few, if any, child care services, making it difficult for women to adapt to new work responsibilities.

What is evident from these two sites is that (1) women experience different levels of vulnerability in very diverse circumstances; and (2) their level of vulnerability increases following a disaster, regardless of place. Cultural norms constrain and potentially silence women more than they do men. In both cases, women are expected to conform to expectations, as demonstrated by Australian women's increased physical labor and Bangladeshi women's desperate search for water. In both cases, women appear to have less ownership and control over resources and, hence, less power over decisions being made about reframed livelihood strategies within the family unit. This also appears to be the case in community decisions (e.g., water supply infrastructure in Bangladesh) and industry decisions (e.g., Australian industry bodies not addressing gender issues). Women in both countries note they continue to monitor the health of their families while largely ignoring their own.

There is clear evidence in these case studies that disaster and water politics are not gender neutral. In both countries, women have fewer opportunities to access positions of influence. This involves women having limited access to decision-making forums in which their views can be heard and their needs factored into policies and processes. In both case studies, in very different contexts, cultural constraints shape the work of women.

Common adaptations are evident across the two countries following a disaster. These include changes in livelihood and adaptation strategies with new ways of accessing income and distributing work. Displacement is also common across cultures, with family members in Bangladesh moving to find work and dairy families in Australia being forced out of the industry. In both countries, families were found to be diversifying their industry base or production processes to stay viable.

However, it is arguable that the current neoliberal policy framework and the dominance of climate change knowledge by scientific research mask social inequalities and inherent vulnerabilities in areas affected by climate disasters. Much adaptation research is based on the fundamentally flawed assumption that adaptation is both possible and desirable in all areas of the world and that with determined effort, the right technology, and adequate funding, the vulnerable will adapt (Tschakert et al., 2012). This linear assessment of adaptive responses presupposes that existing conceptual frameworks are adequate. Yet it is increasingly clear that there are limits and barriers to the capacity of individuals and communities to adapt and that expectations that rational adaptive responses will occur are illusory for a variety of reasons, not least being widespread poverty and gender inequalities (Tschakert et al., 2012).

What is also clear from this research is that neoliberal policies focused on market strategies and economic outcomes have shaped climate responses particularly in highly developed countries. These policies give little or no attention to social impacts of climate events at the household level and in fact assume that households will absorb the shocks of climate events. This mantra creates significant tensions at the household level as gender negotiations around restructured livelihoods take place in a situation of unequal power. Arguably, as the two studies reveal, women are taking on enhanced work roles as a result.

POLICY INTERVENTIONS

Clearly, climate events will continue and in fact are increasing in frequency and intensity (IPCC, 2014). In many cases, this results in reduced access to safe drinking water or water for irrigated agriculture, and this requires major adaptations in livelihood strategies at the household level—adaptations that have significant gendered impacts. It is not sufficient to adopt neoliberal responses to these water challenges and to expect the market to determine outcomes. Social policy interventions are required that address the social implications of climate changes and the uneven gender outcomes at the household level and assist women and men to adapt. Both studies reveal the need to address the ownership of agricultural land and associated resources. They reveal the patrilineal practices that ensure male control of land, and consequently of women's labor, and the need to undo patriarchal power relations that silence women at the same time as so much is demanded of them. Both studies also reveal the need to unpack cultural norms that act to ensure women conform to changed expectations, including a significant increase in their labor. Moreover, they reveal the need for decision-making bodies, including governmental, nongovernmental, and industry bodies, to be gender inclusive to ensure that issues affecting women and men are heard and addressed.

In the Australian case, further required policies include the need for child care and access to services such as mobile phone coverage, transportation, health and education services, employment opportunities, and training. In the Bangladesh case, similar issues arise in more extreme conditions. Access to safe water close to home is essential to the health and well-being of family members and to reducing the amount of time women must spend collecting water. Without ready access, women's time is compromised by having to walk long distances, which further compromises other livelihood strategies and tasks demanding their time. Service access issues are also evident in Bangladesh, with health factors resulting from climate events dominating discussions. Access to health care and other services is essential in both contexts. Visiting village-level health workers, access to education and other services, and access to employment opportunities are just some of the policy interventions that would address gendered vulnerabilities consequent on climate events.

In all cases, gender-sensitive climate policies must be directed to the household, village/community, region, and national levels. Furthermore, to prevent women bearing an unfair burden of climate adaptation, gender issues must form part of global negotiations regarding climate change.

CONCLUSION

This chapter supports existing research on the gendered nature of climate change impacts. Furthermore, what emerges is the notion that water, and access to it, is not a gender-neutral issue. In the two contrasting case studies presented here, water access in the context of climate disasters emerges as an issue fraught with uneven gendered implications at the household level. The Bangladeshi study reveals the significant imposition on women's time and the health consequences of problematic water access. There is no doubt that fresh water access is one of the most critical impacts of disasters and that, in Bangladesh, accessing water is a task that is relegated mostly to women. Addressing this issue in post-disaster responses is critical to addressing women's health and welfare, their adaptive capacity, and their vulnerability to health issues.

The gendered impacts are less evident in the study performed in Australia, where water access for irrigation farmers has been restricted and farms are expected to reshape their enterprises around the new reality of declining water availability. This appears to be a gender-neutral decision and in fact affects farms and businesses in different ways. However, the case study reveals the surprisingly gendered outcomes of adaptation strategies adopted in individual enterprises. Women appear now to be more central to farm livelihood strategies, yet their choices remain limited.

What remains problematic in the Australian case study is the framing of water policies. Stakeholders acknowledge that the water restriction policies introduced in the basin are environmentally necessary, but the resulting policies have been developed in consultation with industry bodies—bodies that have very limited representation by women. Instead, such polices are very much focused on market-based solutions despite the issue causing major social upheavals. As noted above, the policies, despite the precarious position in which they place many families, deal with water access as a private issue rather than a public crisis, which should include the support of the whole community.

Thus, farm families are renegotiating gender roles within enterprises with limited wider community awareness of the consequences. The expectation that this is a personal responsibility to be addressed at the farm level means that there is inadequate policy attention to social vulnerability resulting from major changes to water access. A telling example of this neglect is the lack of attention to child care policies despite evidence that women are central to reframed livelihood strategies.

In Bangladesh, it appears that access to safe water is not receiving the priority it deserves given the health implications and the huge imposition on women's time. There is an expectation that women will collect water regardless of the circumstances and an underlying assumption that women will continue their invisible work accessing water for the family. The lack of attention given to women's time collecting safe water in post-disaster sites illustrates the silence around gender expectations and the invisibility of women's work even when operating in plain sight. It also highlights that the focus of neoliberal policies when applied to climate events is very much shaped by market priorities rather than household health and well-being. Climate-related events such as those described above require significant attention to social policies directed at household, community, regional, and national levels. An expectation that markets can address gender inequalities and that these policies excuse the state from intervening is laughable.

What emerges from this chapter is that water, or the lack of it, is not a gender-neutral issue and that water policies and a lack of actions directed at ensuring safe water access can exacerbate gender inequalities. Fair and just social policies are required that move away from neoliberal, market-based attention to a broader focus on actions designed to address the impacts on people and communities. Policies that rely on markets to solve social crises without an assessment of gender outcomes create significant disempowerment for women.

What is needed? I argue that post-disaster policies require the input of women and men to address the nuances of gender vulnerability. In addition, attention to cultural constraints and the human rights of women is essential for fair and just governance. Climate change will not go away despite the views of conservative politicians and commentators. What is needed is a kinder, gentler polity that acknowledges women as citizens and extends policy responses accordingly.

REFERENCES

Adger, W. N., & Kelly, M. (1999). Social vulnerability to climate change and the architecture of entitlements. *Mitigation and Adaptation Strategies for Global Change, 4*, 253–266.

Alber, G. (2011). *Gender, cities and climate change: Thematic report prepared for Cities and Climate Change Global Report on Human Settlements.* UN Habitat. Retrieved from www.unhabitat.org/grhs/2011

Alston, M. (2015). *Women and climate change in Bangladesh.* Abingdon, UK: Routledge.

Alston, M. (2017). Eco-social work: Reflections from the global south. In A. Matthies & K. Narhi (Eds.), *Ecosocial transitions of society: Contribution of social work and social policy* (pp. 91–104). London, UK: Routledge.

Alston, M., & Whittenbury, K. (2011). Climate change and water policy in Australia's irrigation areas: A lost opportunity for participatory regional development. *Environmental Politics, 20*(6), 899–917.

Alston, M., & Whittenbury, K. (2012). Introduction. In M. Alston & K. Whittenbury (Eds.), *Research, action and policy: Addressing the gendered impacts of climate change* (pp. 3–14). New York, NY: Springer.

Alston, M., Whittenbury, K., & Clarke, J. (2017). Gender relations, livelihood strategies, water policies and structural adjustment in the Australian dairy industry. *Sociologia Ruralis, 57*(S1), 752–768. doi:10.1111/soru.12164

Alston, M., Whittenbury, K., & Haynes, A. (2014). *Gender and climate change in Bangladesh: A report to Monash-Oxfam.* Melbourne, Australia: Monash University.

Botterill, L., & Fisher, M. (2003). Introduction. In L. Botterill & M. Fisher (Eds.), *Beyond drought: People, policy and perspectives* (pp. 1–8). Collingwood, Australia: CSIRO.

Clarke, J., Alston, M., Whittenbury, K., & Gosling, A. (2017). *Social sustainability in dairy communities affected by the Murray–Darling Basin Water Plan.* Melbourne, Australia: Monash University.

Cox, L. (2015, July 13). Other countries "airy-fairy" on climate change, says Tony Abbott, as Australia delays new emissions target announcement. *Sydney Morning Herald.* Retrieved from http://www.smh.com.au/federal-politics/political-news/other-countries-airyfairy-on-climate-change-says-tony-abbott-as-australia-delays-new-emissions-target-announcement-20150713-giazve.html

Dairy Australia. (2013). *2013 Dairy people factfinder*. Retrieved from https://www.thepeopleindairy.org.au/projects/2013%20dairy%20people%20factfinder.pdf

Deputy prime minister Barnaby Joyce faces the reality of climate change. (2016, May 21). *Sydney Morning Herald*. Retrieved from https://www.smh.com.au/national/deputy-prime-minister-barnaby-joyce-faces-the-reality-of-climate-change-20160520-gozlh3.html

Dunlap, R. E. (2010). Comment: Climate change and rural sociology: Broadening the research agenda. *Rural Sociology, 75*(1), 17–27.

Hussey, K. (2014). Using markets to achieve environmental ends: Reconciling social equity issues in contemporary water policy in Australia. In T. Fitzpatrick (Ed.), *International handbook on social policy and the environment* (pp. 300–326). Cheltenham, UK: Elgar.

Intergovernmental Panel on Climate Change. (2001). *Climate change: Third assessment report*. Retrieved from http://www.ipcc.ch/publications_and_data/publications_and_data_reports.shtml#.T8BtkVFpu8U

Intergovernmental Panel on Climate Change. (2014). *Fifth assessment report*. Retrieved from https://www.ipcc.ch/report/ar5/

Mathies, A., & Narhi, K. (2017). Introduction: It is time for social work and social policy research on ecosocial transition. In A. Maathies & K. Narhi (Eds.), *The ecosocial transition of societies: The contribution of social work and social policy* (pp. 1–14). Abingdon, UK: Routledge.

Pelling, M. (2011). *Adaptation to climate change: From resilience to transformation*. London, UK: Routledge.

Pender, J. S. (2008). *What is climate change? And how it will affect Bangladesh*. Church of Bangladesh Social Development Programme. Retrieved from http://www.churchofscotland.org.uk/__data/assets/pdf_file/0003/2982/climate_change_bangladesh.pdf

Schlosberg, D., Collins, L. B., & Niemeyer, S. (2017). Adaptation policy and community discourse: Risk, vulnerability, and just transformation. *Environmental Politics, 26*(3), 413–437. doi:10.1080/09644016.2017.1287628

Tschakert, P., Ziervogel, G., Koelle, B., Sallu, S., Shackleton, S. & Alston, M. (2012). *Barriers and limits to climate change adaptation: A conceptual framework*. Paper prepared by members of the World Universities Network Limits to Adaptation group. Inquiries to Margaret.alston@monash.edu

United Nations Population Fund. (2017). *World population trends*. Retrieved from https://www.unfpa.org/world-population-trends

World Bank. (2000). *Bangladesh: Climate change and sustainable development*. Retrieved from http://documents.worldbank.org/curated/en/906951468743377163/Bangladesh-Climate-change-and-sustainable-development

World Health Organization. (2012). *UN-Water global analysis and assessment of sanitation and drinking-water*. Retrieved from http://www.who.int/water_sanitation_health/monitoring/investments/glaas/en

10

The Indigenous Climate–Food–Health Nexus

INDIGENOUS VOICES, STORIES, AND LIVED EXPERIENCES
IN CANADA, UGANDA, AND PERU

Sherilee L. Harper, Lea Berrang-Ford, Cesar Carcamo,

Ashlee Cunsolo, Victoria L. Edge, James D. Ford, Alejandro Llanos,

Shuaib Lwasa, and Didacus B. Namanya

BACKGROUND: A "CREEPING CATASTROPHE"

Climate change is widely regarded as one of the main challenges facing humanity this century. Herein, the importance of climate change research, mitigation, and adaptation is becoming increasingly clear as the frequency and intensity of climate-related events rise. The impacts of current and projected changes are wide-ranging and include human migration (McMichael, Barnett, & McMichael, 2012), increases in conflict and violence (Theisen, Gleditsch, & Buhaug, 2013), substantial economic consequences (Whiteman, Hope, & Wadhams, 2013), species extinction (Urban, 2015), and serious human health effects (Wang & Horton, 2015). Research is only beginning to examine the potential human health effects of climate change and already indicates significant vulnerabilities (McMichael, 2013). As such, the health-related impacts of climate change have been considered a "creeping catastrophe" (Summerhayes, 2010, p. 410), "the defining issue for the 21st century" (Chan, 2015), and "ultimately, a threat to our biological health and survival" (McMichael & Dear, 2010, p. 9483).

Substantial Climate Change Impacts on Food Security and Health

Evidence suggests that climate change threats related to impacts on food and water security present the largest consequence to human health (Fischer, Shah, Tubiello, & van Velhuizen, 2005; Springmann et al., 2016). Without adaptation actions, increased temperatures and changes in precipitation are expected to have a significant negative net impact on global food security. For instance, for every 1°C of warming, water insecurity is projected to increase by 20%, which will be further stressed by a 40% increase in demand for crop irrigation due to atmospheric and soil moisture deficits (Jiménez Cisneros & Oki, 2014). By 2050, this is projected to result in global net reductions in crop yields by up to 45% for maize, 50% for wheat, 30% for rice, and 60% for soybean (Rosenzweig et al., 2014); lower concentrations of nutrients in these staple foods (Oppenheimer, Campos, & Warren, 2014); and substantial increases in global food prices (Porter & Xie, 2014). Such climate-related impacts to food security are anticipated to significantly affect several determinants of health and well-being, with the World Health Organization (2014) projecting that more than half of future climate-related deaths will be attributable to food. Indeed, recent research projects a 38% increase in prevalence of hunger and malnutrition globally by 2050 (Maharjan & Joshi, 2013). Food-related mortality attributed to climate change "far exceeds" that linked to heat, flooding, malaria, and dengue combined (Springmann et al., 2016).

Climate Change and Indigenous Peoples' Health

Small island developing states, low-income countries, and socioeconomically marginalized populations are projected to experience the strongest climate change impacts and also are highly sensitive to them (Smith & Woodward, 2014; Wang & Horton, 2015). Indigenous populations are particularly at risk, given their close relationships with rapidly changing environments for livelihoods and well-being. This exacerbates existing disparities in socioeconomic, environmental, and health conditions, and it lies "at the heart of indigenous vulnerability to climate change" (Ford, 2012, p. 1262).

To explore how climate change affects the health of indigenous people through food systems, food security, and food safety (Figure 10.1), this chapter profiles research conducted in partnership with three indigenous populations: Inuit in Arctic Canada, Batwa from the Ugandan Impenetrable Forest, and Shawi in the Peruvian Amazon. Drawing from data captured in cohort surveys, focus group discussions, in-depth interviews, and participatory methods, we first characterize food-related climate change exposures, sensitivities, and adaptive capacities in each region. Then, based on these food-related climate change experiences, we examine the critical role of indigenous knowledge, equity, and research in health-related climate change adaptation and policy.

FOOD SYSTEMS

Food Systems include all activities related to the production, distribution, and consumption of food that affect nutrition and health.

FOOD SECURITY

Food Security exists when "all people, at all times, have physical and economic access to sufficient, safe and nutritious food to meet their dietary needs and food preferences for an active and healthy life."

FOOD SAFETY

Food Safety includes activities, processes, and policies encompassing the food chain, aimed at ensuring food is safe for consumption.

FIGURE 10.1 Description of food systems, food security, and food safety, as defined by the Food and Agriculture Organization of the United Nations (1996).

THE INDIGENOUS HEALTH ADAPTATION TO CLIMATE CHANGE PROGRAM: PARTNERS, APPROACH, AND METHODS
Project Partners

The Indigenous Health Adaptation to Climate Change (IHACC) program works with indigenous peoples to gather baseline data on climate-sensitive health outcomes, such as malnutrition, food security, mental health, maternal health, and other infectious diseases. Since 2010, the program has partnered with indigenous communities, organizations, and governments in three locations—Arctic Canada, the Impenetrable Forest in Uganda, and the Amazon in Peru (Figure 10.2)—to develop and implement climate–health research projects. These locations reflect the diverse cultures and livelihoods of remote indigenous populations globally, including within high-, medium-, and low-income countries. Furthermore, these locations reflect diverse biophysical environments, which facilitates the development of broad insights on current and future indigenous vulnerability and health adaptations in a changing climate. These regions also share similarities, including population size, socioeconomic–health inequality, remoteness, dependence on the biophysical environment, and nutritional transitions. The contrast and similarity of these locations underpin IHACC's aim to assess both the generalizability and the context dependence of food-related vulnerability to climate change.

A Participatory Approach: Community-Based Adaptation Research

Historically, researchers have conducted research on indigenous peoples—what some describe as researchers parachuting into communities, collecting data, leaving, and never returning (Castleden, Morgan, & Lamb, 2012; Ford et al., 2016). This practice, though less frequent, still persists and has resulted in skepticism and/or distrust about research in

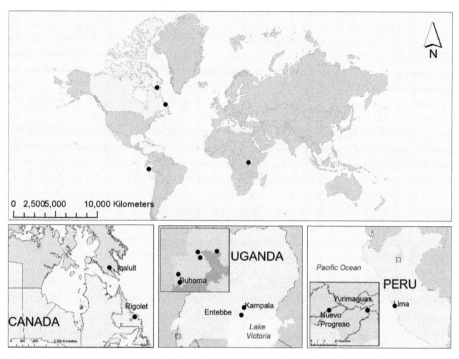

FIGURE 10.2 Maps of the partner communities in the Indigenous Health Adaptation to Climate Change Program (http://ihacc.ca).

many indigenous communities (Castleden et al., 2012). The IHACC program embraced a participatory, community-based research approach, conducting research *with, for,* and *led by* community members as full partners and research leads throughout the research process; drawing on their knowledge and experience; and respecting social norms and decision processes (Ford et al., 2016; Harper, Edge, Cunsolo Willox, & Rigolet Inuit Community Government, 2012). Accordingly, the research was premised on principles of interdisciplinary approaches, community participation, shared decision-making, systems thinking, sustainability, and social equity (Charron, 2012; Harper et al., 2012). Community participation in all phases of research allowed co-development of research design and implementation, which served to address local concerns and needs in a culturally appropriate manner.

Conceptual Framework: Climate Change Exposure, Sensitivity, and Adaptive Capacity

IHACC employs a conceptual model built on the intellectual traditions and approaches embodied in vulnerability science (Ford & Smit, 2004), including values of resiliency. The research team conceptualized climate-related health vulnerability as a function of exposure sensitivity and adaptive capacity (Ebi & Semenza, 2008; Ford, 2009). *Exposure sensitivity* reflects the susceptibility of food systems to conditions that represent risks, manifesting as constrained food access, availability, safety, and quality. Exposure sensitivity is dependent on both the characteristics of climatic conditions and the nature of the food system. *Adaptive capacity* refers to the ability of individuals, households, and institutions to adjust to food-related exposure sensitivities to moderate potential health impacts, take advantage of opportunities, and avoid activities that may increase vulnerability or reduce resilience. *Resilience* is a component of adaptive capacity (Smit & Wandel, 2006) that captures the capacity of social–ecological systems to cope with disturbance; respond in ways that maintain their essential function, identity, and structure; and maintain the capacity for adaptation, learning, and transformation (Stern et al., 2013).

Methods: Meta-Synthesis

The case studies presented in this chapter draw from meta-syntheses (Barnett-Page & Thomas, 2009) of databases created within the three partner regions to characterize the role of gender, social inequities, adaptation, and indigenous knowledge at the climate–health–food nexus. Databases included qualitative and quantitative data from more than 4,000 respondents to longitudinal open cohort questionnaires, more than 500 interviews, and more than 240 focus groups discussions. In addition, we worked with local partners to ensure that the synthesis accurately reflected the lived experience of indigenous peoples in each region; this involved six workshops, 43 semistructured interviews, 8 focus groups, and a series of interdisciplinary discussions across sectors, with governments, policymakers, health practitioners, and indigenous community leaders ($N = 192$ individuals).

INDIGENOUS FOOD SYSTEMS: DIVERSE HUNTER–GATHERER LIVELIHOODS

To understand how climate change affects food-related health outcomes for Inuit, Batwa, and Shawi, it is first necessary to understand their food systems and relationships with food. Though there are similarities, there are also important differences in their food systems and heterogeneity within and among groups.

Inuit Food Systems

Inuit are the original inhabitants of Arctic and sub-Arctic regions in Canada and are among the most remote populations in the world (Figure 10.3). Many of their cultural values and practices are embedded within and dependent on their close relationships with the environment, including the "land" (encompassing arctic tundra and sub-arctic boreal forests, water, ice, flora, and fauna) and the cold climate (Watt-Cloutier, 2015). Inuit have "ecocentric" world views, in which other people, animals, and the

FIGURE 10.3 Photos of Arctic Canada and sub-Arctic communities, food, and people.

Sources (left to right): David Barbour, Sherilee Harper, My Word Digital Media and Storytelling Lab, Sherilee Harper, Inez Shiwak, and Marilyn Baikie.

land are interrelated with and interconnected to the self (Kirmayer, Fletcher, & Watt, 2008). As such, access to and connection with the land—and the food the land provides—are central to Inuit livelihoods, health, and well-being (Cunsolo Willox et al., 2012).

Locally harvested country foods (e.g., fish, caribou, marine mammals, birds, geese, berries, mushrooms, eggs) are an important component of Inuit food systems (Council of Canadian Academies, 2014). The act of harvesting, preparing, sharing, and consuming country food is foundational to many Inuit cultural values and practices (Wenzel, 2013). Health benefits include high nutrition value and associations with mental wellness, cultural continuity, increased physical activity required to hunt and harvest, and decreased obesity (Kuhnlein & Receveur, 2007). Due to colonial legacies and changing climate regimes, Inuit food systems have begun to shift, and the consumption of retail foods has increased, despite the high cost, long shipping distance, and often poor nutritional content.

Batwa Food Systems

The Batwa traditionally inhabited the Bwindi Impenetrable Forest in Uganda. As indigenous "keepers of the forest," the Batwa held sacred hunting, healing, burial, naming, and rainmaking ceremonies in the forest, as well as song, dance, clan and totems, and spirituality. In 1991, however, the Batwa were forcibly evicted from the forest with no compensation to make way for a national park to promote tourism and conserve mountain gorillas. To this day, Batwa are no longer permitted to enter or access resources in their ancestral forest homeland.

This forced relocation fundamentally changed Batwa food systems: They had to transition from subsistence seminomadic hunter–gatherers to settled agrarian livelihoods (Figure 10.4). The Batwa traditional seminomadic lifestyle in the forest enabled relocation when food sources were scarce, and it required minimal storage of surplus of resources to facilitate mobility. Furthermore, similar to other hunter–gatherer societies, Batwa did not perceive time as linear but, rather, circular around the present. As such, the forced transition to a settled agrarian lifestyle required not only new agricultural capacity, knowledge, and skills development but also a significant shift in underlying world views to conform to Western notions of time, planning, and resource management. Within this transition, Batwa food systems have changed from a meat and root vegetable diet in the forest to a diet with little diversity (e.g., beans, maize flour) outside of the forest. The current diet is supported by bartering food in exchange for heavy manual labor, trading with other farms, or earning cash from low-paying heavy manual labor to purchase food at the market (Patterson et al., 2017).

FIGURE 10.4 Photos of Bwindi Impenetrable Forest, agricultural fields alongside the forest, food, and Batwa people in Uganda.

Sources (left to right): Sherilee Harper, James Ford, Will Vanderbilt, Will Vanderbilt, Sherilee Harper, and Sherilee Harper.

Shawi Food Systems

Shawi (previously known as Chayahuita) traditionally lived inland from riverbanks and more recently settled in remote indigenous communities predominately located along the riverbanks in the Loreto and San Martín regions in the Amazon in northeastern Peru (Figure 10.5). Spiritual cosmology, kinship, and reciprocity continue to play a key role in Shawi relationships with the environment. Shawi agro-fishing livelihoods are gendered: Both men and women participate in slash-and-burn agriculture, whereas only men participate in hunting and small-scale fishing (Odonne et al., 2009, 2013). Small-scale cultivation of some commercial crops (e.g., yucca, banana) provides the main source of income, and important food crops include sweet cassava, plantain, and yams.

CLIMATE CHANGE PROJECTIONS: DIVERSE CLIMATE CHANGE EXPOSURES

Arctic Canada, Uganda, and Peru have already experienced climate change, which will continue to accelerate by the end of the century (International Panel on Climate Change [IPCC], 2013). Though climate change will manifest differently in each region, the resultant impacts on the local environment, ecosystems, flora, and fauna have important implications for the food systems for Inuit, Batwa, and Shawi.

A Warmer, Ice-Free Arctic

The Arctic is experiencing the fastest and most dramatic warming in the world—more than twice the annual global average and more than four times the winter global average—with projected increases in annual mean surface temperature of 2°–8°C by 2081 (IPCC, 2013). In the near term, warming will be amplified, resulting in accelerated thinning of sea ice, reduction of sea ice coverage and extent, decreases in spring snow cover, decreases of northern high-latitude springtime snow cover, and less near-surface permafrost (IPCC, 2013). Longer term projections indicate an ice-free summer by 2040 (Holland, Finnis, & Serreze, 2006) or sooner (Wang & Overland, 2012) and an ice-free Arctic by 2100 (IPCC, 2013).

These changes will affect vegetation, mammals, fish, and birds; however, impacts will vary by location due to differences in social systems, biophysical characteristics, and associated drivers of change (IPCC, 2014). Approximately one-third of the pan-Arctic has already greened with tall shrubs and grasses in many locales, and approximately 4% has browned as the tree line continues to move northward in most areas (Xu et al., 2013). Elmendorf and colleagues (2012) project a significant decrease in mosses and lichens coverage and overall species diversity, leading to an estimated 50% of tundra being displaced by forest by 2100 (Callaghan et al., 2005). Moreover, marine mammals (Laidre et al., 2008), fish and shellfish (Poloczanska et al., 2013), and caribou populations are highly vulnerable to climate change (Vors & Boyce, 2009).

FIGURE 10.5 Photos of the Amazonian landscape, river, food, and Shawi in Peru.

Sources (left to right): Alejandra Busalleu, Mya Sherman, Mya Sherman, Mya Sherman, Irene Hofmeijer, and Mya Sherman.

A Warmer, Drier Climate in Uganda

Africa is expected to experience greater warming than the global annual mean in all seasons, as well as increased floods, droughts, heat waves, and high-impact rainfall events (IPCC, 2013). Uganda has experienced significant seasonal warming since 1960 (Funk, Michaelsen, & Marshall, 2012), which is expected to increase significantly by 2100 (IPCC, 2014). Rainfall is also projected to significantly decrease during the rainy season in the near term; longer term precipitation projections are less clear but indicate a continuation of the current drying trend (Funk et al., 2008; Williams & Funk, 2011).

Warming temperatures and precipitation changes will reduce already stressed water availability in Africa (IPCC, 2014). Such impacts will negatively affect cereal crop, high-value perennial crop, and livestock productivity (IPCC, 2014). For instance, in Uganda there is a projected reduction in coffee (Jaramillo et al., 2011), maize (Thornton, Jones, Alagarswamy, & Andresen, 2009), bean, potato, and cassava production (Jarvis, Ramirez-Villegas, Campo, & Navarro-Racines, 2012). Overall, sub-Saharan Africa food insecurity is anticipated to more than double from 24% to 50%–75% by 2080; however, the actual magnitude and impact of food insecurity and malnutrition will largely depend on socioeconomic developments (Schmidhuber & Tubiello, 2007).

A Wetter Peruvian Amazon

The climate in the Amazon is projected to experience an increase of 2°C in annual mean surface temperature by 2040 and a 4°C increase by 2070 (Marengo et al., 2012). Future rainfall will vary substantially by region, with eastern Amazon becoming much drier (Cook, Zeng, & Yoon, 2012; Marengo et al., 2012) and western Amazon substantially wetter (Cook et al., 2012).

In Peru, an unprecedented intensification of weather and hydrological patterns has been documented since 2003, including extreme weather events and patterns that do not align with El Niño–La Niña cycles (Santa Cruz, Mujica, Álvarez, & Leslie, 2013). This has generated concern about the high risk of flooding and resultant damage in the region (Marengo, Jones, Alves, & Valverde, 2009), with projections indicating that the flooding area in the Peruvian Amazon basin will increase by one-third (Langerwisch et al., 2013), and annual discharge will increase by 20%–100% in the Requena basin (Lavado Casimiro, Labat, Guyot, & Ardoin-Bardin, 2011). Despite the increased rainfall, soil moisture is projected to decrease in the region, reflecting warmer temperatures leading to increased evapotranspiration and heavy rainfall not penetrating soil due to run-off (Lavado Casimiro et al., 2011). Such examples of climate change have consequences for agro-fishing livelihoods, including impacts on catfish migration and spawning (Zulkafli et al., 2016), and swamp–forest ecology.

CLIMATE–FOOD–HEALTH NEXUS: SENSITIVITIES

Though indigenous food systems and climate change exposures differ in each region, the fundamental pathways through which climate change will affect food-related health outcomes have similarities. Through indigenous voices, lived experience, and wisdom, this section highlights how social, cultural, and economic conditions influence climate change impacts on food and health systems of the Inuit, Batwa, and Shawi.

Food Systems in Transition

The three IHACC partner regions are experiencing food system shifts linked to social, economic, and political transitions, which climate change will exacerbate. In all regions, the acts of harvesting, preparing, sharing, and consuming traditional foods are foundational to cultural values (Berrang-Ford et al., 2012; Hofmeijer et al., 2013; Wenzel, 2013). As such, Inuit, Batwa, and Shawi have expressed concern regarding their ability to adapt their food systems to climate variability (Berrang-Ford et al., 2012; Ford, 2009; Hofmeijer et al., 2013). An Inuit woman described this amplification as a "ripple effect," explaining (Harper et al., 2015),

> I guess it's all the pieces, like dominoes, all touches each other. I mean everything you do, [our] Inuit way of life and our way of thinking is all intertwined and interconnected [to the environment]. So, something as significant as changes in the temperature, and in snow and rain and that kind of thing, it's all going to have a ripple effect.

One Inuit youth described concern over the rate of changes, and another expressed concern for her elderly father (Petrasek MacDonald et al., 2013, p. 6):

> It kind of worries me how fast it is going to happen. Are my kids going to be able to go off to the cabin in the wintertime on skidoo? . . . It seems that might not happen when I get old. It seems like it is happening so fast.
>
> I just keeps thinking, man, what did he think about these changes? He must feel like he just got picked about at one place and put right and somewhere like on a different planet.

Similar comments were made by Shawi when discussing climate change-related challenges to their agro-fishing food systems (Hofmeijer et al., 2013). Two Shawi explained that

Now any crop dries. Before we planted the beans with the bananas so as to protect them, but that's useless now, they dry up anyways.

The corn dries up rapidly [nowadays]. Before we know when it was its season [to be harvested], now we have to look at it all the time to make sure the plants don't die.

For Batwa, the difficulties in transitioning to an agrarian livelihood are being compounded by climate change. One Batwa described the transition as necessary for their survival as a people, and another described climate-related challenges with this transition:

Today we've learned digging and growing crops to get food compared to when we were in the forest. . . . This tells that in future and after adopting farming we may not lack food for our families. Because we are trying to adapt to the new life. (Patterson et al., 2017, p. 9)

Our crops are no longer growing very well. We used to get good harvests but now they don't grow so well because of the sunshine. We get more sunshine than there was before and we don't get enough food. (Donnelly, 2016).

Research is only beginning to examine how local adaptations might offset the impacts of long-term change on food systems, with many projections indicating severe challenges ahead (IPCC, 2014).

Existing Food Insecurity Challenges

Food insecurity is a fundamental challenge that all three regions are facing, increasing sensitivity and constraining adaptive capacity to deal with climate change. Inuit experience the highest rates in Canada; in Nunavut, an Inuit territory, the food insecurity prevalence rate is nearly 70%—the highest rate for any indigenous population residing in a high-income country (Egeland, 2011). Batwa and Shawi households are experiencing the highest levels of food insecurity globally—a staggering rate of greater than 95% (Patterson et al., 2017; Zavaleta et al., 2017).

Challenges to food security are complex. They include socioeconomic factors, such as unemployment, low income, increasing cost of hunting, environmental dispossession, and cost of retail foods (Ford, 2012). Environmental changes, such as animal migration patterns, food animal quality and quantity, and new travel hazards, also pose challenges to food security. Finally, sociocultural changes—reduced sharing of food, decreased number of active hunters, and decreased transfer of traditional hunting knowledge—contribute to food insecurity. These factors affect food quality, access, and availability. Moreover, they are highly sensitive to climatic conditions, as is evident in all three regions.

Indigenous Knowledge and Food Systems

Founded on generations of environmental observations and reciprocal relationships with the environment, indigenous knowledge and practices are critical for adaptation to climate change impacts on food systems and health (Savo et al., 2016). Global social, economic, and political transformations raise concern regarding the "erosion" of indigenous knowledge (Ford, 2012), which resonated for Inuit, Batwa, and Shawi in the face of climate change. For instance, the traditional practice of food sharing is common in all three regions, which serves as an important adaptation (Berrang-Ford et al., 2012; Ford, 2009; Hofmeijer et al., 2013). Two Shawi explained this practice and how it is increasingly challenging in light of climate change (Zavaleta, 2018):

> When we find a big animal, we share with our brother and his family, this is our custom. The same when he finds a big amount of fish; he shares with us. That is how we Shawi eat.
>
> When my son finds something to eat in the forest, either fish or meat, he invites me to eat, or sends a little piece for me, but sometimes there is not enough for me.

In Arctic Canada, indigenous knowledge plays vital roles in navigating the environment, as well as knowing how to select, hunt, harvest, and prepare foods. An Inuit hunter described how indigenous knowledge is dynamic and will change with climate change (Harper et al., 2015):

> It's different because when you're growing up, you're taught where to go and where not to go 'cause there's bad parts of the ice. Ah, it seems like today or this past winter, you had [bad] places that are existing where they shouldn't be, where they weren't before.

As such, Inuit described that traditional knowledge is still passed on; however, how it is applied and adapted becomes a question. Another Inuit explained that "it's almost always the same message . . . the general part of it is still there, you just have to apply it differently now 'cause things have changed" (Harper et al., 2015).

Health Impacts of Climate Change

Climate change impacts on indigenous food systems have important implications for human health. Ranging from direct to indirect, such impacts have consequences for physical, emotional, mental, and spiritual health (Figure 10.6). Here, through the lived experience of Inuit, Batwa, and Shawi, we describe how climate change has already affected indigenous food-related health.

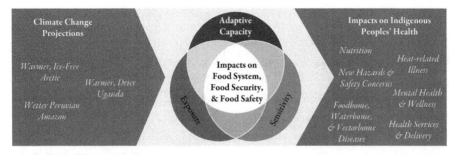

FIGURE 10.6 Climate change will impact food-related indigenous health outcomes via food system exposure, sensitivity, and adaptive capacity.

Nutrition

Climate change adds additional stress on existing nutritional challenges experienced in some indigenous households. For instance, 58% of Batwa children aged younger than 5 years suffer from extreme malnutrition (Lewnard et al., 2014; Patterson et al., 2017), 65% from anemia (65%), and 39% from stunting (Zavaleta et al., 2017). A Shawi woman explained food security challenges in the context of current climate and environmental changes (Zavaleta et al., 2017, p. 77): "There are not animals as there were in the past. What are we going to do? There is nothing."

For Inuit, climate change disrupts access to foods that are locally hunted, trapped, and gathered (Ford, 2009). These traditional foods are highly nutritious (Egeland, Johnson-Down, Cao, Sheikh, & Weiler, 2011) and healthier than retail food. An Inuit Elder explained (Harper et al., 2015),

> Last year we had no blueberries. And I mean blueberries are almost a staple. They're so good for you and they're so high in the antioxidants. There were none. And there is none because it got really hot in the spring and the berry, the bushes fried up. But to have no blueberries, it's unheard of. You know, to have that happen [long pause].

Going further, another Inuit woman explained the low nutritional value of retail food (Harper et al., 2015):

> The conditions were horrible. People didn't get what they normally get for caribou and then you rely on store [retail] food junk, because what other option do you have when you live in a remote fly-in only community? And, the foods sources that you usually get to, you can't reach. There is not enough snow, there is not enough ice. It's alarming that we are just seeing the beginning of climate change. . . . And if the weather is down [bad] for five weeks, how do you get in and out of your community to access services? How do you get food in there? . . . [The grocery store's] stock was down to bare bones because there was no way to get food in.

Nutrition is one of the most common health implications of climate change impacts on food systems. When the quantity, diversity, quality, and accessibility of food are affected, malnutrition and hunger are natural results, as described by Inuit, Batwa, and Shawi.

Unintended Injury

Climate change is altering environments to the point that they pose increased risk of injury on land and water (Clark et al., 2016). For Shawi, extreme hydrological events have affected hunting, fishing, and small-scale agriculture; increased risk of injury from flooding, erosion, and landslides; and led to higher water levels and flow rates (Hofmeijer et al., 2013; Zavaleta et al., 2017).

For Inuit, climate change has affected land and ice safety, and hunters have reported increased and new hazards on land, linked to reduced strength, duration, and extent of sea ice, as well as unpredictable weather and ice conditions (Durkalec, 2012). For instance, Inuit hunters reported that "you really don't know what is safe and what isn't out there [anymore]" and consequently "the ice is not predictable, it is not stable, people don't trust it" (Harper et al., 2015). But because hunting, trapping, and fishing are vital to Inuit culture and food security, Inuit explained that they are "jeopardizing their lives going out on unstable elements" and "people going through the ice" (Harper et al., 2015). These unstable and unpredictable conditions can result in negative health outcomes such as increased self-reported accidents, hypothermia, and frostbite (Harper et al., 2015).

Mental Health and Wellness

Mental health consequences of climate change range from extreme anxiety reactions (e.g., post-traumatic stress disorder) to symptoms of chronic loss and failure (e.g., depression and generalized anxiety) (Cunsolo & Ellis, 2018). Landscapes altered or degraded by climate change have important mental health implications for indigenous populations, including depression, distress, anger, anxiety, fear, and loss of solace or a sense of belonging (Cunsolo & Ellis, 2018).

Worried about their family members hunting in unstable conditions or fishing on thin ice, more Inuit women report such mental health implications than men (Harper et al., 2015). For instance, an Inuit woman explained,

Every conversation [this winter] was around the ice was thin, it was unsafe to go, then they added some worry to that because people were still craving to get out on their skidoos on thin ice, with people going through the ice, and then there were family members that was off [hunting] and didn't come back. So, a lot of extra anxiety and disappointment, and unfulfilled needs. . . . It [the weather] was definitely different than it was expected here normally.

Another Inuit woman explained,

> Horrible, horrible, horrible. So, that is my first thought [about climate change] . . . already look at what has happened with people losing that sense of identify and pride and people feel proud of bringing that fish home and that caribou home and they share it with people. So, losing the ability to provide that, and give that satisfaction from giving and sharing and feeding your family—it is going to continue to erode.

Though less studied in Uganda and Peru, Batwa and Shawi have described similar mental health implications associated with climate change. For instance, one Shawi reported that "for us, going to the forest is like for non-Shawi people going to the market to obtain food. . . . We are worried about what we will eat. Where will we find food?" (Patterson et al., 2017, p. 6). A Batwa community member explained, "We get discouraged that we grow crops and they don't yield . . . even you would get discouraged. If nothing grew, you would give up too" (Patterson et al., 2017, p. 8).

Heat-Related Illness

Heat-related illness is an unequivocal health consequence of climate change (Huang et al., 2011). Individuals who work outdoors are the most vulnerable to heat-related health consequences of climate change. When air temperatures exceed 35°C, the body "can only maintain normal core body temperature by the heat-reducing mechanism of sweat evaporation," which "in certain climatic conditions, even if very light clothing is worn, sweat evaporation is not sufficient to maintain core body temperature and a health-threatening increase in core body temperature will occur" (Kjellstrom, 2009, p. 1).

In Uganda, Batwa participate in a variety of heavy agricultural labor, and, similar to other agricultural laborers in low-income tropical countries (Kjellstrom, 2009), are at heightened risk of heat-related illness. A Batwa participant explained that health consequences of heat extend beyond heat stroke and mortality: "Digging in hot temperatures makes dust come into our nose, and then flu comes" (Berrang-Ford et al., 2012, p. 1072).

In Arctic Canada, Inuit have also reported increased heat-related illness while out on the land hunting and fishing, particularly for elders and seniors, that has been attributed to climate change. For instance, three Inuit elders explained (Furgal, Martin, & Gosselin, 2002, p. 271),

> This past summer while we were up at OKak [a popular fishing location out on the land] we had one full week, if not more, of hot hot weather. I don't ever remember it being that hot . . . it was shocking.

I almost suffocated because of the heat, I had to keep splashing myself with water and in the afternoon, I couldn't stay on land because it was so hot. I had to stay in the water to stay cool . . . my breathing was even shallow.

Foodborne Diseases

Many foodborne diseases, such as diarrheal disease, have transmission pathways (e.g., water, food, exposure to animals) that are climate sensitive. Seasonal trends in diarrheal disease occur globally, which suggests that weather factors play a role in transmission. In Arctic Canada, for instance, cases of campylobacteriosis and salmonellosis specifically occur more frequently in the late summer and early fall (Pardhan-Ali et al., 2012), and diarrhea-related clinic visits occur more frequently in summer and fall months (Harper et al., 2011).

Though climate-related foodborne disease is a concern for Batwa (Berrang-Ford et al., 2012; Clark et al., 2015) and Shawi (Hofmeijer et al., 2013), more research has been conducted in Arctic Canada. Inuit in Canada have the highest rates of self-reported enteric illness in the world among indigenous peoples, with unique retail and country food risk factors (Harper et al., 2016). Shipping retail food to Northern remote communities poses additional challenges, including the increased distance the food must travel, perishability, appropriate handling, and maintaining proper temperature. For country foods, warming temperatures enable infectious agents and animal hosts to survive winter temperatures, potentially resulting in the increased risk of zoonotic diseases (Parkinson & Butler, 2005).

CRITICAL COMPONENTS OF INDIGENOUS CLIMATE–FOOD–HEALTH ADAPTATION

Through the IHACC research program, we identified and characterized common underlying food-related climate change exposures and sensitivities pathways for Inuit, Batwa, and Shawi. In grappling with these current climate–food–health challenges, Inuit, Batwa, and Shawi have already displayed considerable adaptive capacity (Berrang-Ford et al., 2012; Ford, 2009; Hofmeijer et al., 2013). Though research documenting, monitoring, and characterizing this adaptive capacity and adaptation efforts is growing, it is still generally underrepresented in indigenous contexts (Berrang-Ford, Ford, & Paterson, 2011; Ford & Pearce, 2010). What is clear, based on the experiences shared in this chapter, is that indigenous knowledge, values, and practices must be at the heart of successful health-related climate change policy interventions (Ford et al., 2014). Understanding climate change impacts on Inuit, Batwa, and Shawi food systems through indigenous voices, lived experience, and wisdom is central to adaptation, as policy interventions must (Ford et al., 2010)

(i) support the teaching and transmission of environmental knowledge and land skills, (ii) enhance and review emergency management capability, (iii) ensure the flexibility of resource management regimes, (iv) provide economic support to facilitate adaptation for groups with limited household income, (v) increase research effort to identify short and long term risk factors and adaptive response options, (vi) protect key infrastructure, and (vii) promote awareness of climate change impacts and adaptation among policy makers. (p. 177)

CONCLUSION

This chapter synthesizes data on food-related health impacts of climate change in Arctic Canada, Uganda, and Peru. By characterizing climate change exposures, food system sensitivities, potential impacts on human health, and adaptive capacity, we hope to offer important information for public health planning, prioritization, and programming when working with and for indigenous populations. Indeed, government, nongovernmental organizations, and health care providers will need to consider climate change in all food-related planning, policy, and program development (Bradbear & Friel, 2013). More generally, programming at the nexus of food and health that does not consider indigenous, cultural, and climate change contexts risks inefficiency and increases inequities in indigenous health.

REFERENCES

Barnett-Page, E., & Thomas, J. (2009). Methods for the synthesis of qualitative research: A critical review. *BMC Medical Research Methodology, 9*, 59.

Berrang-Ford, L., Dingle, K., Ford, J. D., Lee., C., Lwasa, S., Namanya, D. B., . . . Edge, V. (2012). Vulnerability of indigenous health to climate change: A case study of Uganda's Batwa pygmies. *Social Science and Medicine, 75*(6), 1067–1077.

Berrang-Ford, L., Ford, J. D., & Paterson, J. (2011). Are we adapting to climate change? *Global Environmental Change, 21*, 25–33.

Bradbear, C., & Friel, S. (2013). Integrating climate change, food prices and population health. *Food Policy, 43*, 56–66.

Callaghan, T., Björn, L. O., Chapin, F. S., Chernov, Y., Christensen, T. R., Huntley, B., . . . Shaver, G. (2005). Arctic tundra and polar desert ecosystems. In C. Symon, L. Arris, & B. Heal (Eds.), *Arctic climate impact assessment* (pp. 243–352). Cambridge, UK: Cambridge University Press.

Castleden, H., Morgan, V. S., & Lamb, C. (2012). "I spent the first year drinking tea": Exploring Canadian university researchers' perspectives on community-based participatory research involving indigenous peoples. *The Canadian Geographer, 56*(2), 160–179.

Chan, M. (2015, December 8). WHO Director-General addresses event on climate change and health [Speech].

Charron, D. F. (2012). *Ecohealth research in practice: Innovative applications of an ecosystem approach to health*. Ottawa, Ontario, Canada: Springer.

Clark, D. G., Ford, J. D., Berrang-Ford, L., Pearce, T., Kowal, S., & Gough, W. A. (2016). The role of environmental factors in search and rescue incidents in Nunavut, Canada. *Public Health, 137,* 44–49.

Clark, S., Berrang-Ford, L., Lwasa, S., Namanya, D. B., Edge, V. L., IHACC Research Team, & Harper, S. (2015). The burden and determinants of self-reported acute gastrointestinal illness in an indigenous Batwa pygmy population in southwestern Uganda. *Epidemiology & Infection, 143*(11), 2287–2298.

Cook, B., Zeng, N., & Yoon, J.-H. (2012). Will Amazonia dry out? Magnitude and causes of change from IPCC climate model projections. *Earth Interactions, 16,* 1–27.

Council of Canadian Academies. (2014). *Aboriginal food security in Northern Canada: An assessment of the state of knowledge.* Expert Panel on the State of Knowledge of Food Security in Northern Canada. Retrieved from https://foodsecurecanada.org/resources-news/resources-research/report-northern-aboriginal-food-insecurity

Cunsolo, A., & Ellis, N. (2018). Towards a science of ecological grief and loss: New insights in climate change research. *Natural Climate Change,* in press.

Cunsolo Willox, A., Harper, S. L., Ford, J. D., Landman, K., Houle, K., Edge, V. L., & Rigolet Inuit Community Government. (2012). "From this place and of this place": Climate change, sense of place, and health in Nunatsiavut, Canada. *Social Science Medicine, 75*(3), 538–547.

Donnelly, B. (2016). *Indigenous health, livestock, and climate change adaptation in Kanungu District, Uganda* (PhD dissertation). Department of Geography, McGill University, Montreal, Quebec, Canada.

Durkalec, A. (2012). *Understanding the role of environment for Indigenous health: A case study of sea ice as a place of health and risk in the Inuit community of Nain, Nunatsiavut* (MA dissertation). Trent University, Peterborough, Ontario, Canada.

Ebi, K. L., & Semenza, J. C. (2008). Community-based adaptation to the health impacts of climate change. *American Journal of Preventive Medicine, 35*(5), 501–507.

Egeland, G. M. (2011). IPY Inuit Health Survey speaks to need to address inadequate housing, food insecurity and nutrition transition. *International Journal of Circumpolar Health, 70,* 444–446.

Egeland, G. M., Johnson-Down, L., Cao, Z. R., Sheikh, N., & Weiler, H. (2011). Food insecurity and nutrition transition combine to affect nutrient intakes in Canadian arctic communities. *Nutrition, 141*(9), 1746–1753.

Elmendorf, S. C., Henry, G. H. R., Hollister, R. D., Bjork, R. G., Bjorkman, A. D., Callaghan, T. V., . . . Wookey, P. A. (2012). Global assessment of experimental climate warming on tundra vegetation: Heterogeneity over space and time. *Ecology Letters, 15*(2), 164–175.

Fischer, G., Shah, M., Tubiello, F., & van Velhuizen, H. (2005). Socio-economic and climate change impacts on agriculture: An integrated assessment, 1990–2080. *Philosophical Transactions of the Royal Society B, 360,* 2067–2083.

Food and Agriculture Organization of the United Nations. (1996). *Rome declaration on world food security and world food summit plan of action.* Retrieved from http://www.fao.org/docrep/003/w3613e/w3613e00.htm

Ford, J. (2012). Indigenous health and climate change. *American Journal of Public Health, 102,* 1260–1266.

Ford, J., Willox Cunsolo, A., Chatwood, S., Furgal, C., Harper, S., Mauro, I., & Pierce, T. (2014). Adapting to the effects of climate change on Inuit health. *American Journal of Public Health, 104,* 9–17.

Ford, J. D. (2009). Vulnerability of Inuit food systems to food insecurity as a consequence of climate change: A case study from Igloolik, Nunavut. *Regional Environmental Change, 9*, 83–100.

Ford, J. D., & Pearce, T. (2010). What we know, do not know, and need to know about climate change vulnerability in the western Canadian Arctic: A systematic literature review. *Environmental Research Letters, 5*, 14008.

Ford, J. D., Pearce, T., Duerden, F., Furgal, C., & Smit, B. (2010). Climate change policy responses for Canada's Inuit population: The importance of and opportunities for adaptation. *Global Environmental Change, 20*(1), 177–191.

Ford, J. D., & Smit, B. (2004). A framework for assessing the vulnerability of communities in the Canadian Arctic to risks associated with climate change. *Arctic, 57*, 389–400.

Ford, J. D., Stephenson, E., Cunsolo Willox, A., Edge, V. L., Farahbakhsh, K., Furgal, C., . . . Sherman, M. (2016). Community-based adaptation research in the Canadian Arctic. *Wiley Interdisciplinary Review of Climate Change, 7*, 175–191.

Funk, C., Dettinger, M. D., Michaelsen, J. C., Verdin, J. P., Brown, M. E., Barlow, M., & Hoell, A. (2008). Warming of the Indian Ocean threatens eastern and southern African food security but could be mitigated by agricultural development. *Proceedings of the National Academy of Sciences of the USA, 105*(32), 11081–11086.

Funk, C., Michaelsen, J., & Marshall, M. T. (2012). Mapping recent decadal climate variations in precipitation and temperature across Eastern Africa and the Sahel. In B. D. Wardlow, M. C. Anderson, & J. P. Verdin (Eds.), *Remote sensing drought: Innovative monitoring approaches* (pp. 331–357). Boca Raton, FL: CRC Press.

Furgal, C., Martin, D., & Gosselin, P. (2002). Climate change and health in Nunavik and Labrador: Lessons from Inuit knowledge. In I. Krupnik & D. Jolly (Eds.), *The earth is faster now* (pp. 266–300). Washington, DC: Arctic Research Consortium of the United States.

Harper, S. L., Edge, V. L., Cunsolo Willox, A., & Rigolet Inuit Community Government. (2012). "Changing climate, changing health, changing stories" profile: Using an ecohealth approach to explore impacts of climate change on Inuit health. *Ecohealth, 9*(1), 89–101.

Harper, S. L., Edge, V. L., Ford, J., Cunsolo Willox, A., Wood, M, IHACC Research Team, . . . McEwen, S. A. (2015). Climate-sensitive health priorities in Nunatsiavut, Canada. *BMC Public Health, 15*, 605.

Harper, S. L., Edge, V. L., Ford, J., Thomas, M. K., Pearl, D. L., Shirley, J, . . . McEwen, S. A. (2016). Acute gastrointestinal illness in two Inuit communities: Burden of illness in Rigolet and Iqaluit, Canada. *Epidemiology & Infection, 143*(14), 3048–3063.

Harper, S., Edge, V. L., Schuster-Wallace, C. J., Berke, O., & McEwen, S. A. (2011). Weather, water quality and infectious gastrointestinal illness in two Inuit communities in Nunatsiavut, Canada: Potential implications for climate change. *Ecohealth, 8*, 93–108.

Hofmeijer, I., Ford, J. D., Berrang-Ford, L., Zavaleta, C., Carcamo, E., Llanos, E., . . . Namanya, D. (2013). Community vulnerability to the health effects of climate change among indigenous populations in the Peruvian Amazon: A case study from Panaillo and Nuevo Progreso. *Mitigation and Adaptation Strategies for Global Change, 18*(7), 957–978.

Holland, M., Finnis, J., & Serreze, M. (2006). Simulated Arctic Ocean freshwater budgets in the twentieth and twenty-first centuries. *Journal of Climate, 19*, 6221–6242.

Huang, C., Barnett, A. G., Wang, X., Vaneckova, P., FitzGerald, G., & Tong, S. (2011). Projecting future heat-related mortality under climate change scenarios: A systematic review. *Environmental Health Perspective, 119*(2),1681–1690.

International Panel on Climate Change. (2013). *Climate Change 2013: The Physical Science Basis.* Contribution of Working Group I to the Fifth Assessment Report of the Intergovernmental Panel on Climate Change. Retrieved from http://www.ipcc.ch/report/ar5/wg1

International Panel on Climate Change. (2014). *Climate Change 2014: Impacts, adaptation, and vulnerability. Part A: Global and sectoral aspects.* Contribution of Working Group II to the Fifth Assessment Report of the Intergovernmental Panel on Climate Change. doi:10.1017/CBO9781107415324.004

Jaramillo, J., Muchugu, E., Vega, F. E., Davis, A., Borgemeister, C., & Chabi-Olaye, A. (2011). Some like it hot: The influence and implications of climate change on coffee berry borer (*Hypothenemus hampei*) and coffee production in East Africa. *PLoS One, 6,* 24528.

Jarvis, A., Ramirez-Villegas, J., Campo, B. V. H., & Navarro-Racines, C. (2012). Is cassava the answer to African climate change adaptation? *Tropical Plant Biology, 5*(1), 9–29.

Jiménez Cisneros, B. E., & Oki, T. (2014). *Freshwater resources.* International Panel on Climate Change. Retrieved from https://www.ipcc.ch/pdf/assessment-report/ar5/wg2/WGIIAR5-Chap3_FINAL.pdf

Kirmayer, L. J., Fletcher, C., & Watt, R. (2008). Locating the ecocentric self: Inuit concepts of mental health and illness. In L. J. Kirmayer & G. G. Valaskakis (Eds.), *Healing traditions: Mental health of Aboriginal Peoples in Canada* (pp. 289–314). Vancouver, British Columbia, Canada: UBC Press.

Kjellstrom, T. (2009). Climate change, direct heat exposure, health and well-being in low and middle-income countries. *Global Health Action, 2,* 1–2.

Kuhnlein, H. V., & Receveur, O. (2007). Local cultural animal food contributes high levels of nutrients for Arctic Canadian Indigenous adults and children. *Nutrition, 137,* 1110–1114.

Laidre, K. L., Stirling, I., Lowry, L. F., Wiig, O., Heide-Jorgensen, M. P., & Ferguson, S. H. (2008). Quantifying the sensitivity of Arctic marine mammals to climate-induced habitat change. *Ecological Applications, 18,* 97–125.

Langerwisch, F., Rost, S., Gerten, D., Poulter, B., Rammig, A., & Cramer, W. (2013). Potential effects of climate change on inundation patterns in the Amazon basin. *Hydrology Earth Systems Sciences, 17,* 2247–2262.

Lavado Casimiro, W. S., Labat, D., Guyot, J. L., & Ardoin-Bardin, S. (2011). Assessment of climate change impacts on the hydrology of the Peruvian Amazon–Andes basin. *Hydrology Process, 25,* 3721–3734.

Lewnard, J., Berrang-Ford, L., Lwasa, S., Namanya, D. B., Patterson, K. A., Donnelly, B., Kulkarni, M. A., . . . IHAAC Research Team. (2014). Relative undernourishment and food insecurity associations with *Plasmodium falciparum* among Batwa pygmies in Uganda: Evidence from a cross-sectional survey. *American Journal of Tropical Medicine and Hygiene, 91*(1), 39–49.

Maharjan, K. L., & Joshi, N. P. (2013). *Climate change, agriculture and rural livelihoods in developing countries.* New York, NY: Springer.

Marengo, J. A., Chan, S., Gillian, C., Alves, L. M., Pesquero, J. F., Soares, W. R., . . . Tavares, P. (2012). Development of regional future climate change scenarios in South America using the Eta CPTEC/HadCM3 climate change projections: Climatology and regional analyses for the Amazon, Sao Francisco and the Parana River basins. *Climate Dynamics, 38*(9–10), 1829–1848.

Marengo, J. A., Jones, R., Alves, L. M., & Valverde, M. C. (2009). Future change of temperature and precipitation extremes in South America as derived from the PRECIS regional climate modeling system. *International Journal of Climatology, 29,* 2241–2255.

McMichael, A. J. (2013). Impediments to comprehensive research on climate change and health. *International Journal of Environmental Research and Public Health, 10*, 6096–6105.

McMichael, A. J., & Dear, K. B. G. (2010). Climate change: Heat, health, and longer horizons. *Proceedings of the National Academy of Sciences of the USA, 107*(21), 9483–9484.

McMichael, C., Barnett, J., & McMichael, A. J. (2012). An ill wind? Climate change, migration, and health. *Environmental Health Perspective, 120*, 646–654.

Odonne, G., Bourdy, G., Castillo, D., Estevez, Y., Lancha-Tangoa, A., Alban-Castillo, J., . . . Sauvain, M. (2009). Ta'ta', Huayani: Perception of leishmaniasis and evaluation of medicinal plants used by the Chayahuita in Peru: Part II. *Ethnopharmacology, 126*(1), 149–158.

Odonne, G., Valadeau, C., Alban-Castillo, J., Stein, D., Sauvain, M., & Bourdy, G. (2013). Medical ethnobotany of the Chayahuita of the Paranapura basin (Peruvian Amazon). *Ethnopharmacology, 146*(1), 127–153.

Oppenheimer, M., Campos, M., & Warren, R. (2014). *Emergent risks and key vulnerabilities.* International Panel on Climate Change. Retrieved from https://www.ipcc.ch/pdf/assessment-report/ar5/wg2/WGIIAR5-Chap19_FINAL.pdf

Pardhan-Ali, A., Wilson, J., Edge, V. L., Furgal, C., Reid-Smith, R., Santos, M., & McEwen, S. A. (2012). A descriptive analysis of notifiable gastrointestinal illness in the Northwest Territories, Canada, 1991–2008. *BMJ Open, 2*(4), 1–11.

Parkinson, A. J., & Butler, J. C. (2005). Potential impacts of climate change on infectious diseases in the Arctic. *International Journal of Circumpolar Health, 64*, 478–486.

Patterson, K., Berrang-Ford, L., Lwasa, S., Namanya, D. B., Ford, J., Twebaze, F., . . . Harper, S. L. (2017). Seasonal variation of food security among the Batwa of Kanungu, Uganda. *Public Health Nutrition, 20*(1), 1–11.

Petrasek MacDonald, J., Harper, S. L., Cunsolo Willox, A., Edge, V. L., & Rigolet Inuit Community Government. (2013). A necessary voice: Climate change and lived experiences of youth in Rigolet, Nunatsiavut, Canada. *Global Environmental Change, 23*(1), 360–371.

Poloczanska, E. S., Brown, C. J., Sydeman, W. J., Kiessling W., Schoeman, D. S., Moore, P. J., . . . Richardson, A. J. (2013). Global imprint of climate change on marine life. *Nature Climate Change, 3*, 919–925.

Porter, J. R., & Xie, L. (2014). *Food security and food production systems.* International Panel on Climate Change. Retrieved from https://ipcc.ch/pdf/assessment-report/ar5/wg2/WGIIAR5-Chap7_FINAL.pdf

Rosenzweig, C., Elliott, J., Deryng, D., Ruane, A. C., Muller, A. A., Boote, K. J., . . . Jones, J. W. (2014). Assessing agricultural risks of climate change in the 21st century in a global gridded crop model intercomparison. *Proceedings of the National Academy of Sciences of the USA, 111*(9), 3268–3273.

Santa Cruz, F., Mujica, M., Álvarez, J., & Leslie, J. (2013). *Informe sobre Desarrollo Humano Perú 2013.* Cambio climático y territorio, Desafíos y respuestas para un futuro sostenible, Lima, Peru.

Savo, V., Lepofsky, D., Benner, J. P., Kohfeld, K. E., Bailey, J., & Lertzman, K. (2016). Observations of climate change among subsistence-oriented communities around the world. *Nature Climate Change, 6*, 462–473.

Schmidhuber, J., & Tubiello, F. N. (2007). Global food security under climate change. *Proceedings of the National Academy of Sciences of the USA, 104*, 19703–19708.

Smit, B., & Wandel, J. (2006). Adaptation, adaptive capacity and vulnerability. *Global Environmental Change, 16*, 282–292.

Smith, K. R., & Woodward, A. (2014). *Human health: Impacts, adaptation, and co-benefits.* International Panel on Climate Change. Retrieved from https://www.ipcc.ch/pdf/assessment-report/ar5/wg2/WGIIAR5-Chap11_FINAL.pdf

Springmann, M., Mason-D'Croz, D., Robinson, S., Garnett, T., Godfray, H. C. J., Gollin, D., ... Scarborough, P. (2016). Global and regional health effects of future food production under climate change: A modelling study. *Lancet, 387*(10031), 1937–1946.

Stern, P. C., Ebi, K. L., Leichenko, R., Olson, R. S., Steinbruner, J. D., & Lempert, R. (2013). Managing risk with climate vulnerability science. *Nature Climate Change, 3,* 607–609.

Summerhayes, C. (2010). Climate change: A creeping catastrophe. *Bulletin of the World Health Organization, 88*(6), 410–411.

Theisen, O. M., Gleditsch, N. P., & Buhaug, H. (2013). Is climate change a driver of armed conflict? *Climate Change, 117*(3), 613–625.

Thornton, P. K., Jones, P. G., Alagarswamy, G., & Andresen, J. (2009). Spatial variation of crop yield response to climate change in East Africa. *Global Environmental Change, 19,* 54–65.

Urban, M. (2015). Accelerating extinction risk from climate change. *Science, 348*(6234), 571–573.

Vors, L., & Boyce, M. (2009). Global declines of caribou and reindeer. *Global Change Biology, 15,* 2626–2633.

Wang, H., & Horton, R. (2015). Tackling climate change: The greatest opportunity for global health. *Lancet, 386,* 7–13.

Wang, M., & Overland, J. E. (2012). A sea ice free summer Arctic within 30 years: An update from CMIP5 models. *Geophysical Research Letters, 39,* L18501.

Watt-Cloutier, S. (2015). *The right to be cold: One woman's story of protecting her culture, the Arctic and the whole planet.* Toronto, Ontario, Canada: Penguin.

Wenzel, G. W. (2013). Inuit and modern hunter–gatherer subsistence. *Études/Inuit/Studies, 37,* 181–200.

Whiteman, G., Hope, C., & Wadhams, P. (2013). Vast costs of Arctic change. *Nature, 499,* 401–403.

Williams, A. P., & Funk, C. (2011). A westward extension of the warm pool leads to a westward extension of the Walker circulation, drying eastern Africa. *Climate Dynamics, 37,* 2417–2435.

World Health Organization. (2014). *Quantitative risk assessment of the effects of climate change on selected causes of death, 2030s and 2050s.* WHO Press, Geneva, Switzerland.

Xu, L., Myneni, R. B., Chapin, F. S., Callaghan, T. V., Pinzon, J. E., Tucker, C. J., ... Stroeve, J. C. (2013). Temperature and vegetation seasonality diminishment over northern lands. *Nature Climate Change, 3,* 581–586.

Zavaleta, C. (2018). *Food insecurity and climate change adaptation among Peruvian Indigenous Shawi* (PhD dissertation). McGill University, Montreal, Canada.

Zavaleta, C., Berrang-Ford, L., Llanos-Cuentas, A., Carcamo, C., Ford, J., Silvera, R., ... IHACC Research Team. (2017). Indigenous Shawi communities and national food security support: Right direction, but not enough. *Food Policy, 73,* 75–87.

Zulkafli, Z., Buytaert, W., Manz, B., Rosas, C. V., Willems, P., Lavado-Casimiro, W., ... Santini, W. (2016). Projected increases in the annual flood pulse of the western Amazon. *Environmental Research Letters, 11*(1), 14013.

PART V

Conclusions and Future Directions

11

Moving Forward for Community Inclusion and Policy Change

Lisa Reyes Mason and Jonathan Rigg

⌐⌐ ——

TAKING THE BOOK as a whole, what can we say about examining vulnerability and adaptation in context, broadening how we think about climate change, and moving toward policy changes that advance social justice? In this chapter, we revisit core themes from the opening chapter, synthesizing how the chapters of the book address them and point us toward intentional and meaningful work for and with communities to address the wicked problem of climate change.

COMMUNITY REALITIES

In a critical review, Aiken, Middlemiss, Sallu, and Hauxwell-Baldwin (2017) remind us that the very concept of "community" is contested, inside and outside of climate change discourse. Communities can be based on geography (i.e., space, place) or identity (e.g., ethnicity, gender, age); have "membership" with different levels of commitment and activity; and have diverse experiences, viewpoints, and preferences within themselves (Birkenmaier & Berg-Weger, 2017).

Indeed, we see examples of such contestation and diversity in many chapters of this book due to the different kinds of questions that the authors ask and deep methods of inquiry that they use. For water insecurity and gender, for example, we see the importance of taking an intersectional view of how gender also overlaps with age, economic class, geography, and other characteristics (Chapters 3 and 9)—an approach that is critically needed when thinking about gender and climate to avoid homogenizing "women" and "men" as just two groups (Demetriades & Esplen, 2010). Though "indigenous groups" may be discussed as though they have much in common, experiences and expertise between and within their members will undoubtedly vary (Chapters 6, 8, and 10).

Also arising from the chapters is a critical question of how outside researchers (or practitioners or policymakers) may impose labels of "vulnerable" or "marginalized" on some groups, who in turn reject these terms or feel further oppressed by them. Lower income residents in Phoenix, Arizona (Chapter 2), for example, have their own visions of sustainability and awareness of their strengths as a community, questioning whether outsiders are using the community to "rally people" around the cause of climate change. In Santa Fe, Argentina (Chapter 5), some residents of a land sacrificed to flooding argue for their own right and choice to live there, although at the same time the chapter argues that such "normalization of risk" is, at least in part, a byproduct of government discourse that intentionally places responsibility on individuals in lieu of the state.

The critique of a neoliberal approach to vulnerability, raised in the introduction, also resurfaces here as we think about complex community realities. As Aiken and colleagues (2017) note, the rational, market-oriented, individual economic actor approach of neoliberalism is in stark contrast to calls for collective action that consider, reach out to, and give space for community voices. But as these "calls" for action continue to be made, we must ask: Whose voices? Through what channels? And to what ends? The examples of older adults in England (Chapter 4), United Houma Nation tribal members in the United States (Chapter 6), and community-based resistance groups in Indonesia (Chapter 7) all point to the too common practice of overlooking—or intentionally excluding—the viewpoints of some communities from policy decisions, even (or, perhaps, especially) when it is those groups' land, livelihood, or well-being that is directly at stake.

CLIMATE REDUCTIONISMS REVISITED

Revisiting the five climate reductionisms from the introduction—disciplinary, participatory, experiential, teleological, and species—we also ask in what ways the book has contributed to "un-narrowing" the debate about climate change, its consequences, and potential ways to respond. And where, for each, do we go from here?

Certainly, the chapters speak from *disciplinary* diversity and with heavy emphasis on data and research methods grounded in people's lived experiences. In contrast to the privileging of natural or predictive science, or technical expertise, the lens of this book is shaped especially by disciplines such as social work, geography, sociology, international development, and public health. Also notable is that some chapters or projects described herein are in close collaboration with hard science or other more technical disciplines, including climatology, ecology, and medicine. We are not naive enough to argue that socially informed approaches alone will "solve" climate change or protect the people it affects but, rather, that the privileging of some disciplines over others must continue to be challenged, with other ways of knowing and collaborating valued as well. As Castree and colleagues (2014) write, "Which facts are worth knowing, and which solutions worth pursuing, are partly a function of whose values (moral, spiritual, aesthetic) count and where the power to realize them lies" (p. 766).

Following closely, many of the chapters support the call to address *participatory* reductionism. People's wisdom of a lifetime—or in some cases, lifetimes passed down through generations—of responding to environmental change or to juggling the many stressors of life should be viewed as an invaluable resource for identifying policy changes that would reduce vulnerability. In some cases, this means making it a priority in the policy process to understand people's experiences and preferences for change. In others cases, it means going further by looking to people's resilience and creating policies that further bolster or protect them. In all cases, we challenge those in formal positions of power to not just use what Burton and Mustelin (2013, p. 406) call the "rhetoric of inclusivity" but also genuinely seek active, creative, and intentional participation of diverse groups.

In several cases, chapters make an *experiential* widening of our understanding of how climate change "ranks" in people's concerns about their everyday lives. Climate change is a global process but with a local signature, and at the local level it needs to be understood relationally—in relation to the other threats (and opportunities) that people face. But there is also a second facet to this relational lens, where climate change at once enjoins us to have a "sense of planet," but alongside a "sense of place" (Devine-Wright, Price, & Leviston, 2015). "A critical finding" of Devine-Wright and colleagues' research in Australia is that it is not attachment "at the global level per se that is important, but the interplay between global and national attachments, showing the necessity for future research to adopt a relational approach to multiple forms of belonging, rather than seeing each as discrete" (p. 76).

A *teleological* narrowing is challenged by several chapters in this book, particularly those that trace the historical roots of structural discrimination that have produced today's vulnerability for some groups more than others. Though climate change, unchecked and unmitigated, may indeed have "doomsday" outcomes for many peoples and communities, policymakers must not be so blinded by this one projection that they create policies that lead to maladaptation and worsen quality of life for affected groups (Adger, Barnett, Brown, Marshall, & O'Brien, 2012). Also related is the need to envision new and alternative futures that challenge the neoliberal, individualistic, market-oriented approach to development, and in ways that are grounded in capabilities thinking (Schlosberg, 2012): How do we structure society so that all people have capacities to not just cope with their changing environment but also thrive and live meaningful, productive lives?

Finally, *species* reductionism is challenged in every chapter of this book, with each case detailing how people in settings as different as highly industrialized England and the Peruvian Amazon experience the consequences of climate change in different ways. These differences need to be continually documented and detailed so that the "sense of planet" noted above does not become a generalized, reductionist call to "do something" but, rather, a nuanced, locally relevant, and tuned diversity of interventions.

PARTNERSHIP FOR POLICY CHANGE

Where do we go from here for policy change? Each chapter, in ways specific to the details and context of its case, identifies policy implications or recommendations. We organize these by scale and theme in Table 11.1. Though we do not claim that these are comprehensive recommendations for "solving" vulnerability to the consequences of climate change across the contexts and cases included, they do point to specific changes that could be developed, implemented, and studied for their effectiveness over time as a place to start.

Of course, it is one matter to generate a list of policy prescriptions. It is another to put such policy changes in place. If there is one theme that pervades this book, it is the important role that community voice, engagement, and participation can bring to improved understanding of how climate change affects people's everyday lives and how to reduce vulnerability and increase resilience. If communities are truly to be valued in the policy process, then partnerships for and with communities must be deliberate, inclusive, and ongoing.

Climate change, as noted in the opening chapter, is a wicked problem. Partnerships for policy change might, thus, be conceived as a wicked "solution"—they will inevitably be fraught with uncertainty, complexity, and change. They will involve many stakeholders, there is little precedent for how to make them successful, and there are still questions of whether they are needed in all phases of the policy process or for all policy decisions (Vogel & Henstra, 2015). To help move this field forward, we offer four essential principles for partnership in conclusion of this book.

Seek Local Expertise

Communities are experts in their own conditions, experiences, and visions of the future. Also, differences of opinion exist within communities; they are not homogeneous. Local expertise must be sought for policies to be appropriately designed, implemented, and sustained. To accomplish this, efforts to "include" communities in the policy process must be meaningful, implemented in ways that community members prefer, and not add another burden of effort to already overburdened communities. What this looks like will undoubtedly vary by context and issue. We encourage policymakers to intentionally and thoughtfully build relationships with local communities, be open to more "bottom up" ways of seeking community members' expertise, and build time into the planning process for such activities. Local grassroots groups and community-based nonprofit organizations can be invaluable in this process, as can partnerships with researchers who are steeped in rich, engaged, participatory methods with communities. In writing this, we do

TABLE II.I

Policy Implications or Recommendations Across Chapters

Scale	Themes (Chapters)
Community	Draw on accumulated wisdom and experience of members (4, 6, 8, 10).
	Advocate for own vision and priority of needs (2, 4).
	Advocate for meaningful inclusion in policy and planning (6, 7).
	Support women's voices in public policy (9).
	Question and challenge patriarchal cultural norms (9).
	Question and challenge materialistic and capitalistic norms (3).
City government[a]	Conduct careful, detailed social assessments (7).
	Reorder priorities to focus on basic needs of most vulnerable (2, 7, 10).
	Provide energy/weatherization subsidies to cope with heat (2).
	Implement legal protections for renters (2).
	Review and improve emergency management sector (e.g., expand the "first responder" network) (4, 10).
	Invite organized groups, even "resistance" groups, to the policy table (7).
	Look beyond technical reductions of risk (e.g., zoning and land use) (5).
	Diversify decision-making bodies, particularly by gender (9).
	Use engaged, participatory planning processes (3, 5–8, 10).
State, regional, or national government	Challenge policies that ban climate or sustainability focused legislation (2).
	Question reliance on market-driven policies (3, 9).
	Allow national policies to be tailored to states or regions (8).
	Allow flexible resource management (8, 10).
	Provide funding for local-level adaptation, including for tribal governments (6, 10).
	Avoid relocation of groups without consent (6).
	Reconsider ways of working with tribal governments, including when federal recognition is not yet in place (6).
	Address multiple policies that support resilience (e.g., child care, employment, health care, housing, and transportation) (2, 9).
Other sectors	Engage public health sector in more advocacy (2).
	Improve linkages between the health care and social service sectors (4).
	Integrate industry into water policy discussions, and diversify industrial boards by gender (9).

[a]Also applies at the state, regional, or national level.

not suggest that the answers lie solely with local communities; there are many aspects of climate change that surpass past experience. Even so, we are certain—and the chapters in this book provide ample evidence—that climate change policy and action that does not take local communities seriously will be a denuded and likely ineffective response.

Prioritize Justice

When justice is prioritized, policymakers address basic needs of the most vulnerable and aim to equalize opportunities for all. Legacies of systematic and structural discrimination are addressed, and people are not blamed for their own vulnerability. How do we move justice to the fore in policymaking? Amplifying calls for social justice at local and state (or regional) levels is one way forward because compared to national governments, these levels of government may be more open to influence from local advocates. Also, we need continued research—and translation of research into policy (discussed below)—that sheds light on structural explanations for inequality and thus structural solutions. In some cases, using the language of capabilities and opportunities may help advance social justice goals, in terms with more appeal across the political spectrum (i.e., left to right, liberal to conservative). In other words, framing of policy communication matters, and advocates of climate and social justice should consider which frames will be most effective for each policy effort.

Design Science to Inform Policy

Both the predictive (i.e., natural) and interpretive (i.e., social, humanities) sciences are guilty of avoiding policy debates, holding to an ideal of policy-neutral science (Castree et al., 2014). But science purely for the sake of knowledge, at least in the realm of climate change and social justice, is not and should not be value-free. Though the need for boundary organizations to help bridge the science to policy or practice gap remains (Graham & Mitchell, 2016), we also call on scholars to embrace some of this work themselves. Scholars in many disciplines should challenge themselves to thoughtfully build more application into their work by asking how their work can inform critical policy questions, or in some cases put an issue on the policy agenda, and how their work can be disseminated more widely and influence the policy process. This may require new ways of training future scholars for this work, improving the abilities of current scholars, and working to change public and policy perceptions of the role and value of science in society.

Collaborate Widely

Finally, neither technical nor social, top-down nor bottom-up, or national or local approaches to vulnerability and adaptation will "solve" climate change alone. Partnerships must be new, creative, with perhaps "unusual bedfellows" who may not yet know how to communicate or work best with each other but who are willing to try. Together, we must pursue these new and diverse collaborations, with shared commitment to people's well-being and resilience and to a socially just world, in the face of a changing climate.

REFERENCES

Adger, W. N., Barnett, J., Brown, K., Marshall, N., & O'Brien, K. (2012). Cultural dimensions of climate change impacts and adaptation. *Nature Climate Change, 3*(2), 112–117.

Aiken, G. T., Middlemiss, L., Sallu, S., & Hauxwell-Baldwin, R. (2017). Researching climate change and community in neoliberal contexts: An emerging critical approach. *Wiley Interdisciplinary Reviews: Climate Change, 8*(4). doi:10.1002/wcc.463

Birkenmaier, J., & Berg-Weger, M. (2017). *The practice of generalist social work* (4th ed.). New York, NY: Routledge.

Burton, P., & Mustelin, J. (2013). Planning for climate change: Is greater public participation the key to success? *Urban Policy and Research, 31*(4), 399–415.

Castree, N., Adams, W. M., Barry, J., Brockington, D., Büscher, B., Corbera, E., . . . Newell, P. (2014). Changing the intellectual climate. *Nature Climate Change, 4*(9), 763.

Demetriades, J., & Esplen, E. (2010). The gender dimensions of poverty and climate change adaptation. In R. Mearns & A. Norton (Eds.), *Social dimensions of climate change: Equity and vulnerability in a warming world* (pp. 133–144). Washington, DC: World Bank.

Devine-Wright, P., Price, J., & Leviston, Z. (2015). My country or my planet? Exploring the influence of multiple place attachments and ideological beliefs upon climate change attitudes and opinions. *Global Environmental Change, 30*, 68–79.

Graham, A., & Mitchell, C. L. (2016). The role of boundary organizations in climate change adaptation from the perspective of municipal practitioners. *Climatic Change, 139*(3-4), 381–395.

Schlosberg, D. (2012). Climate justice and capabilities: A framework for adaptation policy. *Ethics & International Affairs, 26*(4), 445–461.

Vogel, B., & Henstra, D. (2015). Studying local climate adaptation: A heuristic research framework for comparative policy analysis. *Global Environmental Change, 31*, 110–120.

INDEX